BGP

BGP

Iljitsch van Beijnum

Beijing · Cambridge · Farnham · Köln · Sebastopol · Tokyo

BGP
by Iljitsch van Beijnum

Published by O'Reilly Media, Inc., 1005 Gravenstein Highway North, Sebastopol, CA 95472.

O'Reilly Media, Inc. books may be purchased for educational, business, or sales promotional use. On-line editions are also available for most titles (*safari.oreilly.com*). For more information contact our corporate/institutional sales department: (800) 998-9938 or *corporate@oreilly.com*.

Editor:	Jim Sumser
Production Editor:	Mary Anne Weeks Mayo
Cover Designer:	Ellie Volckhausen
Interior Designer:	David Futato

Printing History:

September 2002:   First Edition.

ISBN: 978-0-596-00254-1
[LSI]   [2011-03-25]

Table of Contents

Preface

This is a book about connecting to the Internet as reliably as possible. This means eliminating all single points of failure, including having just one Internet service provider (ISP). By *multihoming* to two or more ISPs, you can remain connected when either ISP (or your connection to them) experiences problems. However, there is a catch: if you are a regular customer, your ISP makes sure your IP addresses are known throughout the Net, so every router connected to the Internet knows where to send packets addressed to your systems. If you connect to two ISPs, you'll have to do this yourself and enter the world of *interdomain routing* via the Border Gateway Protocol (BGP). The majority of this book deals with BGP in a practical, hands-on manner.

My involvement with BGP started in 1995, when I entered a darkened room with a lot of modem lights blinking and was told, "This box connects to both our ISPs, but it doesn't do what we want it to. Maybe you can have a look. It's called a Cisco. Here are the manuals." It didn't take me long to figure out that we needed to run BGP to make this setup work as desired, but getting information on how to do this properly was a lot harder: very little of the available BGP information takes actual interdomain routing practices into account. In this book, I intend to provide an insight into these practices, based on my experiences as a network engineer working for several small multihomed ISPs and a large ISP with many multihomed customers, and as a consultant in the area of routing in general and interdomain routing in particular.

Intended Audience

The audience for this book is everyone interested in running BGP to create reliable connectivity to the Internet. It caters specifically to the needs of those who have to determine whether BGP is the right solution for them, and if so, how to go about preparing for and then implementing the protocol. The latter topic occupies most of the book. A lot of the information applies to everyone who needs reliable Internet-connectivity: end-user organizations, application service providers, web hosters, and smaller ISPs. Later in the book, the focus shifts to topics that are mainly of interest to ISPs: interconnecting (peering) with other networks and providing BGP transit services.

The network operations and engineering people at large ISPs should already be well aware of all the issues discussed in this book. However, the sales engineering, provisioning, and support staff should find its information useful when dealing with customers who run or want to run BGP.

Specific prior knowledge isn't required for reading this book, but some exposure to basic networking theory (such as the OSI model), the IP protocol, and relevant lower-layer protocols such as Ethernet would be useful for putting everything in the right perspective. References to books on these topics are spread throughout the text. The configuration examples in this book are all for Cisco routers.* It proved impossible to provide a useful number of configuration examples for additional router brands without doubling the size of the book and having to change the title to *A Comparative Analysis of BGP Implementations and Their Configuration*. When using non-Cisco equipment, the book can be used alongside the sections on BGP configuration and IP filtering (access lists) in the router's manual.

What's in This Book?

The book contains pretty much everything you need to know to run BGP for regular IPv4 routing in all but the largest networks. But there is a lot of related information that is *not* in the book: the intent of this book is to help you achieve common BGP-related goals, such as reliability and balancing traffic over multiple connections, and provide an introduction into the world of interdomain routing. The book is by no means a reference on the BGP protocol or BGP configuration on a Cisco router. Consult the Cisco documentation at *http://www.cisco.com* for additional details on Cisco's BGP implementation and IOS in general. For more details on the internals of BGP and other protocols, see the relevant RFCs. Lower-layer protocols such as Ethernet, ATM, and SONET, aren't covered in the book.

Chapter 1, *The Internet, Routing, and BGP*, sets the scene with some (often misunderstood) history and a discussion of how ISP networks connect together to form the worldwide Internet. It continues with an overview of TCP/IP design principles, the consequences of those principles, and how they make routing protocols necessary. There is a short overview of the IP header and an explanation of why there must be interdomain routing protocols in addition to intradomain (interior) routing protocols.

---

* Configuration examples are based on Cisco IOS Version 12.0 and should run on all Cisco BGP-capable platforms.

Chapter 2, *IP Addressing and the BGP Protocol*, is about IP addressing and the inner workings of the BGP protocol, including the multiprotocol extensions and the BGP route selection algorithm. The chapter ends with a discussion of previous versions of BGP and other interdomain protocols.

Chapter 3, *Physical Design Considerations*, discusses the physical side of the network: higher availability through redundancy, router hardware, and network topology. There are also sections on calculating bandwidth requirements and selecting ISPs.

Chapter 4, *IP Address Space and AS Numbers*, discusses the various types of IP address space, their limitations, and how to get those addresses. This chapter also covers renumbering IP addresses and introduces the Routing Registry system.

Chapter 5, *Getting Started with BGP*, explains in detail how to configure external BGP (eBGP) to a single ISP and how to determine whether your address block shows up on routers in other networks. The chapter provides examples of how to use a second router to connect to a second ISP and how to configure internal BGP sessions. The chapter also describes a setup in which two BGP routers run the Cisco Hot Standby Routing Protocol (HSRP) so the network remains usable if one router fails. Finally, the chapter provides information on minimizing the impact of link failures and an explanation of eBGP multihop.

Chapter 6, *Traffic Engineering*, explains how to take advantage of having two connections to the Internet by optimizing the traffic flow for input and output traffic. The chapter provides many examples of how to configure the mechanisms that influence route selection, such as manipulation of the AS path, the Multi Exit Discriminator, and communities. Chapters 5 and 6 include Routing Policy Specification Language (RPSL) examples for several routing policies described in these chapters.

Chapter 7, *Security and Integrity of the Network*, discusses the best way to secure access to your routers, the use of Telnet versus SSH, and software weaknesses. But the main topics of the chapter are protecting BGP against problems caused by other networks, intentionally or unintentionally. This includes extensive information on using BGP to deflect (Distributed) Denial of Service attacks.

Chapter 8, *Day-to-Day Operation of the Network*, talks about the requirements interdomain routing imposes on the Network Operations Center and how to manage day-to-day BGP operation. This includes a discussion of the Simple Network Management Protocol (SNMP) management and configuration examples for the popular Multi Router Traffic Grapher (MRTG) software. This chapter also provides suggestions for router names.

Chapter 9, *When Things Start to Go Down: Troubleshooting*, starts with a small section on managing the troubleshooting process and then explains how to troubleshoot physical and datalink layer problems and, in detail, interdomain routing and reachability problems.

Chapter 10, *BGP in Larger Networks*, examines the challenges of designing a large, stable network. It discusses BGP peer groups, use of loopback addresses for internal BGP (iBGP), iBGP scaling using route reflectors and confederations, and preservation of CPU cycles by dampening route flaps. It also contains examples of how to use OSPF as the interior routing protocol, the pitfalls of route redistribution, and traffic engineering in the internal network.

Chapter 11, *Providing Transit Services*, explains how to provide your multihomed customers with the tools they need to make the best use of their connection to you if you provide transit services. This includes ways for them to deflect Denial of Service attacks and communities for traffic engineering. The chapter also tells you how you can connect non-BGP customers with a backup connection and discusses providing IPv6 and multicast services.

Chapter 12, *Interconnecting with Other Networks*, is mainly about connecting to a public exchange point such as an Internet Exchange, network access point (NAP), or Metropolitan Area Exchange (MAE). It presents the business case for exchanging traffic with other networks (peering), how to connect to an exchange point, and the routing issues associated with connecting to several exchange points. The chapter ends with configuration examples for securing border routers against abusive traffic from peers.

There are three appendixes. Appendix A, *Cisco Configuration Basics*, tells you how to perform configuration changes on a Cisco router and explains a basic IP configuration. Appendix B, *Binary Logic, Netmasks, and Prefixes*, shows how netmasks and prefixes work in their native binary representation. Appendix C, *Notes on the IPv4 Address Space*, is an overview of the IPv4 address space and address ranges reserved for special purposes.

Finally, there is a *Glossary* that defines terminology related to BGP.

How to Read This Book

The book is structured such that it's best read from the beginning to the end. If you are new to Cisco routers, read Appendix A first. If you're unfamiliar with configuring BGP and properly filtering incoming and outgoing routing updates, you should read and understand those sections in Chapter 5 before moving on. Chapter 6 explains how route maps work; they're extensively used in examples in later chapters. Apart from this you can implement individual examples as desired, but remember that the examples are just that: they show how something *could* be done, which isn't necessarily the best way to do it in your particular situation. However, the text should provide you with enough information to be able to adapt the examples to the particulars of your network. Chapters 10, 11, and 12 are mostly of interest if you work in an ISP environment, but they should be informative for others as well, if not immediately applicable.

Conventions Used in This Book

Italic is used for:

- Commands, filenames, statements, keywords, and directories
- New terms where they are defined
- Internet addresses, such as domain names and URLs

Constant width is used for:

- IP addresses, subnet masks, error messages, formulas, attributes, prefixes, and BGP communities

Constant width italic is used for:

- Replaceable text

Constant width bold is used for:

- User input

This icon designates a note, which is an important aside to the nearby text.

This icon designates a warning relating to the nearby text.

The word "host" is used for any system implementing TCP/IP that doesn't perform any networking functions on behalf of other systems, such as forwarding packets, i.e., a regular PC or workstation. A "router" is any system performing IP forwarding. A "system" is either a host or a router. All addresses, AS numbers, and domain names used in examples are fictional, and where they are the same as actual numbers or names used on the Internet, this is completely coincidental. Replace those numbers with your own when implementing the examples.

Interdomain routing borrows jargon from different disciplines, resulting in many words being used in different ways by different people. I've tried to be consistent in my use of technical terms, but I'm sure I haven't been completely successful in avoiding the use of different words for the same thing, or the same word for different things. When in doubt, look the word up in the Glossary or the Index.

How to Contact Us

Please address comments and questions concerning this book to the publisher:

O'Reilly & Associates, Inc.
1005 Gravenstein Highway North
Sebastopol, CA 95472
(800) 998-9938 (in the United States or Canada)
(707) 829-0515 (international or local)
(707) 829-0104 (fax)

We have a web page for this book, where we list errata, examples, or any additional information. You can access this page at:

http://www.oreilly.com/catalog/bgp

To comment or ask technical questions about this book, send email to:

bookquestions@oreilly.com

For more information about our books, conferences, Resource Centers, and the O'Reilly Network, see our web site at:

http://www.oreilly.com

Acknowledgments

First of all, I'd like to thank everyone who gave me the opportunity to work on their network over the years, specifically Michel, Sylvia, Joost, Roy, Patrick, Mark, and Irene. I owe another debt of gratitude to the technical reviewers: Elsa Lankford, Frank Pohlman, Jonathan Hassell, Ravi Malhotra, and Nick Vermeulen. The comments from Ravi and Nick were especially valuable. Richard Jimmerson and Job Witteman provided important suggestions as well. And thanks to my editor Jim Sumser for his constant encouragement, and to all the people at O'Reilly who turned this book from a bunch of letters on the screen into something tangible.

CHAPTER 1

The Internet, Routing, and BGP

One of the many remarkable qualities of the Internet is that it has scaled so well to its current size. This doesn't mean that nothing has changed since the early days of the ARPANET in 1969. The opposite is true: our current TCP and IP protocols weren't constructed until the late 1970s. Since that time, TCP/IP has become the predominant networking protocol for just about every kind of digital communication.

The story goes that the Internet—or rather the ARPANET, which is regarded as the origin of today's Internet—was invented by the military as a network that could withstand a nuclear attack. That isn't how it actually happened. In the early 1960s, Paul Baran, a researcher for the RAND Corporation, wrote a number of memoranda proposing a digital communications network for military use that could still function after sustaining heavy damage from an enemy attack.* Using simulations, Baran proved that a network with only three or four times as many connections as the minimum required to operate comes close to the theoretical maximum possible robustness. This of course implies that the network adapts when connections fail, something the telephone network and the simple digital connections of that time couldn't do, because every connection was manually configured. Baran incorporated numerous revolutionary concepts into his proposed network: packet switching, adaptive routing, the use of digital circuits to carry voice communication, and encryption inside the network. Many people believed such a network couldn't work, and it was never built.

Several years later, the Department of Defense's Advanced Research Project Agency (ARPA) grew unsatisfied with the fact that many universities and other research institutions that worked on ARPA projects were unable to easily exchange results on computer-related work. Because computers from the many different vendors used different operating systems and languages, and because they were usually customized to some extent by their users, it was extremely hard to make a program developed on one computer run on another machine. ARPA wanted a network that

---

* The "On Distributed Communications" series is available online at *http://www.rand.org/publications/RM/baran.list.html.*

would enable researchers to access computers located at different research institutions throughout the United States.

Access to a remote computer wasn't a novelty in the late 1960s: connecting remote terminals over a phone line or dedicated circuit was complex but nonetheless a matter of routine. In these situations, however, the mainframe or minicomputer always controlled the communication: a user typed a command, the characters were sent to the central computer, the computer sent back the results after some time, and the terminal displayed them on the screen or on paper. Connecting two *computers* together was still a rather revolutionary concept, and the research institutions didn't like the idea of connecting their computers to a network one bit. Only after it was decided that dedicated minicomputers would be used to perform all network-related tasks were people persuaded to connect their systems to the network. The use of minicomputers as Interface Message Processors (IMPs) made building the network a lot easier: rather than having to deal with a large number of very different systems on the network, each computer had to talk only to the local IMP, and the IMPs only to a single local computer and, over the network, to other IMPs. Today's routers function in a similar way to the ARPANET IMPs.

During the 1970s, the ARPANET continued to evolve. The original Network Control Protocol (NCP) was replaced by two different protocols: the Internet Protocol (IP), which connects (internetworks) different networks, and the Transport Control Protocol (TCP), which applications use to communicate without having to deal with the intricacies of IP. IP and TCP are often mentioned together as TCP/IP to encompass the entire family of related protocols used on the Internet.

Topology of the Internet

Because it's a "network of networks," there was always a need to interconnect the different networks that together form the global Internet. In the beginning, everyone simply connected to the ARPANET, but over the years, the topology of the Internet has changed radically.

The NSFNET Backbone

During the late 1980s, the ARPANET was replaced as the major "backbone" of the Internet by a new National Science Foundation–sponsored network between five supercomputer locations: the NSFNET Backbone. Federal Internet Exchanges on the East and West Coasts (FIX East and FIX West) were built in 1989 to aid in the transition from the ARPANET to the NSFNET Backbone. Originally, the FIXes were 10-Mbps Ethernets, but 100-Mbps FDDI was added later to increase bandwidth. The Commercial Internet Exchange (CIX, "kicks") on the West Coast came into existence because the people in charge of the FIXes were hesitant to connect commercial networks. CIX operated a CIX router and several FDDI rings for some time, but it abandoned those activities and turned into a trade association in the late 1990s. In 1992, Metropolitan Fiber Systems (MFS, now Worldcom) built a Metropolitan Area Ethernet (MAE) in the Washington, DC, area, which quickly became a place where many different (commercial) networks interconnected. Interconnecting at an Internet Exchange (IX) or MAE is attractive, because many networks connect to the IX or MAE infrastructure, so all that's needed is a single physical connection to interconnect with many other networks.

Commercial Backbones and NAPs

Before the early 1990s, the Internet was almost exclusively used as a research network. Some businesses were connected, but this was limited to their research divisions. All this changed when email became more pervasive outside the research community, and the World Wide Web made the network much more visible. More and more business and nonresearch organizations connected to the network, and the additional traffic became a burden for the NSFNET Backbone. Also, the NSFNET Backbone Acceptable Use Policy didn't allow "for-profit activities." In 1995, the NSFNET Backbone was decommissioned, giving room to large ISPs to compete with each other by operating their own backbone networks. To ensure connectivity between the different networks, four contracts for Network Access Points (NAPs) were awarded by the NSF, each run by a different telecommunication company:

- The Pacific Bell NAP in San Jose, California
- The Ameritech NAP in Chicago, Illinois
- The Sprint NAP in Pennsauken, New Jersey (in the Philadelphia metropolitan area, but often referred to as "the New York NAP")
- The already existing MAE East,* run by MCI Worldcom, in Vienna, Virginia

The NAPs were created as large-scale exchange points where commercial networks could interconnect without being limited by the NSFNET Acceptable Use Policy. The NAPs were also used to interconnect with a new national research network for high-bandwidth applications, the "very high performance Backbone Network Service" (vBNS).

The Ameritech (Chicago) NAP was built on ATM technology from the start; the Sprint (New Jersey) and PacBell (San Francisco) NAPs used FDDI at first and migrated to ATM later. MAE East also adopted FDDI in addition to Ethernet at this point, and the (Worldcom-trademarked) acronym was quickly changed to mean "Metropolitan Area Exchange." After decommissioning the last FDDI location in 2001, MAE East is now ATM-only as well. Note that it's possible to interconnect Ethernet and FDDI at the datalink level (bridge), so if an IX uses both, a connection

---

* There was now also a MAE West, interconnected with FIX West.

to either suffices. However, it isn't possible to bridge easily from Ethernet or FDDI to ATM and vice versa. Over the past several years, the importance of the NAPs has diminished as the main interconnect locations for Internet traffic. Large networks are showing a tendency to interconnect privately, and smaller networks are looking more and more at regional public interconnect locations. There are now numerous small Internet Exchanges in the United States, and in addition to Worldcom, two other companies now operate Internet Exchanges as a commercial service: Equinix and PAIX. Figure 1-1 shows the distribution of NAPs, MAEs, Equinix Internet Business Exchanges, and PAIX exchanges.

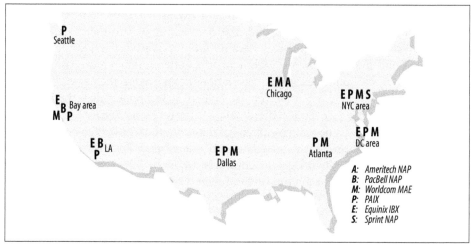

Figure 1-1. Distribution of interconnect locations in the United States

The Rest of the World

The traffic volumes for the Internet Exchanges in Europe and the Asia/Pacific region were much lower at the time the NAPs were being created, so these exchange were not forced to adopt expensive (FDDI) or then still immature (ATM) technologies as the American NAPs were. Because Ethernet is cheap, easier to configure than ATM, and conveniently available in several speeds, most of the non-NAP and non-MAE Internet Exchanges use Ethernet. There are also a few that use frame relay, SMDS, or SRP, usually when the Internet Exchange isn't limited to a single location or a small number of locations but allows connections to any ISP office or *point of presence (POP)* within a metropolitan area.

In Europe, most countries have an Internet Exchange. From an international perspective, the main ones are the London Internet Exchange (LINX), the Amsterdam Internet Exchange (AMS-IX), and the Deutsche Commercial Internet Exchange (DE-CIX) in Frankfurt. Internet Exchanges in the rest of the world haven't yet reached the scale of those in the United States and Europe and are used mainly to exchange national traffic.

Transit and Peering

When a customer connects to an Internet service provider (ISP), the customer pays. This seems natural. Because the customer pays, the ISP has to carry packets to and from all possible destinations worldwide for this customer. This is called *transit service*. Smaller ISPs buy transit from larger ISPs, just as end-user organizations do. But ISPs of roughly similar size also interconnect in a different way: they exchange traffic as equals. This is called *peering*, and typically, there is no money exchanged. Unlike transit, peering traffic always has one network (or one of its customers) as the source and the other network (or one of its customers) as its destination. Chapter 12 offers more details on interconnecting with other networks and peering.

Classification of ISPs

All ISPs aren't created equal: they range from huge, with worldwide networks, to tiny, with only a single Ethernet as their "backbone." Generally, ISPs are categorized in three groups:

Tier-1
> Tier-1 ISPs are so large they don't pay anyone else for transit. They don't have to, because they peer with all other tier-1 networks. All other networks pay at least one tier-1 ISP for transit, so peering with all tier-1 ISPs ensures connectivity to the entire Internet.

Tier-2
> Tier-2 ISPs have a sizable network of their own, but they aren't large enough to convince all tier-1 networks to peer with them, so they get transit service from at least one tier-1 ISP.

Tier-3
> Tier-3 ISPs don't have a network to speak of, so they purchase transit service from one or more tier-1 or tier-2 ISPs that operate in the area. If they peer with other networks, it's usually at just a single exchange point. Many don't even multihome.

The line between tier-1 networks and the largest tier-2 is somewhat blurred, with some tier-2 networks doing "paid peering" with tier-1 networks and calling themselves tier-1. The real difference is that tier-2 networks generally have a geographically limited presence. For instance, even some very large European networks with trans-Atlantic connections of their own pay a U.S. network for transit, rather than interconnecting with a large number of other networks at NAPs throughout the United States. Because tier-1 networks see these regional ISPs as potential customers, they are less likely to peer with them. This goes double for tier-3 networks.

Tier-2 networks, on the other hand, may not peer with many tier-1 networks, but they often peer with all other tier-2 networks operating in the same region and with many tier-3 networks.

TCP/IP Design Philosophy

The fact that TCP/IP runs well over all kinds of underlying networks is no coincidence. Today, every imaginable kind of computer is connected to the Net, even though those connected over the fastest links, such as Gigabit Ethernet, can transfer more data in a second than the slowest, connected through wireless modems, can transfer in a day. This flexibility is the result of the philosophy that network failures shouldn't impede communication between two hosts and that no assumptions should be made about the underlying communications channels. Any kind of circuit that can carry packets from one place to another with some reasonable degree of reliability may be used.*

This philosophy makes it necessary to move all the decision-making to the source and destination hosts: it would be very hard to survive the loss of a router somewhere along the way if this router holds important, necessary information about the connection. This way of doing things is very different from the way telephony and virtual circuit–oriented networks such as X.25 work: they go through a setup phase, in which a path is configured at central offices or telephone switches along the way before any communication takes place. The problem with this approach is that when a switch fails, all paths that use this switch fail, disrupting ongoing communication. In a network built on an *unreliable datagram service*, such as the Internet, packets can simply be diverted around the failure and still be delivered. The price to be paid for this flexibility is that end hosts have to do more work. Packets that were on their way over the broken circuit may be lost; some packets may be diverted in the wrong direction at first, so that they arrive after subsequent packets have already been received; or the new route may be of a different speed or capacity. The networking software in the end hosts must be able to handle any and all of these eventualities.

The IP Protocol

Because the TCP protocol takes care of the most complex tasks, IP processing along the way becomes extremely simple: basically, just take the destination address, look it up in the routing table to find the next-hop address and/or interface, and send the packet on its way to this next hop over the appropriate interface. This isn't immediately obvious by looking at the IP header (Figure 1-2), because there are 12 fields in

---

* "The Design Philosophy of the DARPA Internet Protocols" contains a good overview; it can be found at *http://www.cs.umd.edu/class/fall1999/cmsc711/papers/design-philosophy.pdf*.

it, which seems like a lot at first glance. The function of each field, except perhaps the Type of Service and fragmentation-related fields, is simple enough, however.

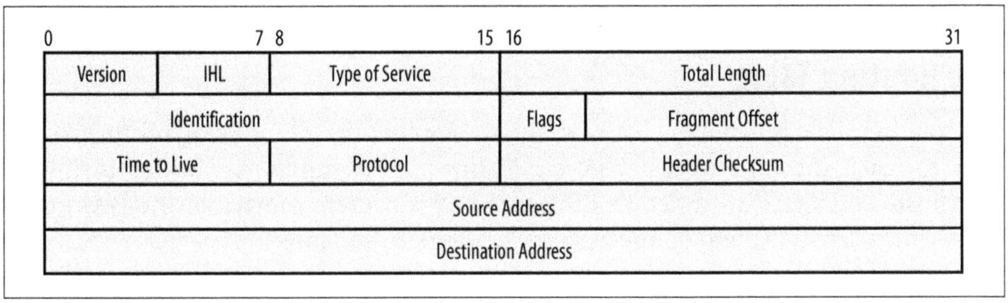

0		7 8	15 16	31

Version	IHL	Type of Service	Total Length	
Identification			Flags	Fragment Offset
Time to Live		Protocol	Header Checksum	
Source Address				
Destination Address				

Figure 1-2. The IP header as defined in RFC 791

The first 32 bits of the header are mainly for housekeeping: the Version field indicates the IP version (4), the Internet Header Length ("IHL"), and the length of the header (usually 5 32-bit words); the Total Length is the length of the entire IP packet, including the header, in bytes. The Type of Service field can be used by applications to indicate that they desire a nonstandard service level or quality of service (QoS). In most networks, the contents of this field are ignored.

The next 32 bits are used when the IP packet needs to be fragmented. This happens when the maximum packet size on a network link isn't enough to transmit the packet whole. The router breaks up the packet in smaller packets, and the receiving host can later reassemble the original packet using the information in the Identifier, Flags, and Fragment Offset fields.

The middle 32 bits contains the Time to Live (TTL), Protocol, and Header Checksum fields. The TTL is initialized at a sufficiently high value (usually 60) by the source host and then decremented by each router. When the TTL reaches zero, the router throws away the packet. This is done to prevent packets from circling the Net indefinitely when there are routing loops.[*] The Protocol field indicates what's inside the IP packet: usually TCP or UDP data, or an ICMP control message. The Header Checksum is just that, and it's used to protect the header from inadvertent changes en route. As with all checksums, the receiver performs the checksum calculation over the received information, and if the computed checksum is different from the received checksum, the packet contains invalid information and is discarded. The final two 32-bit words contain the address of the source system that generated the packet and the destination system to which the packet is addressed.

---

[*] This happens when router A thinks a certain destination is reachable over router B, but router B thinks this destination is reachable over router A. The packet is then forwarded back and forth between the two routers. A routing loop is usually caused by incorrect configuration or by temporary inconsistencies when there is a change in the network.

When there are errors during IP processing, the system experiencing the error (this can be a router along the way or the destination host) sends back an Internet Control Message Protocol (ICMP) message to inform the source host of the problem.

The Routing Table

The routing table is just a big list of destination networks, along with information on how to reach those networks. Figure 1-3 shows an example network consisting of two hosts connected to different Ethernets and a router connecting the two Ethernets, with a second router connecting the network to the Internet.*

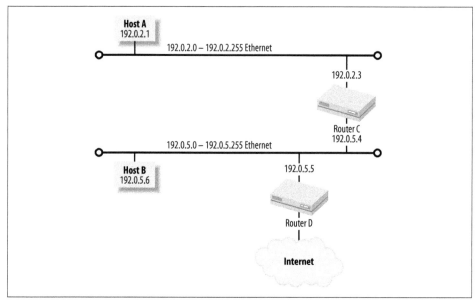

Figure 1-3. A small example network

Each router and host has a different routing table, telling it how to reach all possible destinations. The contents of these routing tables is shown in Table 1-1.

Table 1-1. Routing tables for hosts and routers in Figure 1-3

Destination	Host A	Host B	Router C	Router D
192.0.2.0 net	Directly connected	192.0.5.4 (Router C)	Directly connected	192.0.5.4 (Router C)
192.0.5.0 net	192.0.2.3 (Router C)	Directly connected	Directly connected	Directly connected
Default route	192.0.2.3 (Router C)	192.0.5.5 (Router D)	192.0.5.5 (Router D)	Over ISP connection

---

* To avoid confusion between routers and switches or hubs, Ethernets are drawn in this and other examples to resemble a strand of coaxial wiring with terminators at the ends and with hosts and routers connecting to the coax wire in different places.

The actual routing table looks different inside a host or router, of course. Most hosts have a *route* command, which can be used to list and manipulate entries (routes) in the routing table. This is how the route to host B (192.0.5.6) looks in host A's routing table, if host A is a FreeBSD system:

```
# route get 192.0.5.6
   route to: 192.0.5.6
destination: 192.0.5.0
       mask: 255.255.255.0
    gateway: 192.0.2.3
  interface: xl0
```

Because there is no specific route to the IP address 192.0.5.6, the routing table returns a route for a range of addresses starting at 192.0.5.0. The mask indicates how big the range is, and the gateway is the router that is used to reach this destination. The xl0 Ethernet interface is used to transmit the packets. Hosts usually have a limited number of routes in their routing table, so for most (nonlocal) destinations, there is no specific route to an address range that includes the destination IP address. In this case, the routing table returns the *default route*:

```
# route get 207.25.71.5
   route to: 207.25.71.5
destination: default
       mask: default
    gateway: 192.0.2.3
  interface: xl0
```

Packets match the default route and are sent to the *default gateway* (the router the default route points to, in this case 192.0.2.3) when there is no better, specific route available. The default gateway may have a route for this destination, or it may send the packet "upstream" (in the direction of the elusive core of the Internet) to its own default gateway, until the packet arrives at a router that has the desired route in its routing table. From there, the packet is forwarded hop by hop until it reaches its destination.

Routing Protocols

This leaves just one problem unsolved: how do we maintain an up-to-date routing table? Simply entering the necessary information manually isn't good enough: the routing table has to reflect the actual way in which everything is connected at any given time, the *network topology*. This means using dynamic routing protocols so that topology changes, such as cable cuts and failed routers, are communicated promptly throughout the network.

A simple routing protocol is the Routing Information Protocol (RIP). RIP basically broadcasts the contents of the routing table periodically over every connection and listens for other routers to do the same. Routes received through RIP are added to the routing table and, from then on, are broadcast along with the rest of the routing table. Every route contains a "hop count" that indicates the distance to the destination network, so routers have a way to select the best path when they receive multiple routes to the same destination. RIP is considered a *distance-vector* routing protocol, because it only stores information about where to send packets for a certain destination and how many hops are necessary to get there. Open Shortest Path First (OSPF)* is a much more advanced routing protocol, so much so that it was even questioned whether Dijkstra's Shortest Path First algorithm, on which the protocol is based, wouldn't be too complex for routers to run. This turned out not to be a problem as long as some restrictions are taken into account when designing OSPF networks. Instead of broadcasting all routes periodically, OSPF keeps a topology map of the network and sends updates to the other routers throughout the network only when something changes. Then all routers recompute the topology map using the SPF algorithm. This makes OSPF a *link-state* protocol. Rather than the number of hops, OSPF also takes into account the cost, which usually translates to the link bandwidth, of every link when computing the best path to a destination.

Obviously, periodically broadcasting all the routes or keeping topology information about every single connection isn't possible for the entire Internet. Thus, in addition to *interior* routing protocols such as RIP and OSPF for use within a single organization's network, *exterior* protocols are needed to relay routing information between organizations. Routers, especially routers connecting one type of network to another, were called "gateways" in the early days of the TCP/IP protocol family, so we usually talk about *interior gateway protocols* (IGPs) and *exterior gateway protocols* (EGPs). To confuse the uninitiated even further, one of the older EGPs is named *EGP*. There may be some time-forgotten Internet sites where EGP is still used, but the present protocol of choice for interdomain routing in the Internet is the Border Gateway Protocol Version 4 (BGP-4), a more advanced exterior gateway protocol.

BGP is sometimes called a *distance-path* protocol. It isn't satisfied with a simple hop count, but it doesn't keep track of the full topology of the entire network either. Every router receives reachability information from its neighbors; it then chooses the route with the shortest path for inclusion in the routing table and announces this path to other neighbors, if the routing policy permits it. The path is a list of every *Autonomous System* (AS) between the router and the destination. The idea behind Autonomous Systems is that networks don't care about the inner details of other networks. Thus, instead of listing every router along the way, BGP groups network together within ASes so they may be viewed as a single entity, whether an AS contains only a single BGP-speaking router or hundreds of BGP- and non-BGP-speaking routers. Figure 1-4 shows the differences between the two views: the EGP sees ASes as a whole; the IGP sees individual routers within an AS but is limited to a view of a single AS.

---

* "Open" refers to OSPF being an open standard, not to the openness of the shortest path.

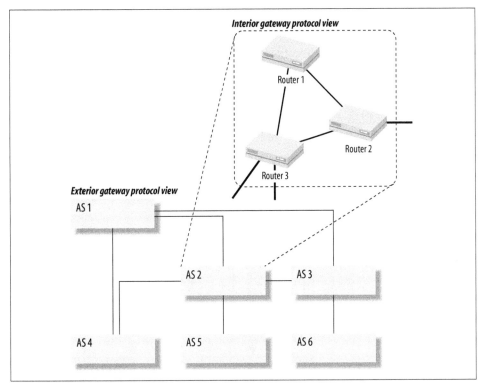

Figure 1-4. The differences between IGP and EGP views

An AS is sometimes described as "a single administrative domain," but this isn't completely accurate. An AS can span more than one organization, for instance, an ISP and its non-BGP speaking customers. The ISP doesn't necessarily have any control over its customers' routers, but the customers do fall within the ISP's AS and are subject to the same routing policy, because without BGP, they have no way to express a routing policy of their own.

It may seem strange that in EGPs, the policies take precedence over the reachability information, but there is a good reason for this. ISPs will, of course, receive all routes from their upstream ISPs and announce all routes to their customers, thereby providing transit services to remote destinations. Someone who is a customer of two ISPs wouldn't want to announce ISP 1's routes to ISP 2, however. And using a customer's infrastructure for your own purposes is usually not considered good business practice. Thus, the most basic routing policy is "send routes only to paying customers." Policies become more complex when two networks peer. When networks are similar in size, it makes sense to exchange traffic at exchange points rather than to pay a larger network for handling it. In this case, the routing policy is to send just your own routes and your customer's routes to the peer and keep the expensive routes from upstream ISPs to yourself. Announcing a route means inviting the other side to send traffic, so this policy is the BGP way of inviting your peering partner to send you traffic with you or your customer as its destination.

Figure 1-5 shows part of the Internet with one large ISP (AS 1), two medium-sized ISPs (AS 2 and AS 3) that resell the AS 1 transit service, and three customers (ASes 4, 5, and 6). Customer 4 is connected to two ISPs, ASes 1 and 2, and is therefore said to be "multihomed." Transit routes are distributed from the top down (from 1 to 2 and 4, from 2 to 4 and 5, and from 3 to 6), and there is a peering connection between ISPs 2 and 3.

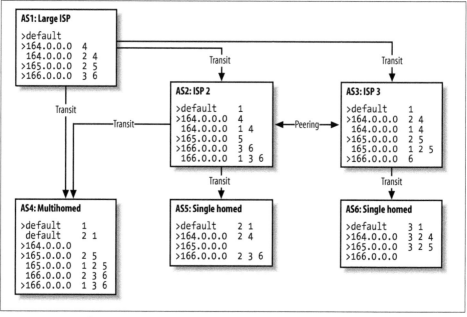

Figure 1-5. Example BGP connectivity between ISPs and customers

For the purposes of this example, there are only four routes: AS 1 announces a default route, indicating that it can handle traffic to every destination connected to the Net; ASes 4, 5, and 6 each announce a single route: 164.0.0.0, 165.0.0.0, and 166.0.0.0, respectively. After all routes have propagated throughout the network, the routing tables* will be populated as illustrated in Figure 1-5. The > character indicates the preferred route when there are several routes to the same destination. The numbers after the destination IP network form the *AS path*, which is used to make policy decisions and to make sure there are no routing loops.

---

* The existence of separate routing tables for BGP processing (BGP table) and forwarding packets ("the routing table" or Forwarding Information Base) is ignored here.

AS 1, the large ISP

The route from AS 4 (164.0.0.0) shows up twice in the AS 1 routing table, because AS 1 receives the announcement from both AS 4 itself and through AS 2. BGP sends only the route with the best path to its neighbors, but it doesn't remove the less preferred routes from memory. In this case, the best path is the one directly to AS 4, because it's obviously shorter. The other route to 164.0.0.0 is used only when the one with the shorter path becomes unavailable.

AS 2, a smaller ISP

The BGP table for AS 2 is a bit more complex than the one for AS 1. AS 2 relays the customer routes 164.0.0.0 and 165.0.0.0 that it receives from ASes 4 and 5 to AS 1, so the rest of the world knows how to reach them. The peering link between AS 2 and AS 3 is used to exchange traffic *to* (and thus routes *from*) each other's customers. So AS 2 sends the routes it received from ASes 4 and 5 to AS 3, but not the routes received from AS 1.

AS 3, another small ISP

The situation for AS 3 is similar to that of AS 2, but AS 3 has only one customer route (from AS 6) to announce to AS 1. The paths for both 164.0.0.0 routes are the same length, but AS 3 will prefer the path over AS 2 (by means that are discussed later in the book) because it's cheaper to send traffic to a peer rather than to a transit network.*

AS 4, a multihomed customer of both AS 1 and AS 2

AS 4 gets two copies of every route: one from AS 1 and one from AS 2. The default route has a shorter path over AS 1, and the 165.0.0.0 has a shorter path over AS 2. For 166.0.0.0, the path is the same length, so in the absence of any policies that instruct it to act differently, the BGP routing process will use several tie-breaking rules to make a choice. The 164.0.0.0 route has an empty path, because it's a locally sourced route, generated by AS 4 itself.

ASes 5 and 6, single-homed customers of ASes 2 and 3, respectively

The routing tables for ASes 5 and 6 are simple: transit routes and a single local route that is announced to their respective upstream ISPs. For networks with only one connection to the outside world, there is rarely any need to run BGP: setting a static default route has the same effect.

Multihoming

Having connections to two or more ISPs and running BGP means cooperating in worldwide interdomain routing. This is the only way to make sure your IP address

---

* The relationship between traffic and cost is usually indirect, but in the long run, it's cheaper to upgrade a peering connection for more traffic rather than a transit connection. The business case for peering with other networks is discussed later in the book.

range is still reachable when your connection to an ISP fails or when the ISP itself fails. Compared to just connecting to a single ISP, multihoming is like driving your own car rather than taking the bus. In the bus, someone else does the driving, and you're just along for the ride. Under most circumstances, driving your own car isn't very difficult, and the extra speed and flexibility are well worth it. However, you need to stay informed about issues such as traffic congestion, and you need to maintain the car yourself.

There are some important disadvantages to using BGP. A pessimist might say that you gain a lot of complexity to lose a lot of stability. Implementing BGP shouldn't be taken lightly. Even if you do everything right, there will be times when you are unreachable because of BGP problems, when your network would have been reachable if you hadn't used BGP. There is a lot you can do to keep the number of these incidents and the time to repair to a minimum, however. On the other hand, if you don't run BGP, and your ISP has a problem in their network or the connection to them fails, there is usually very little you can do, and the downtime can be considerable. So in most cases, BGP will increase your uptime, but only if you carefully correct potential problems before they interfere with proper operation of the network.

CHAPTER 2

IP Addressing and the BGP Protocol

This chapter provides an overview of the IP address architecture and some interdomain routing history, followed by an explanation of the BGP protocol, information on how BGP relates to routing in general, and a discussion of Multiprotocol BGP.

IP Addresses

IP addresses are made up of two parts: the network part and the host part. Because IP addresses are only 32 bits in length, it's not possible to have both a large host part (to accommodate networks with many hosts) and a large network part (to accommodate a large number of networks) at the same time. To get around this, there are three classes of IP addresses:

- Class A addresses, with a 7-bit network part and a 24-bit host part, allow 128 networks with 16 million hosts each. The highest bit is always set to 0 in Class A address, so the first byte of Class A IP addresses ranges from 0 to 127.

- Class B addresses, with a 14-bit network part and a 16-bit host part, allow 16384 networks with 65534 hosts each. The two highest bits are always set to 10 in Class B addresses, so the first byte of Class B IP addresses ranges from 128 to 191.

- Class C addresses, with a 21-bit network part and an 8-bit host part, allow 2 million networks with 254 hosts each. The three highest bits are always set to 110 in Class C addresses so, the first byte of Class C IP addresses ranges from 192 to 223.

Note that the first address in a network (the all-zeros address) is the network address, and can't be used. The last address (with all the bits in the host part set to one) is the network broadcast address and can't be used either. Addresses with a first byte in the 224–239 range are multicast (Class D) addresses, and those in the range 240–255 are reserved for future use. See Appendix C for more information on the IPv4 address space.

Subnetting and VLSM

The network/host structure in IP assumes each network has only a single lower-layer network, such as an Ethernet. Using switches, it's of course possible to build an organization-wide Ethernet, but in practice, most networks consist of several *subnetworks*. To deal with this, IP has the notion of a subnet mask. The *subnet mask* determines how many bits in the address are really used to number hosts and how many are used to number the different subnets within the network. For instance, an organization with a Class B network may use a subnet mask of 255.255.255.0, so that there are eight bits available to number hosts (for a maximum of 254 hosts per subnet) and eight bits to number the subnets.

Having a fixed subnet mask wastes addresses, however: some subnets have only a few hosts in them; others have many hosts. Current routers have no trouble using different subnet masks within the same network. This is called Variable Length Subnet Masks (VLSM). Routing protocols must carry the subnet masks explicitly to support this, however, so routing protocols predating VLSM (most notably RIP) can work only with a single subnet mask per classful network, so all subnets must be the same size.

CIDR: Classless Inter-Domain Routing

The small number of Class A networks hasn't been a problem, because few organizations need to connect more than 65,534 systems within their network. There aren't nearly enough Class B networks, however, to assign one to every organization that needs to connect more than 254 systems to the Internet. The solution was to assign multiple Class C networks to such organizations, because the Class B networks were running out fast in the early 1990s. The unfortunate side effect of this new address-assignment policy was that the number of Class C networks in the routing tables of BGP routers skyrocketed. In the newest version of BGP (the current one, BGP-4), the entire notion of network classes has been abandoned in favor *Classless Inter-Domain Routing* (CIDR). With CIDR, the number of bits for the network part of the address may be chosen freely. Instead of looking at the beginning of the address to see if it's Class A, B, or C, every route has an explicit indication of the number of bits that belong to the network part of the address, either in *prefix* format or as a *netmask*. Table 2-1 shows some network sizes and their prefix and netmask.

Table 2-1. Network/host structure for classless IP addresses

Prefix	Netmask	Net bits	Host bits	Hosts	Equals
/26	255.255.255.192	26	6	62	1/4 Class C
/25	255.255.255.128	25	7	126	1/2 Class C
/24	255.255.255.0	24	8	254	1 Class C
/23	255.255.254.0	23	9	510	2 Class C

Table 2-1. Network/host structure for classless IP addresses (continued)

Prefix	Netmask	Net bits	Host bits	Hosts	Equals
/22	255.255.252.0	22	10	1022	4 Class C
/21	255.255.248.0	21	11	2046	8 Class C
/20	255.255.240.0	20	12	4094	16 Class C
/19	255.255.224.0	19	13	8190	32 Class C
/18	255.255.192.0	18	14	16382	1/4 Class B
/17	255.255.128.0	17	15	32766	1/2 Class B
/16	255.255.0.0	16	16	65534	1 Class B

In addition to CIDR, BGP-4 also supports aggregation. This makes it possible for an ISP to bundle the address ranges of a number of customers into a single, larger range. Some examples of classful and classless addresses and networks follow:

39.0.0.0
> A Class A network; addresses range from 39.0.0.1 to 39.255.255.254 (/8 using CIDR, 255.0.0.0 netmask).

63.23.32.0/20
> A classless 4094-host network, with host addresses from 62.23.32.1 to 62.23.47.254 (255.255.240.0 netmask).

144.16.0.0 mask 255.240.0.0
> A classless 1048574-host network. Most likely, this is an aggregate of 16 Class B networks (/12 using CIDR).

165.3.93.0
> A single address in the 165.3.0.0/16 Class B network. Because 93.0 isn't the first address of the network, it may be used as a valid host address, despite the 0 at the end (this isn't a good idea, however, because some people do over-enthusiastic filtering).

192.0.1.0
> A Class C network, with host addresses from 192.0.1.1 to 192.0.1.254 (/24 using CIDR, 255.255.255.0 netmask).

199.10.0.0/16
> A 65534-host network. These addresses are often allocated to ISPs so they can further assign smaller blocks to their customers and still announce a single route in BGP (255.255.0.0 netmask).

Appendix B has more information on subnetting, prefixes, and masks.

Interdomain Routing History

During the rule of the ARPANET, the original routing protocol between the Interface Message Protocols evolved into the Gateway-to-Gateway Protocol (GGP, RFC 823). This is a distance-vector protocol like RIP, but unlike RIP, it uses a reliable transport mechanism, and routing updates are sent only when there is a change in reachability status for some part of the network.

In 1984, the Exterior Gateway Protocol became formalized in RFC 904. As a routing protocol, EGP isn't very advanced: it doesn't support topologies with loops in them, for instance. The main intended purpose for the protocol was to connect "stub gateways" (routers connecting to a nontransit network) to the rest of the Net and have those stub gateways announce reachability information for their AS. EGP needs the network to have a tree structure, in which information flows either up, in the direction of the core or backbone, or down, in the direction of stub networks. New in EGP was the notion of different routing domains: interior within an autonomous system and exterior between ASes. Within the ARPANET, GGP remained in use as the interior protocol.

In 1989, the new Border Gateway Protocol no longer let routers find neighbors on their own; it required them to be configured manually and ran over TCP. BGP Version 1 (RFC 1105) still had the notion of up, down, or horizontal relationships, as in EGP. This limitation was abandoned in BGP-2 (1163), along with major changes to the message formats. BGP-3 (RFC 1267) introduced, among other things, the BGP identifier field in the open message and defined how to use this field to decide which connection is terminated when two BGP neighbors each initiate a TCP session at the same time (a connection collision). In 1994, BGP-4 (RFC 1654, later RFC 1771) added CIDR, aggregation support, the Local Preference attribute, and a per-connection hold time.

While BGP was still in its infancy, work was being done on an even more groundbreaking approach to interdomain routing: the Inter-Domain Policy Routing (IDPR) protocol (RFC 1479). IDPR tries to look at the policies of a source and destination network and the networks in between and attempts to accommodate user requests for certain services and QoS guarantees. Unlike BGP, IDPR uses a link-state mechanism for distributing routing information. This makes it possible for the source to apply its policies more accurately. But it doesn't stop there: the protocol breaks the fundamental hop-by-hop forwarding paradigm of IP. To do this, all traffic is tunneled. Tunneling hides the network layer: in essence, the source gets to decide how routers further upstream have to route the packet. With IDRP, it's no problem for an ISP to send traffic from one customer over one transit connection and traffic from another customer over another transit connection even if the destination is the same in both cases. An ISP may want to do this if one transit ISP offers a much better service but is also more expensive. One customer may need the better service level, while the other doesn't want to pay too much. With BGP this isn't possible, because hop-by-hop forwarding takes only the destination address into account, and traffic flows that have come together at some point can't be separated later. (At least, they can't be separated without employing special techniques such as policy routing.)

It seems IDPR lost momentum before it could be deployed. The search for QoS guarantees in IP has been picked up elsewhere with the development of the Resource Reservation Protocol (RSVP, RFC 2205). RSVP doesn't break the hop-by-hop paradigm, using a different approach instead: the protocol makes it possible to reserve resources (usually bandwidth) at each router along the way, so individual traffic flows can enjoy a better QoS than regular "bulk" traffic.

The BGP Protocol

BGP uses TCP on port 179 for communication between neighbors. This is unusual: all other routing protocols either run directly on top of IP or use UDP. This makes it possible to send broadcasts or multicasts to discover neighboring routers. This neighbor-discovery functionality isn't required for BGP, however, so running over TCP avoids having to incorporate a significant amount of transport protocol functionality, such as fragmentation, sequencing, and retransmission of data.

 BGP Versions 1, 2, and 3 should be considered completely obsolete. Whenever "BGP" is used, it means BGP-4.

When BGP neighbors establish a TCP session, they start exchanging BGP information in the form of "messages." Each message starts with a header, followed by the contents of the message, as shown in Table 2-2.

Table 2-2. BGP message header format

Marker	Length	Type	Message contents
16 bytes	2 bytes	1 byte	0 - 4077 bytes

The marker usually contains all 1s and is used to check whether the sender and receiver are still synchronized. If the receiver finds an unexpected value in the marker field, something must have gone wrong, so the receiver sends back an error indication and closes the connection. The length field holds the length of the BGP message, which has a minimum length of 19 bytes (just a header with no message) and a maximum of 4,096 bytes. The type indicates the message's purpose: open (1), update (2), notification (3), or keepalive (4) (as defined in RFC 1771, with more message types defined in later RFCs).

Open Message

Both sides send an open message immediately after the TCP session has been established. The open message conveys important information about the BGP speaker's configuration and abilities. The format of the open message is shown in Table 2-3.

Table 2-3. BGP open message format

Version	My AS	Hold time	Identifier	Par len	Optional parameters
1 byte	2 bytes	2 bytes	4 bytes	1 byte	0 - 255 bytes

The first field indicates the BGP version, which would normally be 4. The next field is the sender's AS number. The hold time is the maximum number of seconds the session may remain idle before it's torn down because of a timeout. The lower of the hold times in both open messages is used. The minimum hold time is three seconds; the value zero means the session will never time out. The identifier field contains one of the BGP speaker's IP addresses. A router must use the same identifier for all BGP sessions. The optional parameter length field ("par len") indicates the absence (with a zero value) or length of an optional parameters field. If there are any optional parameters, they are all preceded by a one-byte parameter type and a one-byte parameter length. The optional parameters field negotiates the use of authentication and extended capabilities, such as multiprotocol extensions and route refresh.

If the contents of the open message are to the router's liking, it sends back a keepalive message and start sending over a copy of the BGP routing table (to the extent that configured policies for this peer allow) using update messages. Once this is complete, the router will send only periodic keepalive messages and incremental updates if there are any changes in the routing table.

Update Message

The update message lists withdrawn and new routes. Both are optional, so an update message can withdraw routes, list new routes, or do both. Table 2-4 shows the message format.

Table 2-4. BGP update message format

UR length	Withdrawn routes	PA length	Path attributes	NLRI
2 bytes	Variable	2 bytes	Variable	Variable

The unfeasible routes length ("UR length") field specifies the length of the withdrawn routes field; zero means this field is absent. The path attributes length field and the path attributes field work similarly.

The withdrawn-routes field lists all routes that are no longer reachable as announced earlier. There is no need to explicitly withdraw a route when the attributes change:

an update message with the new attributes and matching NLRI (Network Layer Reachability Information) is sufficient.

Each withdrawn route consists of a length field, indicating the prefix length (in bits), and enough bytes to hold the prefix. The path attributes all begin with a byte containing attribute flags and a second byte indicating the attribute type. The attribute flags are:

Optional bit (bit 0, the most significant bit)
> 0: The attribute is well-known (all BGP routers must recognize it).

> 1: The attribute is optional.

Transitive bit (bit 1)
> 0: The attribute is nontransitive.

> 1: The attribute is transitive or well-known.

Partial bit (bit 2)
> 0: The attribute is complete, nontransitive, or well-known.

> 1: The information in the optional transitive attribute is partial.

> When an optional transitive attribute is relayed by a router that doesn't understand the option, it sets the "partial" bit so routers further downstream know the attribute may not have been processed as desired at all previous hops.

Extended length bit (bit 3)
> 0: The attribute length field is one byte.

> 1: The attribute length field is two bytes.

The remaining bits of the attribute flags byte aren't used. The values and interpretation of the path attribute field itself are determined by the path attribute type:

> Origin (type code 1)
> AS path (type code 2)
> Next hop (type code 3)
> Multi Exit Discriminator (type code 4)
> Local Preference (type code 5)

These path attributes are used to select the most desirable route when a router receives multiple routes to the same destination network (from different BGP neighbors), as explained later this chapter.

The optional/transitive/well-known permutations make it possible to add new path attributes to BGP in such a way that existing BGP implementations know how to handle them without actually knowing what the attributes mean.

The NLRI field is of a variable length, but there is no need to include a length field for it, because it simply occupies whatever space remains in the BGP message following the path-attributes field. This field contains prefixes in the same format as the withdrawn-routes field. All listed path attributes apply to all the prefixes listed in the NLRI field.

The term NLRI is sometimes used outside the context of a BGP update message. It then means simply "a prefix." The word "route" usually indicates the presence of more information than just the prefix/NLRI, such as the next-hop IP address and/or interface. However, the use of terminology in interdomain routing is rather fluid.

Notification and Keepalive Messages

A notification message is generated when a fatal error condition arises. After transmitting the notification, the sender tears down the TCP connection. The message consists of a one-byte error code, a one-byte error subcode, and optional data. keepalive messages are sent when the connection is otherwise idle, to make sure the hold timer doesn't expire. They consist of nothing more than the BGP message header with the type field set to 4, with no additional data.

BGP States

The BGP RFC has a list of specific states a session may be in, as well as a state transition diagram (the BGP "finite state machine"). The behavior of the router is bound by the state a BGP session is in. Also, the BGP MIB defines an SNMP trap message that can be sent when a session goes from a "higher" state into a "lower" state. These states are the following:

Idle
> The router isn't trying to set up a BGP session, and if the neighbor were to attempt to create a session, the TCP connection would be refused. The router waits for a "start" event, typically the user enabling BGP or adding a neighbor or an interface coming up.

Connect
> In this state, the router waits for its own TCP session establishment attempt to complete, and it listens for incoming TCP sessions.

Active
> BGP is waiting for a TCP session.

OpenSent
> The open message has been sent, but an open message hasn't yet been received from the neighbor.

OpenConfirm
> The open message from the neighbor has been received, but not yet the initial keepalive message that completes the BGP session setup phase.

`Established`

The initial keepalive message has been received, and the session is now ready for transmission of update, keepalive, and notification messages.

The state for each neighbor is shown in the output of the *show ip bgp summary* command as the last item on the line with neighbor-specific information. If the router lists the number of prefixes received, the state is "established."

Propagation of BGP Routes

When a BGP router receives a new route in a BGP update message, it executes the following procedure:

1. Checks all incoming filters defined for the BGP session. If the route isn't allowed through by one of the filters, it's ignored, and the procedure stops.
2. Inserts the route in the BGP table.
3. Compares the route to other routes in the BGP table with the same destination prefix (NLRI), and executes the BGP route-selection algorithm. If the new route isn't considered the best route, the procedure stops.
4. Considers the new route best and includes it in the routing table. The old best route is removed.
5. Revokes the old best route in BGP updates to all neighbors that had received a copy of the old best route.
6. Propagates the new best route to BGP neighbors in external ASes, if the filters configured for the neighbor allow it.
7. Propagates the new best route to BGP neighbors in the local AS if that route wasn't received from another BGP neighbor in the local AS. (There is usually no filtering between BGP neighbors in the same AS.)

This procedure can have a paradoxical result: it's possible that the local router receives a better route over BGP but actually revokes (withdraws) the existing route to this destination in updates to BGP neighbors because it's no longer best, without announcing the new best route (because this isn't allowed).

How BGP Selects Routes

To be able to survive network outages, most networks running BGP connect to more than one other network. This means that many destinations are reachable over two or even more BGP neighbors as long as there is no outage. Thus, BGP needs a mechanism to select the best route from the set of available routes from different neighbors. For this purpose, there are several attributes that are communicated from one

BGP speaker to the next, and each attribute may or may not have an impact on the route-selection process. The most important of these attributes are:

Local Preference

> The Local Preference is a value local to an AS communicated over intra-AS BGP sessions. BGP always prefers the route with the highest Local Preference. By default, Cisco routers use a Local Preference of 100 for all routes.

AS path

> The AS path lists all the AS numbers between the local router and the source of the route. This includes the source AS number for nonlocal routes but not the local AS number. The path is used for several things. First, it prevents routing loops: a router ignores any routes it receives from a router in a neighboring AS that contains its own AS number. Second, the path enables the router to make policy decisions based on the presence of certain ASes in the path. Finally, routes with a shorter AS path are preferred over routes with a longer AS path.

Next hop

> The next hop attribute contains the IP address of the router within the remote AS that will accept packets for the current route.

Multi Exit Discriminator

> In older BGP versions, this value was called "Inter AS Metric," and it still shows up as "metric" in some places. The Multi Exit Discriminator (MED) was designed to give a neighboring AS hints about which connection is preferred when there are multiple connections between ASes, but it's often possible to configure the router to compare MEDs between routes received from different ASes. The MED is used late in the route selection process: it's the first tie-breaker when routes are otherwise equal. The route with the lowest Multi Exit Discriminator metric is preferred.

Origin

> This attribute conveys the source of the BGP announcement: an IGP, the EGP protocol, or other means (incomplete). Although this is a mandatory attribute, it doesn't really perform any function in practice.

Communities

> A route may contain one or more communities. A community is a 32-bit value, often expressed in a form such as 701:120, where 701 is an AS number and 120 is a value that has meaning within AS 701. Communities aren't directly used in the route selection process, but they may trigger user-defined actions.

Some attributes behave differently over BGP sessions with other routers within the same AS (internal BGP or iBGP) rather than over BGP sessions with routers in other ASes (external BGP or eBGP). For instance, the Local Preference attribute is communicated only over iBGP, and the next hop and MED attributes aren't updated when transmitted over iBGP.

This is what RFC 1771, "A Border Gateway Protocol 4 (BGP-4)," has to say about selecting the best route from those received from external BGP peers:

> If the route is learned from a BGP speaker in a neighboring autonomous system, then the degree of preference shall be computed based on preconfigured policy information. The exact nature of this policy information and the computation involved is a local matter.

In other words, this is for the network administrator to decide, within the limits imposed by the router vendors.

The route-selection algorithm

In practice, router vendors have decided against implementing a user-defined route-evaluation procedure as outlined in the RFC. They generally implement a decision-making algorithm with several steps, each step taking one or more variables into account. They then provide the user with mechanisms to modify these variables. The general BGP route-selection algorithm, ignoring any possible extra steps a vendor may have included, boils down to this:

- Apply user-configured policies to adjust variables.
- Select the route with the highest Local Preference.
- Select the route with the shortest AS path.
- Select the route with the lowest MED metric, if the routes were received from the same AS or if the router is configured always to compare MEDs.
- Apply the remaining tie-breaking rules.

Cisco routers apply several additional steps throughout the route selection process, but usually these don't change the outcome of the algorithm:

- Before looking at the Local Preference, the router considers the weight of a route. Weight is a Cisco-specific attribute local to a router. By default, locally sourced routes have a weight of 32768, and other routes have a weight of 0. The routes with the highest weight are used.
- Before looking at the AS path, the router first selects locally sourced routes.
- Before looking at the MED, the router considers the origin attribute. Routes with origin IGP are preferred over origin EGP, and both are preferred over an incomplete origin.
- Depending on the IOS version, there are several settings that influence the route-selection process. See the Cisco documentation for more information.

There is no requirement that all routers within an AS agree on how to select the best route. It isn't uncommon for two border routers both to think their link to an external AS is the best route for a certain destination. (If both routes are otherwise equal, it's even standard behavior for each router to select its own exterior route as best.) Thus, packets that arrive at router A will be routed over ISP 1, and packets that arrive at router B, over ISP 2. This isn't a problem, and it may even be desirable in ASes that span large geographic areas.

BGP tie-breaking rules

When the AS path is the same length, several tie-breaking rules are applied, assuming the networks don't have any policies in place to explicitly prefer one route over another. Here are the tie-breaking rules listed in RFC 1771:

1. Select the route with the lowest MED metric from the routes received from a single AS.
2. Select the route with the lowest cost or metric for the next hop address in the interior routing protocol.
3. Select the route advertised by the external BGP peer with the lowest IP address as its BGP identifier.
4. Select the route advertised by the internal BGP peer with the lowest IP address as its BGP identifier.

The tie-breaking process starts with all possible valid routes that are considered equally preferable by the regular BGP route-selection process. Each tie-breaking rule selects the best route. If only a single route remains, this route is selected. The next rule is applied only when two or more routes are considered "best" by the rule.

Often the AS path for two routes is the same length, and there is no specific policy in place to prefer one route over the other. The first tie-breaker is the MED, but MEDs aren't always present. If they are, they are compared only if both routers are received from the same AS or if the router is configured to always compare MEDs. The next tie-breaker is the IGP metric for the next hop address. This one doesn't always help much either, because this metric will be the same for all routes learned in the same location. So, the IP address of the neighboring BGP router can make all the difference. It's possible for one ISP to have consistently lower addresses for its routers than another, so that most networks that peer with both ISPs send their traffic to one ISP. This is usually not the case, and traffic is reasonably balanced.

Multiprotocol BGP

To enable use of BGP with protocols other than just IPv4, RFC 2858 describes a way to encode reachability information for different address families in two new optional nontransitive path attributes. This makes it possible to encode routing information for different address families in BGP-4 without breaking compatibility with older implementations. (However, I can't think of any reason to send a router reachability information for a protocol it doesn't support in the first place.) Table 2-5 shows the first new attribute, MP_REACH_NLRI.

Table 2-5. The MP_REACH_NLRI attribute

AFI	SAFI	NH len	Next hop	SNPAs	SNPA	NLRI
2 bytes	1 byte	1 byte	variable	1 byte	variable	variable

The Address Family Identifier (AFI) does just what it's name suggests. Note the subtle distinction between addresses and protocols, which isn't important for IP and similar protocols, but the multiprotocol extensions can also be used to carry different address families, such as E.164 (phone numbers), which aren't tied to a specific protocol. The Subsequent Address Family Identifier (SAFI) indicates the kind of addresses relative to the AFI. In IPv4 and IPv6, this is used to distinguish among routing information for unicast, multicast, or both.

The next hop field holds the network layer address for the next hop and is preceded by a length field ("NH len"). The next hop address in the format of the specified address family may not be enough information to forward packets or set up connections successfully, so there is also room for Sub-Network Point of Attachment (SNPA) information: in non-OSI terms, one or more MAC addresses for the next hop. The SNPAs field holds the number of SNPAs, and each SNPA is encoded in a somewhat perverted prefix format: rather than counting bits or bytes, the length field with the SNPA is in "semi-octet" (4-bit) units.

The NLRI is in regular prefix format for the IPv4 and IPv6 unicast, multicast, and unicast plus multicast SAFIs. Table 2-6 shows the second new attribute, MP_UNREACH_ NLRI.

Table 2-6. The MP_UNREACH_NLRI attribute

AFI	SAFI	Withdrawn routes
2 bytes	1 byte	Variable

The format of the AFI and SAFI fields is the same as that for the MP_REACH_NLRI attribute, and the withdrawn routes field also uses the same NLRI format for the now unreachable routes.

Multiprotocol extended BGP is often referred to as Multiprotocol BGP (MBGP) or BGP4+ (but not BGP-4+). The new path attributes are defined in such a general way that they can encode addresses for every imaginable protocol and for regular unicast routing, multicast routing, or both. Because using MBGP for IPv4 unicast routing is somewhat redundant, it's used mostly for IPv4 multicast and IPv6 unicast routing.

Routing Multicast

Most information transmitted over a network is relevant only to one destination system. For instance, if a user requests a page from a web server, this page should go only to the user's system, not to any other hosts, which have no use for it. In theory, some information is relevant to everyone. To avoid having to send it to all interested parties individually, a system may simply broadcast it, but this only works in theory. For example, RIP periodically broadcasts the routing table, but only a few hosts are listening to these broadcasts. With multicast, packets are still delivered to multiple destination hosts but, unlike broadcasts, only to those hosts that are actually interested in them. To do this, all multicasts are sent to special multicast or "group" addresses. In IPv4, these are the Class D addresses in the 224.0.0.0/4 range.

At the LAN level, multicasts are well understood and in widespread use. For instance, OSPF uses multicasts for neighbor discovery and link-state flooding, and IPv6 uses multicasts exclusively for all discovery functions. Things are different at the application level. The applications themselves aren't really the problem: live audio and video streaming are, by their nature, excellent candidates for running over multicast, and both client and server applications have been available for years. Providing an interdomain multicast service at the network layer isn't an easy thing to do, however. There are two major problems to overcome: the multicast packets must be flooded through the network in a controlled manner so that there are no loops, and mechanisms must be in place both to extend flooding of groups to new places as soon as the first client there joins the group and to stop when all clients have left. Before the implementation of protocols that did this in a reasonably efficient and scalable way, there was an experimental multicast network tunneled in regular unicast packets: the MBone. There are now several protocols that address all the necessary functions for multicast routing: Multiprotocol BGP, Protocol Independent Multicast (PIM), and Multicast Source Discovery Protocol (MSDP).

It's interesting to note MBGP doesn't actually carry the multicast group (destination) addresses when used for multicast routing. MBGP is mainly used to transport routing information about the *source* addresses from which multicast traffic may stem; these addresses are regular unicast addresses from the Class A/B/C address space. If this seems redundant, it is: these same source addresses are announced as destination addresses by regular unicast BGP routing. Distributing alternative reachability information for multicast purposes makes it possible to have separate infrastructures for unicast and multicast, which is sometimes useful.

The source address information in MBGP is used to perform a reverse path forwarding (RPF) check. If a multicast packet comes in over the interface the router itself uses to transmit a packet to the source, the packet is considered valid and is forwarded on all other interfaces where the multicast group is active. If the packet is received over a different interface, the RPF check fails, and the packet is dropped. In combination with additional prune mechanisms, this check makes sure that multicast packets are forwarded along a virtual tree, so that there are no loops, and each router forwards every packet only once.

In contrast, another protocol, the Border Gateway Multicast Protocol (BGMP), does indeed carry multicast destinations, and it also requires MBGP to carry them as source addresses. BGMP usually creates only a single forwarding tree for each multicast destination address range. Interior multicast routing protocols, on the other hand, maintain trees for all source/destination combinations that don't scale to interdomain sizes. Using a single tree has the disadvantage that packets sourced at a remote branch must travel all the way up the tree until they reach the root (remember, mathematicians hang their trees upside down) and then travel down over other branches. When the multicast source is located at the root of the group distribution tree, however, the packets tend to take the shortest possible path. Also, BGMP uses bidirectional trees: when two branches join, the packet is sent both up, towards the root, and down the other branch. Thus, neighboring networks should enjoy good multicast performance, regardless of their shared connection to the root.

The BGMP protocol structure is heavily influenced by BGP, but the functionality is fundamentally different, so the protocols aren't very similar.

IPv6

In the early 1990s, it became apparent that the 32-bit IP address space would be too limited to provide addresses for every system connected to the Net in the foreseeable future: about an eighth of the available address space was in use by 1990, and this number doubled every five years. At that rate, there wouldn't be any IP addresses left in 2005. The address-depletion problem was the main reason for development of a new version of the IP protocol: IP Version 6 (IPv6, RFC 2460).* IPv6 uses huge 128-bit addresses, so even the tiniest networks can have a thousand billion times more hosts than a current IPv4 Class A network. However, the stringent address-conservation policies in place since the mid-1990s have left enough IPv4 addresses available for most applications, so IPv6 hasn't yet been widely deployed, except in Korea and Japan. The Regional Internet Registries responsible for giving out IP address space have been giving out smaller blocks to new ISPs for further assignment to their customers, and they require a better utilization of the previously assigned address space before assigning more. This makes it more difficult to get IP addresses in large numbers, with the result that many organizations use Network Address Translation (NAT) to enable many hosts to share a single IP address.

It's expected that the next generation of "always on" wireless devices will be the first large-scale application of IPv6. To give every cellular phone and mobile computing device a permanent connection to the Internet over IPv4 would tax the remaining IPv4 address space too much.

Figure 2-1 shows the IPv6 header.

The main and most obvious differences between IPv4 and IPv6 are the addresses: IPv6 addresses are four times as big as IPv4 addresses. The addresses aren't the only

---

* IP Version 5 was used for a non-IP protocol.

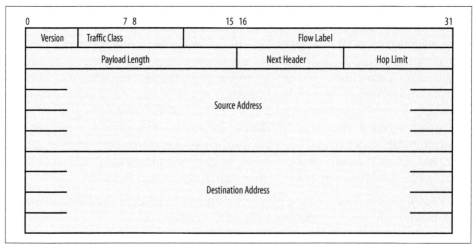

0	7 8	15 16		31
Version	Traffic Class	Flow Label		
Payload Length		Next Header	Hop Limit	
Source Address				
Destination Address				

Figure 2-1. The IPv6 header

things changed in IPv6, however. The header checksum has been removed to allow faster processing; both lower and higher layers provide their own checksums anyway. Support for fragmentation by routers has been removed: if necessary, packets must be fragmented at the source. Alternatively, hosts can limit themselves to sending packets of 1280 bytes or less. The Protocol field is now known as Next Header and the Time to Live field as Hop Limit. The Payload Length field serves the same purpose as the Total Length field in IPv4, but it holds the length of the payload rather than that of the entire IP packet, which also saves some processing. The Flow Label field is new and may be used to optimize the processing of "flows" between two hosts.

IPv6 addresses are written in a new way: instead of four period-separated decimal numbers in the range 0 to 255, there are now eight colon-separated hexadecimal numbers in the range 0 to FFFF. A typical IPv6 address looks like this:

    3ffe:2500:3a10:1:201:2ff:fe29:2640

You may also encounter much shorter IPv6 addresses:

    3ffe:2500:3a10:2::1

The empty space between two consecutive colons is assumed to contain the right number of 0 values to fill up the address to its full length. Only one two-colon sequence per address is allowed. If you're going to do anything with IPv6, it's a good idea to read RFC 2373, "IPv6 Addressing Architecture." This is a complex topic in IPv6: there are many different kinds of IPv6 addresses and special address ranges, and IPv6 makes extensive use of multicasts rather than broadcasts. ARP has also gone the way of the dinosaurs, replaced by the ICMP-based and more general Neighbor Discovery Protocol (NDP). NDP discovers not only MAC addresses for neighbors, but also default routers, link MTUs, and subnet address prefixes. Hosts can construct their own address by combining such a prefix, advertised by a router, with a unique identifier, usually their Ethernet MAC address. Alternatively, routers can tell hosts to use DHCPv6 to obtain their IPv6 address, and it is, of course, still possible to manually configure an address.*

Unlike multicast routing, routing IPv6 works exactly the same way as routing unicast IPv4, with the obvious changes to routing protocols to accommodate the larger addresses.

MBGP and MPLS VPNs

Another use of MBGP is to convey Virtual Private Network (VPN) reachability information across Multiprotocol Label Switching (MPLS) backbones. MPLS is a generic mechanism to do switching over a multitude of lower-layer infrastructures. It borrows from Ethernet VLANs and ATM. Each packet is assigned one or more labels before it enters the MPLS backbone. As long as the packet resides in the backbone and has labels, it's forwarded in accordance with its first label. The network-layer destination address is ignored during this phase. Each MPLS switch replaces the existing label with a new one, just as ATM changes VPI/VCI information in the cell header at each hop. Unlike frame relay or ATM, MPLS doesn't come with its own layer 2 protocol, but it can be used with existing datalink-layer protocols. It even takes advantage of existing labels, such as Ethernet VLAN tags or ATM VCIs.

The original goal of MPLS and its predecessors was to improve packet-forwarding performance. But today's routers are capable of IP forwarding at wire speed for OC-192 (10 Gbps) links, so performance isn't as much an issue as it used to be. (It never hurts to obtain the same speed using cheaper hardware, of course.) However, MPLS has another important advantage: it hides the network layer while retaining the internetworking function, so it's still possible to use different underlying datalink-layer protocols. This enables MPLS to transport different protocols and different instances of the same protocol over a network that isn't end-to-end switched at the datalink layer. For instance, two smaller ISPs could use MPLS service from a larger ISP or from a telco to connect to an exchange point. Any traffic sent from one ISP to the other would first be transported to the exchange point over the MPLS network. The first ISP would forward it to the second using standard peering mechanisms, and the second ISP would use the MPLS network again to transport the traffic back to their own network. It would be impossible to do this using regular IP transit service, because the service-provider network would immediately route the packets to the other ISP, bypassing the exchange point and making it impossible for the two small ISPs to implement the desired peering policies. It would certainly be no problem to deliver the same service using ATM, but this would require the service provider to

---

* For a detailed treatment of IPv6 operation, read *IPv6 Essentials* by Silvia Hagen (O'Reilly & Associates).

operate an end-to-end ATM network. With MPLS, it's possible to combine several datalink technologies (for instance, Gigabit Ethernet, ATM, and Packet over SONET) and still be able to deliver an end-to-end switched service.

When MPLS is used to interconnect different parts of a company network, the company is the proud owner of a VPN. Unlike with frame relay or ATM, where the customer/service provider interface is at the datalink layer, MPLS VPN customers send regular IP packets to the service-provider equipment. The service provider then uses a per-VPN routing table to forward the packet. This is where BGP comes in: the routes for all those routing tables are carried in MBGP. RFC 2547 introduces the "VPN-IPv4" address family for this purpose. The VPN-IPv4 address family adds eight extra bytes to the regular IPv4 address to distinguish routes from different VPNs, even if the destination address prefixes are otherwise identical. This allows the use of the same address range in more than one VPN.

Interior Routing Protocols

There is no requirement for networks running BGP to have an IGP as well. Simple multihomed networks with two routers run just fine without an IGP: a few static routes are all that's needed, because all traffic goes to a directly connected network, to the rest of the world, or to the other router. For larger networks, IGPs are a fact of life. Your only choice for an EGP is BGP-4, but IGPs let you use any interior routing protocol you desire. On a Cisco router, you have the following choices: RIP, IGRP, EIGRP, OSPF, and IS-IS.

RIP

The Routing Information Protocol (RIP) is a simple distance-vector routing protocol. It listens for routing updates from other routers and installs new routes into the local routing table, and it transmits the contents of the routing table every 30 seconds for the benefit of other routers. The metric is a simple hop count with a maximum of 15 hops. RIP is very old, but because it's so simple, it's still the most widely implemented routing protocol. All regular routers support it, but equipment such as terminal servers and many hosts can also do RIP.

RIP is completely unsuitable for applications in which routers must quickly adapt to changes in link status, because it can take several minutes for reachability and (especially) unreachability information to converge throughout the network. RIP can still be useful, however, to convey some limited routing information (such as a default route) to RIP-aware systems that would otherwise need to depend on a static default route.

The original RIP doesn't support VLSM, but RIPv2 can handle different subnet masks within a single classful network. *RIPng* ("next generation") is available for use with IPv6.

IGRP and EIGRP

The Interior Gateway Routing Protocol (IGRP) is a Cisco-proprietary distance-vector protocol. It doesn't support VLSM. Enhanced IGRP (EIGRP) is just what the name says: an enhanced version of IGRP, which does support VLSM. Cisco's goal was to create a routing protocol without the traditional distance-vector limitations, such as slow convergence, but also without the complexity of link-state protocols. They did a reasonably good job, but because EIGRP is available only on Cisco routers, it isn't widely adopted within the IP world, where open standards are appreciated.

OSPF

Open Shortest Path First (OSPF) is a typical link-state protocol, and as such harbors a lot of complexity. OSPF sends out multicast packets on all active interfaces to discover neighbors. A Designated Router and a Backup Designated Router are then selected for every subnet. All other routers on this subnet forward any link state changes to the Designated Router, which in turn redistributes them to all other routers on the subnet. As soon as all the routers have been notified of the current state of the network, each router executes the SPF algorithm to calculate the best route for each destination and installs those routes into the routing table. Because all routers are aware of the state of all links in the network and all use the same algorithm, all the routers agree on the path packets should take through the network, and there aren't any loops.

OSPF was designed by the Internet Engineering Task Force (IETF) to be "the" routing protocol for IP. It supports VLSM, converges quickly, and is available on routers from nearly all router vendors. An IPv6 version of OSPF is in the works.

IS-IS

"Intermediate System to Intermediate System" is the IGP for the OSI Connectionless Network Service (CLNS). It has been extended to support IP also. There are many similarities between OSPF and IS-IS, not just because they are both link-state routing protocols, but also because OSPF was heavily influenced by IS-IS. Network administrators running large networks generally prefer IS-IS over OSPF, but for small- to medium-sized networks, there are no major advantages in using IS-IS rather than OSPF. IS-IS isn't simple to set up because of its OSI inheritance, and it isn't as widely available as OSPF.

Interaction Between Routing Protocols

Each routing protocol has its own way of selecting the best route if multiple routes are available. In RIP, the rule is that the route with the lowest hop count wins: a route over four other routers is superior to one over six hops. OSPF is a bit smarter and assigns a cost value to each connection. This cost is usually derived from the bandwidth of the connection. The total costs of all connections in a path is compared for all paths, and the path with the lowest cost wins. BGP uses a more complex selection algorithm, as we've seen earlier in this chapter. But what happens when there are routes to a destination in more than one routing protocol?

To be able to select the best route from all protocols, the Cisco Internetworking Operating System (IOS) assigns an administrative distance value to every route. When there is more than one route for a destination, the prefix with the lowest distance is used for packet forwarding, if the prefixes are the same size. When prefixes aren't the same size, the *longest match first* rule kicks in, regardless of the administrative distance, and the most specific route (the one with the longest prefix, covering the smallest range of destination addresses) is used for forwarding. Table 2-7 lists the default distances for different routing protocols.

Table 2-7. Routing protocols administrative distance

Routing protocol	Administrative distance
Directly connected	0
Static	1
External BGP	20
Internal EIGRP	90
IGRP	100
OSPF	110
IS-IS	115
RIP	120
External EIGRP	170
Internal BGP	200

To make things more complicated, it's also possible to redistribute routes from one protocol into another. This is necessary when different routing protocols are used in different parts of the network. For instance, OSPF and IS-IS are superior to RIP, but they're generally not available on hosts; RIP is usually the only available routing protocol, if any. Thus, it can be useful to redistribute some routes from OSPF or IS-IS into RIP so that hosts can send traffic for different destinations to different routers, instead of relying on just a default route. A similar situation happens when not all routers are capable of running BGP. If the non-BGP routers need to have access to information learned from BGP, it may be necessary to redistribute BGP routes into an interior routing protocol.

Redistributing routes from exterior protocols into interior protocols and from smart interior protocols (OSPF, IS-IS) into less sophisticated protocols (RIP) should not be a problem, if done with care. Redistributing routes from dumb to smart or from interior to exterior protocols can lead to complex problems, however. Redistributing routes from one protocol into another and back again is extremely dangerous and should be avoided.

It may also be necessary to redistribute interior routes into BGP. This is discussed later in the book.

CHAPTER 3

Physical Design Considerations

"The OC-3 circuit is online again. The telco reports
nettles had grown into the A/C exhaust."

This chapter deals with the costly parts of the network: the physical properties, such as hardware, locations, and topology, and with ISPs and bandwidth.

Availability

There is a lot of theory about network reliability. If you are building a network that has to conform to a specific uptime figure, it's a good idea to spend some time reading up on this. You'll learn how to calculate availability figures for your network using known Mean Time Between Failures (MTBF) and Mean Time To Repair (MTTR) values for your equipment. For a single component, the availability is just the MTTR as a percentage of the MTTR plus the MTBF:

$$\text{availability} = \frac{\text{MTBF}}{\text{MTBF} + \text{MTTR}}$$

A component with a 100,000-hour MTBF (more than 11 years between failures) and an eight-hour MTTR has an availability of 99.992%, statistically. The easiest way to increase this figure is by buying equipment that runs longer before it fails (higher MTBF value) and takes less time to repair or be replaced by a spare (lower MTTR value).

Calculating availability becomes more complex as the number of components increases, but it basically boils down to this: as you add more components that must all be "up" for your network to function, your availability figure drops accordingly. To get the availability for the system as a whole, multiply the availability figures for all components. You can get around the decreasing availability as you add components by having two or more interchangeable components to perform a certain function, so that one of them can fail without impact. This is shown in Figure 3-1. On the left, the figure shows three components, with the middle one decreasing the total availability significantly. On the right, the function of the middle component is performed by two components to get better availability.

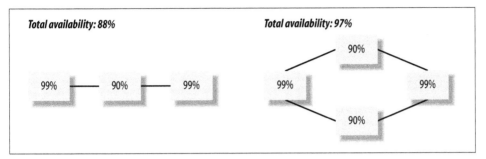

Figure 3-1. Availability figures for different designs

In the design on the right in Figure 3-1, either the left or right component or both middle components have to fail before there is an outage. The two components with 90% availability together function as a single component with 99% availability.

 For connectivity to the Internet, availability calculations don't mean much, because you have to rely on suppliers (the power company, telcos, and ISPs) with largely unknown availability figures. And there are a lot of backhoes out there.

Single points of failure

The simplest way to increase the availability of your Internet connectivity is by eliminating all single points of failure. Assuming every cluster of related components, such as a router, telco connection, and ISP, has a modest availability of at least 99% (which means it's out of order for 3.6 days every year); making sure that there isn't a single component that can bring down the entire network will buy you an availability figure of 99.99%: the network will be down 52 minutes a year. It's hard to do much better without spending a lot of time, effort, and money.

Common sense

As human beings, we are prone to doing stupid things. Some of us are more prone than others, but as a rule, we all do things we know we shouldn't from time to time. Did you ever put a cup of coffee on the edge of a desk, thinking, "I'm not going to knock it over," but then spill it later anyway? I certainly have, and I don't even drink coffee often. The moral of this story is simple: when we do something stupid, we usually know it but rationalize the decision. Don't. And don't do it the wrong way first with the intention to fix it later. Doing it right immediately isn't that much harder, and it keeps the carpeting an even color.

Testing

It's always a good idea to test new equipment, software images, and configurations before exposing the production network to them. In a test setup, you can try all kinds of interesting, dangerous, and even stupid things and see if what you think is true really holds up.

Selecting ISPs

Good ISPs are essential for a reliable connection to the Internet. Not so much because an ISP network should never fail: it shouldn't, but multihoming protects you against problems when this happens. What really matters is whether an ISP is reachable and willing to work with you when there is a problem. The traits that separate the good ISPs from the mediocre and bad are:

- Knowledgeable staff
- Willingness to accept unusual but reasonable BGP address announcements
- Good reachability by email and phone. They should work with you when there is a (distributed) denial-of-service attack.
- Good "Internet citizenship." A good ISP doesn't pollute the Net and discourages others from doing so. Specifically, it filters out packets with spoofed source addresses wherever possible.

 When selecting a second ISP, make sure they don't depend on the same single upstream ISP that your first ISP does.

There are, of course, other minor details, such as an extensive network, good peering, sufficient bandwidth, and price. You may also want to consider the stability of the companies you do business with. Later in the book, there are more in-depth discussions on the cooperation you are likely to need from your ISPs.

 Some ISPs offer Service Level Agreement (SLA) guarantees. This usually means you get some money back when the network performance or uptime isn't what it should be. But don't be too impressed with this: just because a network offers a guarantee, it doesn't mean it can actually deliver the guaranteed service level.

The best way to evaluate an ISP is by talking to their customers, especially a customer with needs similar to your own.

Bandwidth

Bandwidth is the amount of data that can traverse a communication channel per unit of time. On digital circuits, we measure bandwidth in bits per second (bps). When talking about computer memory, a kilobit is 1024 bits, but a "kilobit per second" (Kbps) is 1000 bits per second, or 125 bytes per second. Mbps is 1 million bits (122 KB) per second, and Gbps is 1 billion bits (119 MB) per second. Bandwidth doesn't say much about the actual *speed* of a connection: a 45-Mbps satellite channel has exactly the same bandwidth as an earthbound T3 circuit, but it takes the bits about 120 milliseconds to travel the 45,000 miles to the satellite and back to Earth. This could take as little as a few hundred microseconds for a short terrestrial T3 line. So, when you read "speed" you should think "bandwidth."

Figuring out how much bandwidth to buy isn't usually too much of a problem when you're single-homed. If you aren't yet connected to the Net, anything will be a vast improvement, even if the connection isn't as fast as you'd like. When you are already connected, the decision to upgrade (or downgrade) your bandwidth or to keep things as they are is mostly a matter of weighing the number of complaints about speed against the costs. Determining the necessary bandwidth this way works well in many cases, but it's hardly scientific. More importantly, it won't work for a second line unless you are prepared to bring down the first line to evaluate the speed of the second.

To determine required bandwidth, it's necessary to translate a user experience into numbers. A user doesn't care how many milliseconds it takes a packet to travel from one end of the continent to another; she just wants web pages, email, and files to load quickly. Every one of these applications uses *transactions*: the user starts something, the remote server responds, and data is transferred. From a network-centric viewpoint, only the last stage of the transaction, the transfer of data, is of any interest, but a responsive DNS that doesn't delay the initial connection and a server that can handle user requests fast enough are also essential. It's important to get good values for both the number of transactions and their size. For web servers (and many other types of servers), this information is available in the log file. You can analyze the log file yourself, but a lot of software is also available to do this.

Minimum Bandwidth Required

When you add up the number of bytes that come in and go out every five minutes, every hour, or every day, and convert this to a Kbps figure, this will often seem unbelievably low. Even a 33.6-Kbps dial-up connection is capable of transferring over 300 MB a day in each direction. Thus, it's best to look at the busiest hour of the day. For instance, 200 MB on the busiest hour of the day translates to 209,715,200 bytes in 3600 seconds, or 58,254 bytes per second. At 8 bits per byte and 1000 bits per kilobit, that's 466 Kbps. This is the minimum bandwidth you need. Without it, you're not going to transmit that 200 MB within an hour. In frame relay terms, this is your committed access rate: the amount of bandwidth the network reserves exclusively for you.

There are, of course, many caveats, such as packets getting lost somewhere on the Net, so that they need to be resent and cost you extra bandwidth, but because this isn't an article for an engineering publication, I'm not going to dwell on these issues.

Burst Bandwidth and Queuing Delays

You probably need more bandwidth than 466 Kbps, however. For instance, let's assume this 200 MB is made up of the traffic of 200 users all downloading a 1-MB file, and none of them wants to wait longer than 6 seconds before their download is complete. At 466 Kbps, 1 MB takes 18 seconds, so the solution would appear to be getting three times the bandwidth, 1398 Kbps, to make the downloads three times as fast. In the real world, this would be a 1544-Kbps T1 line. This 1398 or 1544 Kbps is your *burst* bandwidth, excess burst rate (EBR) in frame relay terms. It's also common to express the burst capacity in bytes: in this case, you would want to download a megabyte at the maximum speed, so your burst size would be 1 MB.

At 1544 Kbps, a 1-MB download takes only 5.43 seconds, and downloads are started at an average of 1 every 18 seconds, so this should work out fine. Unfortunately, users aren't in the habit of coordinating their downloads for optimal efficiency, so it's possible that two or even more of them may want to download a file at the same time. When this happens, the download will take longer than the permitted 6 seconds. This can cause problems even if you were careful enough not to guarantee a *maximum* but only an *average* download time of 6 seconds. Queuing theory provides us with a simple formula to calculate the average number of seconds a transaction takes to complete from the average numbers of transactions that are requested and completed in a second:[*]

$$\text{transaction time} = \frac{1}{\text{completed} - \text{requested}}$$

So with 1 / 18 = 0.056 transactions requested per second and 1 / 5.43 = 0.184 transactions completed per second, the average time it takes to download a 1-MB file is 1 / (0.184 - 0.056) = 7.8 seconds. You should increase your burst bandwidth and repeat the calculation until you arrive at an average transaction time that is acceptable.

---

[*] This assumes an exponential distribution of both the requested and completed transactions. This is a reasonable assumption for networks with many concurrent users and/or sessions. See *Computer Networks* by Andrew S. Tanenbaum (Prentice Hall, Inc.) for an introduction into queuing theory.

The usual pricing for bandwidth is based either on the port speed or some percentile of the actual utilization measurements. If you pay for the port speed, either you don't get to burst or you pay for bandwidth that's unused most of the time. Percentile pricing is a better deal. For instance, if you pay for the 95th percentile, you get to burst 5% of the time, and really short bursts don't count because the line utilization is usually measured over 5 minute periods.

A percentage deal is potentially dangerous, because you can't fully control how much traffic others send to you. If you ever experience much more traffic than usual (either legitimate traffic or an attack of some sort), you'll have to pay extra.

Calculating Bandwidth, Step by Step

If you would like to get a better understanding of your bandwidth requirements, it's worth the effort to go through the necessary calculations. Unless your network traffic is extremely predictable, there will probably be some difference between the result of these calculations and real-world performance. But if there is a potential bottleneck, it will quite likely show up after going through these steps:

1. Determine the number and type of "transactions" per hour on the busiest hour of the day. A transaction can be anything: sending or receiving an email message, transmitting or receiving a web page, serving a video stream, and so on. For example, you may receive 35 emails and serve 200 web pages on the busiest hour of the day.

2. Determine the average number of bytes transferred per transaction for every type in each direction. Don't forget the protocol overhead: protocols such as SMTP (mail) and HTTP (Web) add about 10% plus 250 bytes per transaction in each direction in overhead. Also, protocols that send data in one direction also send acknowledgments in the other direction, so add another 5% to the opposite direction.

   For instance, receiving a 20-KB email message uses about 20,480 bytes + 10% of 20,480 bytes + 250 = 22,778 bytes incoming, and it uses 5% of 22,778 + 250 = 1389 bytes outgoing.

   Sending a 50-KB web document over HTTP uses 51,200 + 10% of 51,200 + 250 = 56,570 bytes out and 5% of 56,570 + 250 = 3079 bytes in.

3. Multiply the number of transactions for every type by the averages for that type. Add the totals for each transaction type to get the total incoming and outgoing number of bytes per hour. In our example:

   Mail: 35 * 22,778 = 797,230 in, 35 * 1389 = 48,615 out
   Web: 200 * 3079 = 615,800 in, 200 * 56,570 = 11,314,000 out
   Total in: 797,230 + 615,800 = 1,413,030 bytes per hour
   Total out: 48,615 + 11,314,000 = 11,362,615 bytes per hour

4. Determine the number of requested transactions per second by adding up the number of transactions of each type and dividing by 3600.

> Total transactions: 35 email + 200 web = 235
> 235 / 3600 = 0.065 requested transactions per second

5. Determine the average transaction size by taking the maximum of the total in and the total out and dividing it by the number of transactions per hour.

> Maximum of 1,413,030 and 11,362,615 is 11,362,615
> 11,362,615 / 235 = 48,351

6. Divide the results for incoming and outgoing traffic by 3600 to get bytes per second; multiply by 8 and divide by 1000 to get Kbps. This is the minimum bandwidth you need to transfer all your data, or the committed access rate (CAR) in frame relay terms.

> Total in: 1,413,030 / 3600 * 8 / 1000 = 3.1 Kbps
> Total out: 11,362,615 / 3600 * 8 / 1000 = 25.3 Kbps

7. Select one or more line speeds that are higher than the highest of the totals for input and output.

> Highest of 3.1 and 25.3 is 25.3. Possible line speeds are 56-Kbps leased line or 128-Kbps fractional T1 service.

8. Multiply the line speed by 1000 and divide by 8 to get the number of bytes per second and divide by the average transaction size to get the number of transactions the line can complete per second. (Values below 1 mean it takes more than 1 second to complete a transaction.) Do this for every line speed.

> 56 * 1000 / 8 = 7000, 7000 / 48,351 = 0.14 completed transactions per second
> 128 * 1000 / 8 = 16,000, 16,000 / 48,351 = 0.33 completed transactions per second

- Divide the number 1 by the difference between the number of completed transactions and the number of requested transactions per second. This is the average time it takes to complete a transaction.

> For 56 Kbps: 0.14 - 0.065 = 0.075, 1 / 0.075 = 13.3 seconds per transaction
> For 128 Kbps: 0.33 - 0.065 = 0.265, 1 / 0.265 = 3.8 seconds per transaction

You'll find an online tool to do these calculations at *http://www.bgpexpert.com/bandwidth.php*.

If you have multiple connections to the Net, you should perform the calculation for the total bandwidth and for each of the lines individually, to get an idea of the slowdown you'll experience when a connection fails.

Because users adapt their network use to the perceived speed, predicting how your network will react to changes in available bandwidth is never an exact science. Generally, the network will function better than expected under low-bandwidth conditions and somewhat worse than expected under higher-bandwidth conditions. This means that even if all the transaction time calculations come up with "infinity" (a negative number of seconds per transaction), the network may still be reasonably usable. For instance, if your normal bandwidth requirements are 2 Mbps, and you're doing the calculations for the situation where the failure of one of your two T1s leaves you with just 1.5 Mbps, you'll end up with a negative transaction time. In practice, however, 2 Mbps of bandwidth required with 1.5 Mbps available is workable. In my experience, falling back to 75–100% of the regularly used bandwidth doesn't lead to many complaints, if the difference is noticeable at all. Between 50% and 75%, the network is noticeably slower. Below 50%, the sluggishness becomes annoying, and below 25%, the network is virtually unusable.

First rule of thumb: a reasonable trade-off between wasting bandwidth and having a slow network when one line is down is having two connections that can each handle two-thirds of your average bandwidth use.

Second rule of thumb: a backup of less than 25% of your average bandwidth is of little or no use, unless you use it to allow certain types of traffic (email) to continue even if others (Web) are too slow to be usable.

Router Hardware

When you have decided on the amount of bandwidth you need and the kind of connections to deliver this bandwidth, it's time to go router shopping. Routers share a lot of technology but little economy with regular computers. There are still routers sold that are based on early 1990s technology: it's expensive to design new models, so it's more cost-effective to keep building older models and sell them for a lower price. The most important differences between routers are:

Architecture
  Smaller routers use a single CPU for both packet forwarding and route processing. Some routers use Symmetric Multiprocessing (SMP), in which several CPUs share the route-processing and forwarding functions. Another approach is to distribute these functions over a dedicated CPU for route processing and other CPUs or ASICs (special-purpose chips) that handle forwarding traffic from one or more interfaces each.

Redundancy features
  Many routers have room for redundant power supplies. Some even have room for a second CPU board that kicks in when the first CPU fails due to hardware or software problems. Another important feature is hot swapping. This means that interface cards can be inserted and removed from the chassis without powering down or rebooting the router.

Interfaces

Some smaller routers have a fixed configuration. Most routers can handle a variety of interface cards, but it takes at least a mid-grade model to connect to higher bandwidth connections such as T3 or E3 and OC-3. Only high-end routers can handle Gigabit Ethernet or OC-12 and faster interfaces.

Forwarding speed

Even if high-speed interfaces are available for a router, it doesn't mean the router can fill up all the available bandwidth. This is especially true for LAN interfaces: Fast Ethernet can handle more than 100,000 packets a second in each direction, but the same isn't true for every router that has a Fast Ethernet interface.

Route processing and memory limitations

CPU and memory limitations are important considerations when running BGP with full routing, especially with full routing from multiple BGP peers. A distributed design with separate processors for forwarding and route processing is at an advantage when forwarding packets and processing route information at the same time, but single-processor routers are generally faster when the BGP table is first initialized and no packets are forwarded yet.

Software and features

Some vendors offer only basic IP forwarding and a minimum amount of routing protocols and management, while others support all protocols known to mankind, custom routing protocols, and lots of extra management capabilities. These extra functions are generally not available on every router, however, but only in routers running special software feature sets. Sometimes even the BGP routing protocol requires an additional interdomain routing feature set.

Reliability

The MTBF should be long; the MTTR short.

Space efficiency

Rack space isn't cheap, so the smaller the box, the better.

Table 3-1 lists a number of different router models from different vendors. Most of the values are approximate and will probably change over time as new interface cards and CPU boards come out. Note that the listed model isn't necessarily the fastest within a range or from that vendor. The packet per second (PPS) forwarding rate can vary depending on the configuration of the router.

Table 3-1. Examples of routers

Model	Processors	Redundancy	Interfaces/ Speed	PPS
Cisco 2500	Single	-	3+, max 10 Mbps	6000
Cisco 3600	Single	Power	16+, max 155 Mbps	16-40K
Cisco 7200	Single	Power	16+, max 622 Mbps	225-400K
Cisco 7500	1 / distr.	Power, CPU	50+, max 1 Gbps	220k - 2M

Table 3-1. Examples of routers (continued)

Model	Processors	Redundancy	Interfaces/ Speed	PPS
Cisco 12000	Distributed	Core parts	200+, max 10 Gbps	25-375M
Juniper M5	Distributed	-	16, 1 Gbps	40M
Juniper M160	Distributed	Core parts	128+, 10 Gbps	160M
Nortel BCN	SMP	All parts	100+, 1 Gbps	5M
Foundry NetIron 800	Distributed	Power, CPU	28, 2.4 Gbps	89M
Alcatel 7420 ESR	Distributed	All parts	120+, 622 Mbps	18M
Riverstone RS 8000	Distributed	Power, CPU	32+, 1 Gbps	15M
Charlotte's Web Aranea-1	Distributed	All parts	256, 10 Gbps	384M

It's hard to say anything about prices for these routers, because this depends mostly on the interface cards; the chassis is usually relatively cheap. Router prices start at about the price of a car (a cheap used one for $2,500), go up to a year's salary, and then on to the price of a house. Also, bigger routers are generally more expensive (per port) than smaller ones.

Host-Based Routers

Routing functionality isn't limited to boxes with the word "router" on the front. Many operating systems, particularly Unix variations, can route IP packets if equipped with two or more network interfaces. Interrupting user programs and changing to kernel mode, where IP forwarding takes place, is an expensive operation, so host-based routers need better hardware to reach the same performance level as that of special-purpose routers with dedicated operating systems and potentially special hardware for packet forwarding. There are other types of interfaces for some systems, but only the Ethernet family and ATM at lower speeds are extensively supported as interfaces for hosts. Host-based routers benefit from fast CPUs and large amounts of (virtual) memory, however, and with the Gated or GNU Zebra routing daemons for BGP support, they make good route reflectors. That way, the dedicated routers can be configured as route-reflector clients and offload much of the BGP processing to host-based routers.

A typical host-based router can handle 100-Mbps Ethernet interfaces at full load and/or one or two Gigabit Ethernet interfaces, but those not at the full 1-Gbps load.

Multilayer Switches

Another class of IP routing devices are layer 3 switches or multilayer switches. This is an evolution of the VLAN concept, in which several "virtual LANs" are configured on a switch. The switch switches traffic only between ports that belong to the same

VLAN. To get from one VLAN to the next, packets have to be routed. Connecting a router to numerous VLANs is obviously not efficient, so routers can connect to a VLAN-capable switch over a trunk. With this method, the router uses one physical interface to connect to all VLANs using virtual interfaces, all with their own IP address and other configuration details. The main reason for using VLANs is to prevent certain types of traffic from getting where they don't belong. This was always an expensive or slow setup, because a reasonably priced router performing the routing and filtering between the VLANs could forward packets at nowhere near wire speed. The idea behind a multilayer switch is to get around this limitation by having the router process the first packet that belongs to a certain stream or session. The router then informs the switch how these packets should be handled, and the switch switches the rest of the traffic as per the router's instructions. This couples the performance of switching to the additional benefits of routing, such as intelligent routing protocols and fine-grained access policies. Multilayer switches come in the form of an integrated device, a switch with a router module, or separate routers and switches that work together. Router vendors are building more and more hardware support for packet forwarding into their boxes, while switch vendors put more and more intelligence in the hardware they produce. So the distinction between a multilayer or Layer 3 switch and a "real" router is quickly disappearing, especially since newer Layer 3 switches can do full IP processing and filtering for each individual packet.

Memory and the Routing Table

In early 2001, the global routing table reached 100,000 routes. There are no hard and fast rules about the amount of memory a router needs to handle so many routes; this depends on the software architecture and number of peers. For a Cisco router, 64 MB might be enough to run full routing with a small number of peers, but 128 MB is safer, and it certainly doesn't hurt if a model can take 256 MB or more, even though that much is probably not immediately necessary. There is no real need to carry full routing for networks that aren't part of the *default-free zone*: as long as you pay someone else for transit services, you can simply use default routes and take partial routing only to override the default to optimize routing to a subset of the Internet. But even with filtering in place, the number of routes will continue to grow, and at some point, the amount of available memory in a router can become a problem. Because most routers have only physical memory, and not virtual memory as regular computers do, running under low-memory conditions leads to memory fragmentation. With fragmented memory, processes can't get large enough blocks of continuous memory, and the process fails, even though there seems to be a reasonable amount of free memory. When a router runs out of memory during BGP processing, it usually drops BGP connections, freeing up memory so the connections can be reestablished, and a vicious circle is born. The process that fails doesn't have to be related to BGP processing, however. This problem is discussed later in the book in the section on configuring BGP filters and troubleshooting.

 There is no agreed-upon definition of the concept "default-free zone," but it generally applies to the set of routers that don't have a default route. By necessity, this applies to the core routers of tier-1 ISPs, but many multihomed ISPs and end-user networks also have routers that run defaultless, even though they have one or more transit ISPs they could use as a default route.

Performance

Forwarding or switching packets is a simple process, but router and switch manufacturers employ a wide range of different methods to accomplish this task as fast as possible. These are often called *switching paths*. The simplest way to forward or switch packets is to have a process running on a CPU that reads one packet at a time from a buffer where they are stored as they come in, processes the IP header, applies filters, looks up the next hop in the routing table, and queues the packet for output on the right interface. This is how Cisco's *process switching* works. A regular process has access to the entire software infrastructure of the system, so it's easy to implement complex IP options, filters, and queuing algorithms. Even though router operating systems don't have nearly as much overhead as general-purpose operating systems for hosts, however, there is still a penalty for switching from interrupt mode, in which the packet is read from the interface, to user mode, in which the packet is processed. At the very least, the forwarding process has to contend with other processes for CPU time. So the first step in optimizing packet forwarding is to do it in interrupt mode. This way, when a packet is received, the CPU is interrupted, the packet is processed, and the CPU returns to its original task before the regular processes even notice what's going on. Interrupt code isn't allowed to occupy the CPU for long, because new interrupts must wait until the CPU is finished handling the current one, and there is usually a limited "window of opportunity" for the system to tend to an interrupt generated by the hardware before buffer space runs out.

For this reason, the IP forwarding code running at the interrupt level doesn't implement every possible option. When a packet needs more complex processing than can be done by the interrupt code, it's process-switched by handing it over to the regular IP forwarding process. Cisco's oldest switching path at the interrupt level is *fast switching*, which uses a tree data structure in memory to cache forwarding information. If the fast-switching code can find the destination IP address or network in this route cache, it takes the interface and next-hop MAC header information from there and immediately forwards the packet. If there is no route cache entry, the packet is process-switched, and an entry is created. The route cache entries are removed periodically and when a routing change invalidates them. There is also *optimum switching*, which is an optimized version of fast switching, and *Cisco express forwarding*

(CEF). Unlike fast and optimum switching, CEF creates a full copy of the routing table, consisting of an adjacency table with forwarding information (interface and MAC headers) and a CEF table with reachability (NLRI) information. Because a dedicated process creates these tables, there is no need to process-switch the first packet, so the CEF tables can't really be considered caches.

Fast switching, optimum switching, and CEF all try to optimize the route-lookup phase of the forwarding process. This makes sense, because the number of routes in the routing table can grow very large, and the longest-match-first rule makes it hard to implement a fast way to find the right one. But there are times when looking up the route isn't the problem, in layer 2 (Ethernet) switches, for instance. Under these circumstances, the prime candidate for optimization is the filter part of the switching process. To avoid having to go through the full list of filter rules for each individual packet, many switch and router manufacturers implement some form of *flow switching*. This works by first identifying streams of related packets, such as TCP sessions. Usually, packets with the same source and destination IP addresses (and MAC addresses when switching), source and destination port numbers, protocol, and input interface are considered part of the same flow. Only the first packet of each flow is examined to see if the filters allow it through, and subsequent packets in the same flow are either all allowed or all disallowed based on what happened to the first packet of the flow. This information is contained in a *flow cache*. Cisco supports flow-based switching on some router platforms under the name *netflow*.

 A router using a route cache will perform poorly if packets all go to different destinations. A router or switch using a flow cache will perform poorly if the number of new flows that must be created each second is large, which is typically the case for web traffic in ISP networks. If possible, use a router or switch or a switching mode that doesn't need a route or flow cache.

Anticipating Growth

In pretty much everything relating to the Internet, growth is a given, so buying exactly what you need now and nothing more is probably not a good idea. On the other hand, buying equipment that is much, much faster than you need at the moment costs a lot of money. Waiting until you really need the extra speed will always be cheaper, because prices tend to go down, and performance tends to go up in this business.

If you're an ISP or have an ISP-like network, try to avoid having to rebuild your network completely. This is extremely hard to do, unless you can do it without any customer impact and/or cooperation. Most likely, you'll end up with a partial new network and a partial old network, and you'll need to use ugly hacks to make the two work together. I was in this situation once. We had a beautiful design for a new network, but there was also an old network containing pretty much every router model Cisco ever built, and nearly all those hundreds of routers were in a single OSPF area, of course. The idea was to rebuild one point of presence at a time, but this proved impossible. We had to support both the new network and the old network side by side for many months. Also, the two networks were different (and the old one was fragile), so it took a lot of time to come up with a way to connect both networks intimately enough to be able to move customers (and their IP address ranges) from the old network to the new network, one at a time.

A related issue is standardizing your equipment. Some people like to standardize on one type of router throughout their network. This approach certainly has benefits, but there is also a huge down side: when this type of router becomes obsolete, you'll have a network full of obsolete routers, and you'll have to replace them all. It's better to standardize on two or three types. That way, you can bring in the newest routers where you need them, and you can redeploy the routers that still have some useful lifetime ahead of them in a less demanding part of the network. By buying one new router, you can upgrade two locations in your network, and you don't run the risk of your entire network becoming obsolete and having to be replaced within a short period of time.

 Look for a range of router models that take the same interface cards. Interface cards are the most expensive part of any router configuration, so being able to keep them will save you a lot of money.

Failure Risks

After buying some nice routing and switching hardware, you'll need a good place to put it. The best place would be a data-processing facility specially suited for housing computer and network hardware, with extensive protection against all kinds of hazards, such as fire, water, lightning, riots and civil unrest, tornadoes, earthquakes, and long-term power failure. This isn't always possible, however. If you have to house your equipment under less than ideal circumstances, at least take the time to think about water and power problems, and as always, use common sense.

Water

Water is everywhere. Your equipment can be exposed to it when there is a leaking roof, a broken window, a clogged drain, or broken plumbing. And that's just the small stuff. Rivers and canals sometimes overflow, and if there is a small fire, there is usually more water damage than actual fire or smoke damage. I have personally dealt with water problems twice. Water damage to your equipment is a serious risk.

Water can quickly ruin the building infrastructure or the equipment itself by shorting electrical circuits or, more slowly, by inducing corrosion. Cables dropping down from overhead cable guides may lead the water directly into the equipment. Outlets close to the (raised) floor will short-circuit when there are only a few inches of water present. If possible, cables should be coming in from below a raised floor, and the outlets and connectors should be at least a few inches above floor level. Cabinets should be closed on top, but make sure the temperature inside doesn't get too high. Equipment should never be on the lowest floor of a building, especially not below ground level, because water from floods, leaks, and sprinkler systems will collect there.

Power Failure

In many parts of the world, the power grid is so reliable that installing a cheap uninterruptible power supply (UPS) may actually *increase* the likelihood of power failures to your equipment. The main reason to have UPS, even if it supplies backup power only for a few minutes, is to allow PCs and servers to shut down properly so that open files and the filesystem aren't damaged. This isn't usually an issue for network equipment. After power is reapplied, the routers and switches boot and read configuration data from flash or nonvolatile memory, and they are up and running in half a minute or so. If all the network users will be down when there is a power outage, there is little advantage to having the network equipment connected to an UPS.

A simple UPS with the right VA rating for your equipment will buy you 5 to 10 minutes of backup power. Many power outages last only between a second and a few minutes. By adding more batteries, it's possible to run longer on UPS power; 4 to 8 hours should be enough to survive the majority of utility outages and/or leave enough time to reach the site and fix or bypass local power problems. Depending on your power needs, this can add up to a lot of batteries, which are also heavy. Lower-speed (up to 100 Mbps) communication hardware generally doesn't take too much power compared to computers, with one exception: dial-up and ADSL modem concentrators. These contain many digital signal processors, which are nothing more than specialized CPUs. In particular, dial-up equipment that can handle lots of analog calls uses a lot of power and runs hot.

Unfortunately, it's not enough just to have the power available somewhere in the building. You need to make sure that every piece of critical equipment has power all the time, whatever happens. If the utility power was the only thing that would ever fail, this wouldn't be too much of a problem. But this isn't the case. Other reasons why a router or switch may lose power:

- Too much load on a fuse: the fuse blows.
- A short circuit: the fuse blows.
- Someone trips over a power cable, pulling it out of the socket.
- Someone disconnects the power by accident.
- Something has to be moved; power must be disconnected.

- The UPS fails (even if there is utility or generator power).
- The power supply fails.

The only way to be protected from *all* these eventualities is to use redundant power supplies in critical devices. Most medium- and high-end communication hardware has room for more than a single power supply. One power supply should be directly connected to the utility power, over only a surge protector. The other power supply should be connected to a UPS and possibly a generator. If there is a separate surge protector apart from the UPS, it should not be the same one that handles the other power supply, and they shouldn't have any common fuses in the fuse box.

Building a Wide Area Network

Good redundancy and robustness start at home. Having several connections to the Internet won't do you much good if hosts in your network are unable to use them because of a problem in the internal network. I'm not going to bore you with a detailed description of how to run an inhouse network.* Sure, it can be hard at times, but at least the problems are limited in space, if not in time and complexity, and you're there to solve them. Don't underestimate the difference this makes. Keeping a geographically dispersed network running involves additional challenges.

When you start building a network spanning more than one location, there are many complications, but they all boil down to two things: you have to rely on other people, and everything takes much more time. An example: you make a mess of an access list and can no longer access a router. If this router is in another room in the same building, you can just walk there, connect a terminal to the console and fix the problem. Or you can use the oldest network administrator's trick in the book: reboot the router, so it returns to the configuration you saved before you started making configuration changes. Now imagine this router being 3,000 miles away. You don't want to fly out just because you made a mistake configuring a router. So you need someone in the remote facility to walk up to the router and reboot it.† If the other location is a branch of your own company, this shouldn't be too much of a problem, but things are different if this is a colocation facility. Unless you're particularly fond of airline food, you need remote hands at the colocation facility. But you only want them to reboot your router on your request, and not when anyone else asks them to do this, so this introduces authentication and authorization issues.

Since you are now relying on the services of housing facilitators to colocate your equipment and on telco circuits to connect it all together, you are much more

---

* The book *Designing Large-Scale LANs* by Kevin Dooley (O'Reilly), tells you everything you need to know and more about this subject.

† There are devices that allow you to power-cycle your equipment over the network or over a dial-up connection. This solves some problems, but not all of them.

vulnerable to problems in other organizations. Telcos, large ISPs, and colocation facilitators are all capital-intensive businesses, and they depend on highly trained staff. This means that when the economy is booming, they all have a hard time expanding their services, because their suppliers can't deliver fast enough, and it gets hard to hire the necessary new staff. A dwindling economy paradoxically leads to a similar situation: cost cuts make it impossible to expand services as needed by customer demand (less money doesn't mean less network traffic), and there aren't enough knowledgeable employees because of layoffs.

When it gets really bad, telcos, ISPs, and colocators may literally "pull the plug." Usually, there are warning signs quite a while before this happens, but sometimes the financial people are so creative that nobody notices the problems until it's too late. If you have a choice between doing business with a rock-solid company with lots of money in the bank and doing business with a startup with huge debts, you may want to make your supplier's financial status a factor in your decision. However, the choices aren't usually this clear-cut, and you may be depriving yourself of great service for an excellent price by working only with established players. So make the decision on a case-by-case basis. For example, if you want to peer with other networks on the other side of the continent, you might choose recent startups as a colocation facility and/or a telco. When the colocation facilitator goes out of business, the most you stand to lose is a router, and when the circuit goes down, you lose your peerings, but you can reroute this traffic over your transit connections. On the other hand, if you are looking for a Point of Presence (PoP) location where you can host important servers and connect to customers, using the same colocation facility will be a much bigger risk: if they go belly-up, you not only lose a significant amount of equipment, but you'll also have to move the services to another location, and you'll probably lose customers because it will take a long time to restore service for them. Choosing a less reliable telco increases the risk of a network partition, which is another thing you don't want.

The Likelihood of Concurrent Fiber Cuts

Network partitions lead to all kinds of trouble (more on this in a later chapter), so you'll probably want to make sure they happen as infrequently as possible by building enough redundancy into the internal network. Unfortunately, things aren't this simple. Consider Figure 3-2.

It looks like Chicago is connected to New York and Washington over completely separate paths. In reality, however, the fibers may run through the same trench a good deal of the way, even if the circuits are provided by competing telcos. Telcos often save costs by sharing trenches. Fibers from competitors are often only inches apart, so a single careless backhoe operator can easily cause fiber cuts for a large number of telcos. Figure 3-3 illustrates this risk.

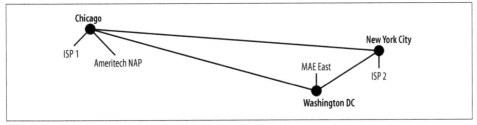

Figure 3-2. A geographically dispersed multihomed network

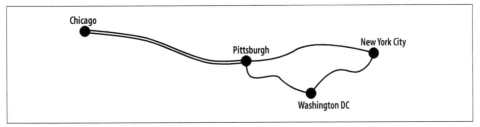

Figure 3-3. Possible long-distance fiber paths

Keep in mind that there are only a few fiber paths between any two locations. This is especially true for long-distance links and for places with many natural barriers, such as deserts, mountains, and rivers. For instance, there are a lot of colocation facilities in Manhattan, but many connections to the rest of the United States run through New Jersey, in addition to the local tails for the large number of transatlantic sea-cable landings there. There are only so many places where you can get a fiber across the Hudson, so if there is a problem with one of those, this will affect many circuits from different telcos.

Getting maps of the actual fiber paths out of telcos is like pulling teeth. More often than not, the sales reps and other people who talk to customers don't really know anything about the internals of the network, but this doesn't preclude them from making definitive statements. Information on paper is usually more reliable. But even if you get an accurate map of the current state of the network from them, there is always reengineering going on, so two circuits that are miles apart at one time may run through the same trench or duct only months later. If you really want to be sure your circuits stay up when there is a fiber cut, you'll have to pay for better than usual service levels for a circuit over a protected SONET ring. Just the promise that the circuit is protected doesn't mean anything: there may be so many fiber cuts in this ring, or the time to repair is so long, that they need the SONET protection to just get ordinary 99.7% uptimes, which still means a day of downtime per year. Good protected circuits can have guaranteed uptimes of up to 99.98%, less than two hours of downtime per year, but this will invariably cost extra. You may want to look at microwave or satellite circuits for backup. They are less reliable, but their failure modes are different from fiber, so they are good backups. Microwave and satellite circuits tend to suffer from atmospheric conditions, so that radio waves get tunneled through the atmosphere and cause interference; heavy rain; snow on the dishes; and, of course, physical problems with the dishes or antennas.

Network Topology Design

There are many books on network design, and they often go into great detail about the different routing protocols, showing nice diagrams of routers and switches and how to connect them. They often fail to address with enough detail the most challenging part, however: coming up with a good topology. Maybe this is because even really bad topologies can work fairly well, if you spend enough time and energy on them. But choosing a better way to connect various parts of the network together will at least save you a lot of time and possibly money.

A Design Model

The first decision in building a network is usually not made on a conscious level: the decision involving which design model, philosophy, or methodology to use. Cisco literature heavily gravitates towards the Hierarchical Design Model illustrated in Figure 3-4.

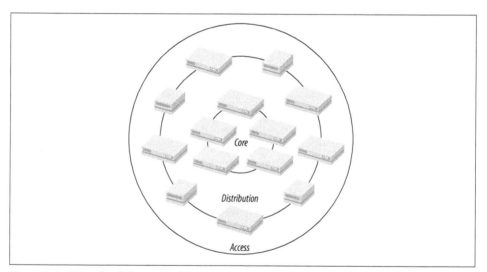

Figure 3-4. Hierarchical Design Model overview

In this design model, the network is divided into three parts: core/backbone, distribution, and access. The core network connects the different parts together with minimal overhead. The access parts of the network connect to the users, and the distribution layer sits between core and access to provide for access and quality of service policies. I'm not entirely comfortable with this way of classifying network components. It seems to me that the Hierarchical Design Model focuses primarily on the internals of large corporate or campus networks, without fitting smaller or ISP networks very well. In my view, each router interface belongs to a certain part of the network: external, core, or access. The backplane of the router is considered a part of the core. Switches shouldn't be considered here, because that would violate the separation between the datalink and network layers.* Each type of interface has specific needs:

External interfaces
> The filters on external interfaces exist to stop traffic that should never enter or leave the network, such as malformed or incorrectly addressed packets.

Access interfaces
> The filters on access interfaces range from a simple filter to block packets with falsified source addresses, to the most stringent filters imaginable, depending on the needs of the systems this specific access interface connects to.

Core interfaces
> Since filtering is already done at the edges of the network, it's redundant for core interfaces, which should be optimized for performance.

This concept works well for small networks, such as the simple multihomed network depicted in Figure 3-5.

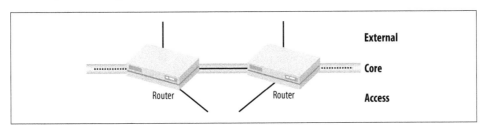

Figure 3-5. Interface function separation in a small network

In larger networks, there will probably be dedicated core routers to handle the aggregate traffic flows between several access and border routers. This is shown in Figure 3-6.

The Topology

In theory, what follows on network topologies applies to LAN, WAN, campus, and mixed networks. The economics are different, however: in a LAN environment, bandwidth is fairly cheap, so redundant links that remain unused until there is an

---

* There is something to be said for mixing switches and routers, however, as often happens in designs following the hierarchical model: switches are now performing more and more functions traditionally performed by routers.

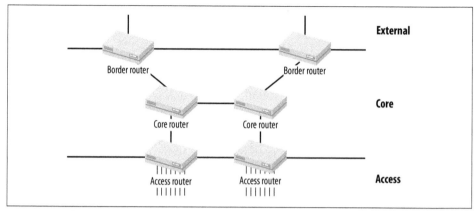

Figure 3-6. A larger network with dedicated core routers

outage aren't a problem. In a WAN environment, network connections are expensive, so the available bandwidth should be used as efficiently as possible. The word "node" in the following list indicates a single location that can connect to the network over more than one link. In a WAN, this would be an office or PoP; in a LAN it would be a wiring closet, equipment rack, or even an individual router or switch. These are the most basic topologies:

Star

When important services are provided at a central facility, the most logical topology is a star: every node in the network is directly connected to a central hub. The advantage of the star is that traffic flow is extremely easy to predict. The disadvantage is that there's no redundancy, and a star topology often doesn't fit the cable layout well; a number of cables may run together for part of their length.

Tree

A tree is much like a star, but rather than having every node connect directly to a hub, nodes can also connect to "upstream" nodes that are closer to the center of the network. There is still only a single path from each node to any other node, so there is no redundancy. A tree is even more susceptible to failure than a star, because when an intermediate node goes down, the network is always partitioned. Trees are efficient, however, since they aggregate multiple downstream connections into a single upstream link, and path lengths are as short as possible.

Ring

A ring has good redundancy and is efficient with respect to the number of connections: just one more than a star. The total length of all the circuits is usually shorter than that of a star. A ring will sometimes fit the physical cable layout, but just as often it will fit quite badly. The main disadvantage of a ring is inefficient bandwidth use: traffic takes up bandwidth over the entire section of the ring between the source and destination.

Full mesh

In a full mesh, every node is connected to every other node. Since this calls for a huge amount of links in all but the smallest networks, a full mesh is rare, especially over real (nonvirtual) circuits. Another problem with full mesh topologies is how to select a backup path when the primary link to a destination fails: all other paths are the same: one extra hop. An advantage of a fully meshed network is that individual connections don't have to be of a high bandwidth.

Partial mesh

The partial mesh covers every other type of topology. A partial mesh is either a tree with some extra links or a full mesh with some links removed. Redundancy and efficiency depend on the actual configuration, and both can vary from minimal to excellent. It's even possible that both are excellent at the same time. A common disadvantage of these networks is that traffic intensity can be high at awkward points in the network that aren't natural candidates for receiving a lot of traffic, but that just happen to be in a place where a lot of links come together. Partially meshed topologies can be hard to manage: when a link is added or removed, the traffic patterns can shift radically. An important advantage is that a partially meshed network can fully follow whatever physical topology is in place.

Figure 3-7 shows the same 14 nodes connected through different network topologies.

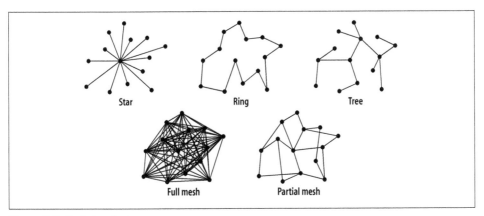

Figure 3-7. Basic topologies

When a network isn't uniform in speed, it can be beneficial to create a high-speed "backbone" with one of the base topologies and add extra nodes and redundant links using lower-bandwidth connections. Backbone links should be readily available for transit traffic, while second-tier connections are strictly for "local" traffic and possibly backup purposes. For example, suppose you operate a large network throughout the United States. New York City and Washington, DC, are both part of the backbone, but Philadelphia, which connects to both, is not. As a result, when the connection between New York and Washington fails, traffic from New York to Washington will not flow over Philadelphia, even if this means it has to take a detour over the West Coast. This is desirable if the path over Philadelphia doesn't have enough bandwidth available to carry the traffic between New York and Washington. This rerouting over the West Coast is accomplished by setting the IGP metric for the second-tier links much higher than metric for the backbone links, regardless of the link bandwidth, on which the metric is based by default.

Here are some possible combined topologies. I've tried to give them descriptive names.

Triangled or ringed star

The easiest way to add some redundancy to a star topology is to connect each non-hub node to another. This leads to a topology that looks like a lot of triangles connecting in the middle. Another approach is connecting all nonhub nodes in a ring, creating a ringed star or wagon wheel topology. The hub/backbone node remains a single point of failure. There is, of course, little need to keep the network running if all the important services are located at the hub, and this location is no longer available. This is a dangerous way to connect to the Internet, however: networks have lived to regret such a topology.

Dual star

A good way to provide full redundancy and still keep some of the advantages of a star topology is simply to have two stars: every node connects to two hub nodes forming the backbone. Each hub node should then be able to provide all the necessary services independently. For instance, the main servers are located at one hub and the backup servers at another, and both hubs have their own connection to the Internet. There should also be a somewhat higher bandwidth connection between both backbone nodes. This way, when a link from a remote node to one of the backbone nodes goes down, the node can still reach this backbone site over the other backbone hub and the interhub backbone link. One of the hub locations can function as the primary center of the network with the other backbone node as a backup, or they can be more or less equal. In the first case, nodes may connect to the backup hub over lower-bandwidth connections, because these connections will be idle during normal operation. In the latter case, you'll want to balance the traffic over two lines of more or less equal bandwidth. A dual star is an excellent choice if you have to build a network on top of a datalink technology that provides virtual circuits, such as frame relay or ATM, because then there is no need for a huge number of router interfaces at the hub locations.

Ringed triangles

In this topology, there is a high-speed backbone ring that touches all nodes where important services are located and all nodes that connect to external networks. Every nonbackbone node connects exactly two backbone nodes. This is one of my favorite topologies: it's easy to understand but still flexible, with excellent redundancy properties. Balancing traffic needs some attention, but it's doable. This is actually a variation of ringed rings, with a limitation on the second-tier rings: they may only have a single nonbackbone node. This makes the second-tier rings easier to manage.

Then there are "fractal topologies" that repeat themselves at lower levels:

Stars

A backbone star that connects other stars together is easy to manage and can be a good choice when redundancy isn't an issue.

Rings

Rings that connect rings together are common in fiber infrastructure. Balancing traffic gets harder as the number of nodes per ring increases, but when there is bandwidth to spare, this is a good way to keep the topology of a large network simple and still have good redundancy.

Full meshes

Since full meshes are feasible only among a small number of nodes, it makes sense to separate the network into a number of fully meshed subnetworks and create another backbone mesh between those. The problem with hard-to-manage traffic flows when direct links fail is still present, however, and connecting a submesh to the backbone without introducing a single point of failure adds extra complexity.

Partial meshes

Since partial meshes aren't well-defined topologies to begin with, the actual difference between a partial mesh of partial meshes and a "pragmatic topology" without any set rules will be rather small.

Trees

Trees always repeat themselves, so a "tree of trees" is no different than just a tree.

Figure 3-8 shows several combined topologies. As you can see, a starred stars fractal topology looks a lot like a tree, and ringed rings look like a partial mesh.

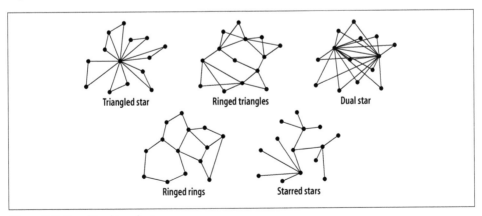

Figure 3-8. Combined topologies

Don't let a quest for the perfect network topology stand in the way of building a solid network: even if you can design such a perfect topology, real-world limitations, such as bandwidth availability, money, and hardware restrictions, will prevent you from implementing it. On the other hand, you should build your network with *some* topology in mind, so when there are necessary exceptions, they stay exceptions, and they don't slowly but surely add up to a big mess. If you add a "convenient" link between two busy locations in the network, attracting a lot of traffic, you may have to adjust a lot of metrics to make sure the new link doesn't attract more traffic than it can handle. But then, when this link fails, the new metrics for the remaining links may cause the network to fail to take proper advantage of the remaining capacity.

There are basically two types of network topology: the type where traffic is never balanced to any noticeable degree, so you just have to buy the bandwidth needed between two nodes in the network, and the type where traffic will balance itself over the available connections, at least to some degree, so you can adjust IGP metrics to adjust this balancing. Full meshes are a good example of the former, along with wagon wheels and all nonredundant topologies, such as stars and trees. Rings and especially partial meshes are open to metric tinkering to adjust traffic balancing.

I favor the ringed-triangle topology because it allows for relatively straightforward traffic balancing, compared to a nonstructured partial mesh. It works like this. First, the second-tier connections (the "triangle" parts) must have metrics that are at least a factor of 10 higher than those for the backbone connections (the "ring" part). This makes sure that the second-tier connections aren't overloaded when a backbone link fails, but traffic stays on the backbone ring. There are always two ways to get to a certain node over the backbone ring: clockwise and counterclockwise. By default, the routers will send packets over the route with the smaller number of hops. This may lead to poor traffic balancing, but it's relatively easy to just increase the IGP cost of the busy links a little, and some traffic will be rerouted over the other leg of the ring. There is an example of how to do this at the end of Chapter 10.

CHAPTER 4

IP Address Space and AS Numbers

All IP addresses aren't created equal. Which kind of IP addresses to announce over BGP is an important decision: it has a large impact on the reachability of your network, and it also has important financial consequences. The main decision is whether to keep using ISP-based addresses or to apply for an independent address range of your own. This poses an important question: where do IP addresses come from, if not from your ISP?

The Internet Assigned Numbers Authority (IANA) is responsible for assigning the protocol numbers used on the Internet. This includes IP addresses and AS numbers, but the IANA has delegated these activities to three Regional Internet Registries (RIRs):

APNIC: http://www.apnic.net
> The Asia-Pacific Network Information Centre in Brisbane, Australia, serves most of Asia, Australia, and the Pacific.

ARIN: http://www.arin.net
> The American Registry for Internet Numbers in Chantilly, Virginia, United States, serves North America.

RIPE NCC: http://www.ripe.net
> The Réseaux IP Européens Network Coordination Centre in Amsterdam, The Netherlands, serves Europe, the Middle East, and the former Soviet Union countries.

Work is currently underway to establish two additional RIRs: one serving the region of Latin America, and the other serving continental Africa. For the time being, ARIN serves Latin America, the Caribbean, and Africa south of the Sahara, and the RIPE NCC serves Africa north of the Sahara.

In turn, the RIRs delegate responsibility for assigning IP address space to Local Internet Registries (LIRs) or directly to ISPs (which are also considered LIRs by RIPE).

When an ISP requests address space for the first time, the RIR *allocates* a relatively large block of address space, usually a /20. Then the RIR *assigns* a smaller range of addresses from this allocation to the ISP. The ISP now gets to announce the full allocation over BGP, but actual use is limited to the addresses that are actually assigned. If the ISP requests more address space for their own use or for customers, further assignments are made from the initial allocation. New blocks of address space are allocated to ISPs from which to draw further assignments if necessary. These allocations are called Provider Aggregatable (PA) address blocks, because an ISP can aggregate several address ranges assigned to customers into a larger range and so announce a relatively small number of routes (one per PA block) over BGP.

The Different Types of Address Space

The IP address assignment policies the RIRs use themselves and impose on LIRs and ISPs are based on RFC 2050, "Internet Registry IP Allocation Guidelines." These IP address assignment guidelines were developed in coordination with user communities, the Internet Engineering Steering Group (IESG), and the Internet Engineering Task Force (IETF). They have three main goals:

- Conservation, to let the remaining IPv4 address space last as long as possible
- Routability, to make sure that assigned addresses are reachable throughout the Internet
- Registration, so every assignment is unique and to aid troubleshooting

Unfortunately, the conservation and routability objectives are at odds with each other. Conservation calls for assigning the smallest possible number of addresses, while routability is best served by keeping the total number of assigned address ranges to a minimum by assigning large blocks to avoid fragmentation of the IP address space. For regular single-homed organizations, there isn't much of a problem; ISPs can assign small address ranges from a PA block to such organizations, keeping the number of routes in the global routing table relatively small—one for each PA block. For this reason, it's hard to get IP addresses from a RIR directly for organizations that connect only to a single ISP: this unnecessarily breaks aggregation. Multihomed networks, on the other hand, can't get around this and have three options:

Request "Provider Independent" (PI) address space
PI space can't be aggregated by an ISP, so it must always be announced over BGP "as is." This was often done in the past, and it's still possible (but not easy) to get even small blocks of PI space at the time of this writing. It seems this is discouraged, and/or the policies on this may change, but don't take "no" for an answer too easily when requesting PI space.

Act as an ISP and request a PA block of their own
This is hard to do and expensive, but if you have enough ISP-like traits, it can be worth it, because this is the "highest quality" address space.

Request address space from an ISP's PA block but announce it as PI space

This is sometimes called "shooting holes" in the ISPs PA block. Since BGP uses a *longest-match-first* route lookup algorithm, a long prefix (smaller block) will always be preferred over a shorter one. So if your ISP announces a /19 and has assigned you a /23 out of that block, you can announce the /23, and other networks will use that route, regardless of the presence or status of the /19.

The routability of these three types of addresses is potentially very different. Some people feel the current global routing table is already too large with more than 100,000 entries: it takes relatively long to initialize the routing table when a router connects to its BGP peers, and convergence of routing updates across the globe is slower than it should be. Others feel the current situation isn't problematic, and reasonable growth of the global routing table is possible. There is probably no magic limit where backbone routers stop functioning altogether, but it's likely that more and more of the larger networks will install filters to minimize the number of routes in their network, just as Sprint did in 1995.

That year, Sprint decided to filter out any prefixes longer than 18 bits in the 206.x.x.x and higher Class C address space. This means that Sprint routers allowed routes in the routing table only for networks the size of 64 Class C's or larger: if you had a 32 Class C or smaller aggregate in this range, you were unreachable for Sprint customers.

Since 1995, the increase in router CPU speed and memory size has been higher than the growth of the global routing table, so even midrange routers can comfortably handle full routing, and there is little need for such a policy right now. It seems the global routing table is growing exponentially again since late 1998, though not alarmingly fast yet. Before that, it had been growing at a more modest linear rate since the introduction of CIDR in 1993.* There is a possibility that transit networks will start filtering out long prefixes (small address ranges) in the future. The three different ways to get address space for use with BGP each have pros and cons with regard to possible filters.

Provider-Independent Address Space

Since more than half the global routing table consists of /24 announcements, those are the first candidates for being filtered. More aggressive filters may even filter out everything smaller than the smallest assigned PA blocks, possibly with some exceptions for "the swamp," the part of the Class C space assigned in pre-CIDR days (192.x.x.x and part of 193.x.x.x). The currently allocated smallest PA blocks are /20, but much of the Class C space is allocated to ISPs in /19 and larger blocks. With this kind of aggressive filtering, you will be completely unreachable from many parts of the Internet if you depend on a small PI block announcement. Since the RIRs won't assign you

---

* "Analyzing the Internet's BGP Routing Table," by Geoff Huston (*http://macross.dynodns.net/idr/4-1-bgp.pdf*).

a larger PI block if you can't demonstrate the need for the number of addresses in question, using a PI block smaller than /20 (especially a /24 or even smaller block) is a dangerous proposition. As RFC 2050 states:

> Note that addresses issued directly from the IRs, (non-provider based), are the least likely to be routable across the Internet.

This of course also applies to PI address space requested through an ISP.

Your Own Provider Aggregatable Block

The best way to avoid being filtered is getting a PA block of your own. Since you aren't expected to use the entire block yourself, you can get a much larger block than would be possible with PI space under similar circumstances. Also, PA blocks are the least likely to be filtered. They are only assigned to ISPs and "enterprise registries," but if this isn't too much of a stretch for your business, you can become one by selling connectivity to daughter organizations or to other companies within the same building. ARIN charges a $2,500 fee for assigning /19 or less address space, either PI or PA. Startup and renewal fees apply depending on the situation. An organization requesting address space directly from the RIPE NCC must become a LIR (in other words, a RIPE member) which costs 1,800 euros a year for small ISP and enterprise registries, and there is a one-time 2,100-euro startup fee. APNIC also requires membership and charges an annual membership fee of $1,250 to very small members holding /22 worth of address space or less and a "resource application" fee of $2,500 for the first IP address assignment. All fees are from fee schedules for the year 2002.

The RIR might refuse to allocate you a PA block if they think you are too small an ISP to start using those addresses for yourself and your customers in the near future. (RIPE requires you to demonstrate the need for a /22.) It's never a good idea to misrepresent the truth when dealing with a RIR, since they will review any previous IP address assignments whenever you submit a new request. Any inconsistencies between the old requests and the current status of the subsequently assigned addresses will, at the very least, delay the processing of the new request. In more severe cases, the new request may be turned down, or previous assignments may even be revoked. On the other hand, nobody can predict the future, so erring on the optimistic side—within reason—when filling in the three-month, one-year, and/or two-year growth figures in the request shouldn't be a problem.

It's possible that the IP addresses you currently hold will be pinged to determine whether they are in use. If you filter ICMP echo and/or echo reply packets, you may want ask your ISPs or RIR if they do this and allow their *ping* packets through your firewall if necessary.

Address Space From an ISP

If you can't get a PA block or a sufficiently large PI block to avoid being filtered, the only alternative is to use IP addresses assigned by an upstream ISP from their PA block: the same kind of address space single-homed organizations use. You can announce those addresses over BGP, even though your upstream ISP also announces the larger block. Announcements like this are likely candidates for filtering elsewhere on the Net, but unlike the situation in which PI space is filtered, this isn't immediately catastrophic; the larger announcement for the ISP PA block is still in place, so you are still reachable in the regular, single-homed way. ISPs would rather not have any holes in their PA blocks, but most will cooperate with such a setup. If your new ISPs allow it, it's also possible to keep using addresses from an ISP you are no longer connected to. But this should be avoided: when your route is lost, all traffic to your network starts to flow over the old ISP, which can't send it to you, so you are unreachable. If some other networks filter your announcements, some of your traffic will end up at the old ISP, where either it gets filtered, which you won't like, or it's forwarded to one of your current ISPs, which your old ISP won't like, because you are using bandwidth on their network without paying for it.

 Many ISPs have policies on what kind of announcements that fall within the PA range of a different ISP they will accept from their customers. These policies don't always make sense. Sometimes they don't accept this kind of announcement at all; sometimes they will accept them only if the ISP the addresses came from has no objections.

When you are in the process of selecting ISPs, and when you decide from which ISP you're going to take address space, it's important to review the interconnection between both ISPs and the route filtering policies they use. Some ISPs won't announce a prefix out of another ISP's PA block or will do so only if the other ISP doesn't object. It's essential that your ISPs accept the prefix you announce not only from you, but also from the other ISP. This may not be the case if one ISP filters. Figure 4-1 shows why this is important.

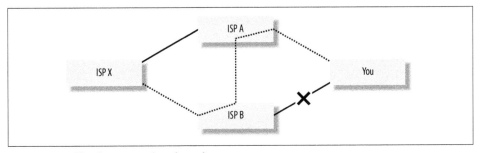

Figure 4-1. Fallback routing when depending on an aggregate

If ISP X filters your announcement, they will send traffic to your network only to the ISP that announces the aggregate your addresses fall in, ISP B in this case. But when your connection to ISP B is down, ISP B can't deliver the traffic. As long as ISP B peers with ISP A and accepts your announcement from them, the traffic will simply flow over the peering link, and you're still reachable.

Requesting Address Space

If you have decided you want to use addresses from the PA space of one of your ISPs, you should discuss this with both ISPs to make sure they're on board with what you want to do. It's a good idea to get this in writing. Then you can proceed to request the addresses from your ISP.

PI addresses can be requested directly from a RIR, but in most cases, it's better to request them through one of your ISPs or at least consult with the ISP first. They'll have to forward your request to the RIR anyway, but involving an ISP will most likely save you time. Your ISP can make sure the request is in order before forwarding it, and the RIRs have more trust in an ISP they've worked with before than in someone they don't know. It may also save you some fees. Make sure your ISP understands you're talking about provider-independent address space, since this isn't all that common; few organizations qualify for a large enough block of PI space to avoid filtering.

If you want a PA block of your own, consult your RIR's web site.

As an end-user organization, you will be asked to provide a full list of subnets with the projected immediate and future use of each subnet when requesting IP address space. Example 4-1 shows how this would appear in the ARIN request form.

Example 4-1. A list of subnets as required for ARIN address requests

```
------------------------------------------------------------
Subnet#  Subnet Mask       Max  Now  1yr   Description
------------------------------------------------------------
1.0      255.255.255.192    64   36   49   Wired PCs
1.1      255.255.255.224    32   15   30   Wireless PCs
1.2      255.255.255.240    16    7   10   Web servers, DNS
1.3      255.255.255.248     8    8    8   Dial-up modems
1.4      255.255.255.248     8    2    2   Firewall DMZ
------------------------------------------------------------
Totals                     128   68   99
------------------------------------------------------------
```

The first number ("Subnet#") doesn't mean anything: it's just to keep the subnets apart in later discussions. Note that the "Max" number is the total number of addresses in the subnet, including the normally unusable first (network) and last (broadcast) address, but the "Now" and "1yr" numbers include only the number of addresses actually used for hosts and other systems that require an IP address, such as routers. When compiling the list, start with the largest subnet, so that all subnets automatically start on the proper bit boundaries. See Appendix A for more information on (sub)netmask calculations. The use of Variable Length Subnet Masking (VLSM) and subnet zero are mandatory, but this shouldn't be a problem for today's routers. There are also policies about giving each virtual web server its own IP address and giving dial-up, ADSL, and cable users fixed IP addresses. These policies boil down to something like, "Please use dynamic addresses, but if you insist on using static addresses, we'll assign them, for now."

If you are in the RIPE or APNIC regions, don't forget to request delegation of the DNS reverse mapping of your new IP addresses, using the appropriate request forms.* The ARIN IP address request form has room for two name servers, so if your name servers will not move to the newly requested address range, there is no need to request delegation separately. If it's necessary to change this information later, send in a request based on a template that is mentioned in the IP address request form. Due to the structure of the *in-addr.arpa* zone, the delegation may have to come from the RIR even for IP addresses assigned by an ISP. Ask your ISP if this is the case. It's also possible just to request delegation from the RIR; they will inform you if your ISP is responsible for delegating authority over this part of the *in-addr.arpa* space.

The information about IP address assignments and allocations is recorded in publicly accessible databases, one for each RIR. These databases can be queried using the *whois* protocol, which is, of course, implemented in the *whois* command, available on every Unix system. There are also versions for most other operating systems, and if all else fails, you can use the *whois* query tool on each RIR's web page. (URLs are at the beginning of the chapter.) If you haven't done this before, you might want to look up your current IP address in the appropriate regional registry's database:

```
whois -h whois.apnic.net <address>
whois -h whois.arin.net <address>
whois -h whois.ripe.net <address>
```

The *whois* server will then give you the details of the organization the addresses are assigned to, as well as contact information for the administrative and technical contacts for this organization. (This could be you!) The RIR databases contain similar information about Autonomous System numbers, which can be queried by doing a *whois* query on the AS number (preceded by "AS" for RIPE and APNIC). Much more information about ASes is present in the Routing Registries, discussed later this chapter.

---

* The reverse mapping is the special domain *in-addr.arpa* in the DNS system that makes it possible for a name server to find the name associated with an IP address. To create a reverse mapping for your IP addresses, authority over the appropriate part of the *in-addr.arpa* domain must be delegated to your DNS servers.

Renumbering IP Addresses

Obviously, you need to renumber IP addresses when switching to a newly requested PI or PA block of your own. But renumbering is also advisable when using multiple address ranges from an ISP: it's better to announce a single, large block than to announce several small ones. Announcing as few routes as possible keeps the size of the global routing table down, which is good for everyone. Also, the larger your announcement, the less likely your route will be filtered, which is good for you. This means asking your ISP to exchange several small address ranges for a single larger one.

Renumbering is a lot of work, but there are some ways to make it as painless as possible to reconfigure the network equipment and deal with users and other departments who also have to make changes:

Make a plan
> That way you don't forget anything. And if you update the plan when you find something unexpected, you'll have a much better plan if you ever have to renumber again. (Knock on wood.)

Use the new and old addresses side by side for a while
> It's next to impossible to change everything at once, so you need some overlap between the moment the new addresses become available and the moment the old addresses are decommissioned.

Register the new DNS IP addresses as soon as possible
> You need to register the IP addresses for your name servers with the RIR and/or your ISPs for the reverse mappings, and with InterNIC/NSI and all other registries where you have registered domain names, including the registries for any country TLD domains you have. This may take some time, so start this process as soon as your name servers are able to respond to queries sent to the new addresses. Also, all name servers that run as secondaries for your domains, or that are primaries for domains you are secondary for, need to be configured with the new addresses.

Make the translation from the old to the new numbers as simple as possible
> It's much easier to remember and explain that 123.56.7.x becomes 213.75.6.x than arbitrary individual mappings from old addresses to new ones. You will probably make some subnets larger and other smaller, so there will be exceptions to the basic rule, but having a rule with a number of exceptions is still better than having no rule at all. For instance, if you have two Class Cs with about 100 addresses in use, only a few of which with a host address over 128, you might want to merge them into a single new /24 like this: "123.56.7.1 through 123.56.7.126 become 213.75.6.x. 123.56.8.1 through 123.56.8.126 become 213.75.6.x+128. Contact me when your IP address ends in a number higher than 126."

Start using DHCP for PCs and other workstations

If PCs and workstations use the Dynamic Host Configuration Protocol (DHCP) to obtain an IP address and other information automatically, you have to reconfigure only one or a few DHCP servers when renumbering. Since you have to renumber anyway, it may be worthwhile to switch to DHCP at this point. You can also switch to DHCP first and renumber later, but this is probably hard to do without having a large enough number of spare addresses in the old range. Switching to DHCP but keeping the current address isn't advisable, because you can't determine whether the change was successful.

Transitioning the servers painlessly

There are two ways to make the address transition as painless as possible for hosts that run services such as HTTP. It's best to run with two addresses temporarily. That way, there is no down time and no name server problems. Not all systems support multiple IP addresses on the same interface, however, and some servers, especially HTTP servers, require extensive configuration per IP address, which may be hard to duplicate temporarily.

The alternative is to set the Time To Live (TTL) in the DNS zone file to a low value, such as 300 seconds, a day or more before the transition. This is accomplished by adding the number 300 between the hostname and the "IN" in the zone file. For example:

```
test    300    IN    A    192.0.2.17
```

With a lower TTL, remote name servers cache the name-to-address mapping for just 5 minutes instead of the usual 24 hours or more. You can then change the IP address for the server and update the name server, and the new address will be used almost immediately. Without changing the TTL, some systems will connect to the old address and some to the new address for as long as the old information is cached in some remote name servers. Don't forget to set the TTL back to the default, or the load on your name server will be higher than necessary.

Don't forget firewalls and other IP-based access restrictions

Most firewalls and many other kinds of access restrictions filter based on IP address. Make a list of every system you have access to, including those on remote networks that aren't renumbered, and see if you have to configure the new IP addresses somewhere. Use the Unix *grep* command to find places where IP addresses are mentioned, if necessary. Keep a list of all the places the IP addresses are, so that you can remove the old addresses more easily later. You may want to use DNS names rather than IP addresses in your filters, but do this only when you are certain the DNS replies are always trustworthy enough to depend on for this purpose.

Communicate the new settings to users as soon as they work, but not before

Some users will immediately reconfigure their systems after you've told them the new settings for the IP address, netmask, default gateway, and name server, so don't give them this information until the new addresses actually work. This also saves you from having to inform users again when you have to make changes to the address deployment plan.

Don't take too much time
> If you take six months to complete the address transition, many of the necessary changes that must take place at the end of the transition period (or have been put off) will be forgotten. It's better to create and maintain some momentum by keeping the transition period short. Two weeks should be enough for users and other departments to do the necessary reconfiguring. This period is, of course, communicated in advance and doesn't coincide with any busy periods.

Log (attempted) use of the old addresses
> By logging the use of old addresses, you can monitor the progress of the renumbering operation. Towards the end of the transition period, you can see who hasn't renumbered yet and again ask them to do so.

Test decommissioning the old addresses
> Disabling the old addresses for a while is a good way to flush out anyone or anything that still uses the old addresses. It's usually easier to deal with this after enabling the old addresses again for a while: this takes the pressure off. So don't wait until the last moment to decommission the old addresses, but rather test this a few times in advance.

Test if the addresses have been removed completely
> After decommissioning the old addresses, do a few traceroutes to see if the network is really free of them and they are properly routed to the outside.

There is an RFC about renumbering, mostly from a router point of view: RFC 2072 "Router Renumbering Guide."

The AS Number

The next step towards running BGP is requesting an AS number. The IANA has reserved the AS numbers from 64512 to 65535 for private use, similar to the 10.0.0.0/8, 172.16.0.0/12, and 192.168.0.0/16 IP address ranges for private networks.[*] Note that, unlike networks that use RFC 1918 address space, a network using a private AS number can still enjoy full connectivity to the entire Internet. The use of a private AS number isn't limited just to private networks but is also useful in cases where a network is fully connected to the Net, but the actual way in which this is accomplished doesn't have to be communicated throughout the world. For example, a company can have two connections to the same ISP and use BGP to route traffic over those connections in a fault-tolerant way. An AS number is needed to run BGP in this setup, but it can be a private one: the ISP can leave out the specific

---

[*] RFC 1918, "Address Allocation for Private Internets" (formerly RFC 1597), and RFC 1930, "Guidelines for creation, selection, and registration of an Autonomous System (AS)."

route to this customer, because this information is covered by an aggregate. Another example would be two companies that independently connect to the Internet but also have a private connection and want to use BGP to exchange routing information between them. In these situations, it's still important to coordinate the AS numbers to be used with all parties involved, so everybody uses a different AS number.

Multihomed networks connecting to two or more ISPs need a "real" (or rather unique) AS number, which can be obtained from the RIRs, in a way similar to obtaining IP addresses. ARIN charges a one-time fee of $500 and a small yearly maintenance fee per AS. The only fees RIPE charges are the membership and startup fees; there is no extra charge for assigning an AS number. RIPE allows nonmember organizations to submit a request for an AS number to one of their ISPs, who will forward the request to the RIPE NCC. The main requirement for getting an AS number is being multihomed. The RIRs check on this by requiring you to list the ASes you will be connecting to using BGP.

Routing Registries

When running BGP, it's a good idea to register your routing policy in a Routing Registry (RR). These RRs exist for two purposes:

To aid in troubleshooting
> When there is a problem related to your network, others can check the policies to see whether the current routing is the way it should be.

To create filters
> Many networks filter routing updates they get from neighboring networks to avoid black holes and routing instability. Filters can be automatically created using the contents of the RRs.

Some ISPs require their customers to register their routing policy in a particular RR, usually their own. Many of the registries replicate each other's data, so registering at a single RR should be enough. The oldest RRs are the ones at RIPE and the Routing Arbiter Project, along with several run by ISPs. The Routing Arbiter Project was funded by the National Science Foundation from 1994 to 1998 to research leading-edge routing in the United States and to develop tools for routing. The Routing Arbiter Database (RADB) is still operational, now funded by a cost-recovery fee charged to those who register their data in the RADB. The database can be queried at *http://whois.radb.net/*. ARIN runs a RR separate from their regular database at *http://www.rr.arin.net/*. The APNIC database also holds some routing information, but it isn't a full RR. A comprehensive list of RRs is available at the Internet Routing Registry, *http://www.irr.net/*.

Routing Policy Specification Language

For many years, the data in the RRs was in a format described in RIPE document 181, but most RRs now use the Routing Policy Specification Language (RPSL) defined in RFC 2622, which can define a broader set of routing policies.

 The Routing Policy Specification Language isn't part of the BGP protocol. The actual implementation of a routing policy on a set of routers is done with filters and route maps, as discussed in Chapters 5 and further.

A simple routing policy in RPSL format and a ROUTE object to link a block of IP addresses to this policy look like this:

```
whois -h whois.ripe.net 222.33.48.0/20
route:        222.33.48.0/20
descr:        Joes PA block
origin:       AS60000
mnt-by:       JOESWEBFARM-MNT
changed:      joe@joeswebfarm.co.uk 20001020
source:       RIPE
whois -h whois.ripe.net as60000
aut-num:      AS60000
as-name:      JOESWEBFARM-AS
descr:        Joes Web Farm Autonomous System
import:       from AS60001 accept AS60001
import:       from AS60002 accept AS-NANCYSNET
import:       from AS60003 accept ANY
export:       to AS60001 announce AS60000
export:       to AS60002 announce AS60000
export:       to AS60003 announce AS60000
admin-c:      JB600-RIPE
tech-c:       JB600-RIPE
notify:       joe@joeswebfarm.co.uk
mnt-by:       JOESWEBFARM-MNT
changed:      joe@joeswebfarm.co.uk 20001020
source:       RIPE
```

The routing databases use a hybrid object-oriented/relational model, where different kinds of objects are connected through relationships formed by one object referencing another. For example, the AUT-NUM object has a TECH-C field that links to a PERSON object, rather than containing all the information about the technical contact in the AUT-NUM object itself. The most important objects are:

AS-SET

An AS-SET is used to group a number of ASes together. For instance, all the ASes an ISP announces to other ISPs (this includes the ISP's own AS and ASes of BGP-speaking customers). If the ASes you speak BGP with accept the AS-SET rather than just your AS number from you, you can later add more AS numbers without neighboring ASes needing to update their ROUTE objects. Naming for AS-SET objects is AS-<name>.

AUT-NUM

The object that describes an Autonomous System. Naming: AS<number>.

MNTNER

Referring to this object protects other objects from being changed by unauthorized persons. The MNTNER (maintainer) object indicates the type of authentication to be used for all objects. Naming: <name>-MNT.

PERSON

This object holds the details about a single person. The "name" of a PERSON object is the NIC handle: <initials><number>-<registry>.

ROLE

This object is similar to a PERSON object, but it applies to a group of people that share a common role, such as a help desk or a network operations center (NOC). ROLE objects use NIC handles like PERSON objects.

ROUTE

The ROUTE object defines which AUT-NUM objects an IP address range belongs to. ROUTE objects are identified by a prefix: <network>/<bits>.

It isn't necessary to spend a lot of time learning RPSL—many of the objects are fairly self-explanatory, and examples of routing policies will be given later in this book—but RFC 2650, "Using RPSL in Practice" is a good introduction to the Routing Policy Specification Language. Your first interactions with a RR after requesting an AS number should be along these lines:

1. Select a Routing Registry. This should be the RIPE Database in the RIPE region.

2. Select a name for your network in the RR, and check if the name is free. The restrictions on these names are similar to those of domain names, and you can't use names that begin with AS-, RS-, RTRS-, FLTR-, or PRNG- and some names that are words used in policy expressions, such as ANY, NOT, or INBOUND.

3. Find out how to register a MNTNER object and create one. Instructions are available on the RR's web site under "Routing Registry" or "database."

4. Find out how to update the database. Emailing new or modified objects to a special email address usually does this.

5. If you are now, or may ever be, in the position to provide IP transit service to another AS, register an AS-SET object containing just your own AS number in the set.

6. Create an AUT-NUM object for your AS.

7. Create ROUTE objects for your address blocks.

It's a good idea to protect your objects in the RR database by using DES or PGP authentication. If you don't, anyone who knows how to falsify the *From:* header in an email address can update or delete information about your network. PGP uses strong encryption, but it's rather complex: installing it just for this purpose is probably overkill, but if you already have it installed, use it. DES encryption works the same way as a traditional Unix *passwd* file: once the password is encrypted, it can no longer be decrypted. Checking whether a supplied password is correct is done by encrypting this password with the same seed and checking whether the result is identical. This means the encrypted password is listed in the MNTNER object, but when updating any object that links to this maintainer, you have to supply the clear text password in a *password:* line.

 This type of DES password authentication is open to password-guessing attacks, the passwords can be intercepted on their way over the network, and updating Route Registry information is usually done using unencrypted email.

If you are the administrator of a Unix machine, the easiest way to create a DES-encrypted password is to change the password for a test user with the *passwd* command and then copy the encrypted password from the */etc/passwd* file. However, some Unix systems use the MD5 algorithm rather than DES. RIPE provides more tips and a link to a web page where you can encrypt passwords on the RIPE Database FAQ page: *http://www.ripe.net/ripencc/faq/database/qa5.html#5.*

CHAPTER 5

Getting Started with BGP

In this chapter I'll take a basic non-BGP Cisco router configuration (see Appendix A for an example configuration) and turn it into a full BGP configuration for a small, multihomed network, step by step. Figure 5-1 shows the Autonomous Systems and the network connections between them that are used for examples in this chapter.

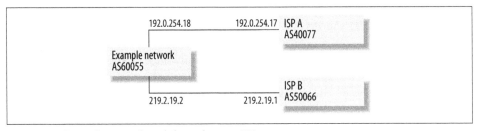

Figure 5-1. Example network multihomed to two ISPs

Enabling BGP

It's common to use *ip unnumbered* for point-to-point (leased line) connections to an ISP, as shown in Example 5-1.

Example 5-1. Unnumbered configuration for a leased line

```
!
interface Ethernet0
 ip address 192.0.2.65 255.255.255.192
!
interface Serial0
 description ISP A
 ip unnumbered Ethernet0
!
ip route 0.0.0.0 0.0.0.0 Serial0
!
```

Without BGP, there is no need to assign a small subnet to the leased line "network," because the remote system is already uniquely identified by the fact that it's the only system at the other side of the point-to-point link. There must still be an IP address present to enable IP processing for the interface, however. The *ip unnumbered* command "borrows" the address from another interface (in this case *Ethernet0*) for this purpose. All traffic to the entire Internet is then directed to the Serial0 interface by using the command *ip route 0.0.0.0 0.0.0.0 Serial0* to create a default route, without any need to know the actual address of the router on the other side of the Serial0 interface. Using *ip unnumbered* is appropriate for a non-BGP setup, and BGP can be configured to work this way, but it's easier to configure and debug BGP routing when there is a dedicated subnet for the leased line, as shown in Example 5-2. This way the router automatically knows how to reach its neighbor by virtue of sharing a subnet.

Example 5-2. "Numbered" configuration for a point-to-point interface

```
!
interface Serial0
 ip address 192.0.254.18 255.255.255.252
!
```

A /30, as indicated by the 255.255.255.252 netmask, is the smallest possible regular subnet in IPv4, with four addresses in it, two of which are usable. This fits exactly: one for the local router (192.0.254.18 in this example), one for the remote router (192.0.254.17), and the remaining two addresses are the network and broadcast addresses (192.0.254.16 and 192.0.254.19, respectively). The advantage of using a subnet is that the router always automatically knows where to find its BGP peer without having to rely on static routes. The four-address subnet is usually assigned from the address space of the upstream ISP. Don't forget to include these extra addresses in the anti-spoofing filters (access lists 101 and 102 in the configuration from Appendix A).

How to Announce an Address Block

There are two ways to announce an address block over BGP: by redistributing an internal routing protocol or by statically configuring that a certain prefix be announced. Redistributing is a risky proposition: if something goes wrong with the internal routing, BGP suffers as well. But the opposite isn't necessarily true: after the internal routing has been fixed, BGP may still not work because of flap dampening elsewhere on the Net. Also, the IGP doesn't handle the full address block but rather the many smaller blocks it's divided into. This makes it hard to announce just a single aggregate without leaking more specific routes under all circumstances. For these reasons, it's better to list all prefixes to be announced explicitly in the BGP configuration.

You have to be extra careful if the prefix you want to announce over BGP is already present in the global routing table. This happens in the situation where your ISP announced your address block but you now want to announce it yourself. Because a path to you, over your ISP, is always longer than a path to that ISP, your announcement will not be visible until your ISP stops announcing the same prefix. However, if something is misconfigured, the prefix is lost from the global routing table, and you are unreachable. This situation calls for close coordination with the ISP involved.

This applies only when you're going to announce the exact same address block/prefix your ISP was announcing and not a smaller (or bigger) one.

Note that the address blocks you announce over BGP don't have to match the way the address space is used internally. For instance, if the organization has been assigned the range 192.0.2.0/24, but the ranges actually in use are 192.0.2.0/26 and 192.0.2.64/26, the announcement over BGP should still be 192.0.2.0/24.

Configuring the Router

We now have an AS number and address space, we know how we want to announce it, and we have a "numbered" network interface, so let's configure BGP:

1. The first step is to enter configuration mode and enable BGP:

   ```
   router bgp <AS number>
   ```

   The router should now show a *(config-router)#* instead of a *(config)#* prompt.

2. Add the address prefix to be announced:

   ```
   network <network address> mask <network mask>
   ```

   Note that the mask part doesn't show up in the configuration if the entered network/mask combination matches a valid classful net. In other words, *network 96.0.0.0 mask 255.0.0.0* simply shows as *network 96.0.0.0*.

3. Add the address and AS number of a neighboring router to the configuration:

   ```
   neighbor <ip address> remote-as <remote AS number>
   ```

4. Allow only routes that originate here to be announced to the neighboring AS:

   ```
   neighbor <ip address> filter-list 2 out
   ```

5. Just to be safe, also filter on IP address for outgoing updates:

   ```
   neighbor <ip address> distribute-list 3 out
   ```

6. Leave the BGP configuration mode and go back to regular configuration mode:

   ```
   exit
   ```

7. Add a static route that matches our BGP announcement. If there is no matching route in the routing table, the prefix won't be announced. Routing an address range to the Null0 interface makes sure BGP will always announce our prefix:

   ```
   ip route <network address> <network mask> null0 250
   ```

250 is the administrative distance value. A high administrative distance ensures this static route doesn't get in the way of routes learned from routing protocols.

8. After this comes the outgoing AS path filter. The local AS number is added to the path *after* processing outbound AS path access lists, so we have to check for an empty path if we want to announce only our own locally sourced routes. An AS path filter list that allows only an empty AS path is a simple regular expression that matches the beginning of the line (^), immediately followed by the end of the line ($). Everything that isn't explicitly permitted is implicitly denied at the end of the access list, as with all Cisco access lists.

```
ip as-path access-list 2 permit ^$
```

9. The address filter is a regular IP access list:

```
access-list 3 permit host <network address>
```

Example 5-3 lists all the previously discussed changes necessary to create a full BGP configuration. It should be merged with the configurations from Appendix A and Example 5-2 to create a working configuration.

Example 5-3. Configuration changes to enable BGP

```
!
router bgp 60055
 network 192.0.2.0 mask 255.255.255.0
 neighbor 192.0.254.17 remote-as 40077
 neighbor 192.0.254.17 description BGP session to ISP A
 neighbor 192.0.254.17 filter-list 2 out
 neighbor 192.0.254.17 distribute-list 3 out
!
ip route 192.0.2.0 255.255.255.0 null0 250
!
ip as-path access-list 2 permit ^$
!
access-list 3 permit host 192.0.2.0
!
```

Monitoring BGP

If the other side has also configured BGP, a session should come up shortly after entering the BGP configuration commands. The *show ip bgp summary* command makes the Cisco router show the current BGP statistics, including for each neighbor a line that shows its current status, as shown in Example 5-4.

Example 5-4. Partial output of the show ip bgp summary command

```
BR1#show ip bgp summary
Neighbor        V    AS   [...]  Up/Down  State/PfxRcd
192.0.254.17    4 40077  [...]  never    Active
```

The last part of this line, "State/PfxRcd", is what concerns us here. If this shows a number, the BGP session is active, and the number indicates the number of routes received from the neighboring router. If it says Idle, there's a problem; probably the interface used to reach the neighbor is down. If the status is Active, the router is trying to initiate a BGP session, but the other side has not (yet) responded. OpenSent or OpenConfirm means the connection is being initialized.

Once the BGP session is established, the output of *show ip route* should list many routes starting with a B, indicating they have been learned from BGP:

```
BR1#show ip route
B    192.1.0.0/16 [20/0] via 192.0.254.17, 1w2d
B    192.5.4.0/23 [20/0] via 192.0.254.17, 1w2d
B    192.18.224.0/20 [20/0] via 192.0.254.17, 1w2d
```

Closer inspection of one of those routes doesn't show much BGP-specific information. Example 5-5 shows the route to the F.ROOT-SERVERS.NET root name server.

Example 5-5. A BGP-learned route in the routing table

```
BR1#show ip route 192.5.5.241
Routing entry for 192.5.4.0/23, supernet
  Known via "bgp 60055", distance 20, metric 0
  Tag 40077, type external
  Last update from 192.0.254.17 1w2d ago
  Routing Descriptor Blocks:
  * 192.0.254.17, from 192.0.254.17, 1w2d ago
      Route metric is 0, traffic share count is 1
      AS Hops 3
```

The BGP table, however, shows a wealth of BGP information. Example 5-6 uses the *show ip bgp* command to show BGP information for the route from Example 5-5.

Example 5-6. An entry in the BGP table

```
BR1#show ip bgp 192.5.5.241
BGP routing table entry for 192.5.4.0/23, version 3116521
Paths: (1 available, best #1)
  Not advertised to any peer
  40077 30099 3557
    192.0.254.17 from 192.0.254.17 (192.0.251.83)
      Origin IGP, localpref 100, valid, external, best, ref 2
```

Because we have configured only a single BGP peer so far, one of the most important differences between the routing table and the BGP table isn't visible: the BGP table stores all routes from all peers, but the routing table stores only one copy of each route for a certain destination prefix: the one the BGP route selection algorithm considers to be best.[*]

---

[*] Exceptions to this are possible when BGP is configured for load balancing.

Clearing BGP Sessions

Traditionally, after making changes to a BGP configuration that affect how routes to or from a neighbor are processed, the BGP session to that neighbor has to be cleared so that it's reinitialized. For instance, after updating an inbound AS path filter, clearing the session makes the remote router send all its routes so that the new filter can be applied. This is accomplished by issuing the *clear ip bgp* command followed by the IP address or AS number of the neighbor. However, resetting BGP sessions is disruptive; it causes all existing routes received from the BGP neighbor in question to be removed from the BGP and routing tables. Then there is a period of time during which there is no connectivity, or packets are diverted over an alternate path. When the routers decide to reestablish the session, the BGP and routing tables are repopulated, and connectivity is restored. (That is, if the entire process didn't trigger flap-dampening further upstream.)

Soft Reconfiguration Inbound

Having to go through all this just because of a minor routing policy change isn't much fun, so to avoid performing the full session-reestablishment procedure, Cisco implemented a soft reconfiguration option. When enabled for a peer, copies of all routes received from that peer are stored separately from the regular BGP table. After configuring a policy change, it's then possible to apply the new policy to the stored copies of the BGP information without having to reset the session. Soft reconfiguration is enabled as follows:

```
!
router bgp 60055
 neighbor 192.0.254.17 remote-as 40077
 neighbor 192.0.254.17 soft-reconfiguration inbound
!
```

A soft reconfiguration is then executed using the *clear ip bgp ... in* command. This works well, but it has a major disadvantage: it takes a lot of memory.

Route Refresh

Alternatively, most 12.0 and later versions of IOS implement the route refresh capability described in RFC 2918. This makes it possible to ask a peer to resend all its routes with the *clear ip bgp ... in* command if the peer also supports route refresh. You can check this with *show ip bgp neighbors*. The router will then show the neighbor's BGP capabilities for all BGP sessions:

```
Neighbor capabilities:
  Route refresh: advertised and received
  Address family IPv4 Unicast: advertised and received
```

You can also send your own routes again using *clear ip bgp ... out*, or you can refresh the routes in both directions with *clear ip bgp ... soft*. The route-refresh feature doesn't have to be configured or enabled: it's simply available if both the local and the remote routers support it.

Filtering Routes

The BGP routing table is getting quite large these days, so if you are using a somewhat older router, it's likely that it doesn't have enough memory to keep one or more copies of the entire BGP table (one for each peer). One solution would be to install more memory or to get a bigger router, but filtering out some routes is a good alternative. Cisco has three different filters that can be applied on incoming or outgoing BGP updates: filter lists, distribute lists, and prefix lists.

 If you filter out some incoming BGP routes, you need a default route to be able reach the filtered destinations.

Filter Lists

A filter list uses simplified regular expressions to filter AS paths. A good way to use AS path filters is to filter out all paths that are longer than a certain length. Because Cisco's implementation of regular expressions is rather limited, a regular expression that matches seven (or more) AS numbers must consist of seven times the sequence that matches one or more characters (.+) separated by the character that matches (among other things) a space (_). The regular expression .* means "anything": . is any character, * means "match the previous character or multicharacter expression zero or more times." This results in the following filter:

```
!
router bgp 60055
 neighbor 192.0.254.17 filter-list 1 in
!
ip as-path access-list 1 deny .+_.+_.+_.+_.+_.+_.+
ip as-path access-list 1 permit .*
!
```

Filtering on the number of ASes in the path is rather arbitrary, and the limit of seven or more AS numbers in the path even more so. But if a possible path is long, it's unlikely that it's the best path anyway, so if you have to filter, this is a reasonable way to do it. A limit of seven AS hops seems to work well in most cases, but this will vary from network to network. Experiment if necessary.

Distribute Lists

Distribute lists are regular access lists that filter on IP address and are available for all IP routing protocols. *Standard* access lists are numbered from 1 to 99 or 1300 to 1999 and can match only a source address for filtering packets or the destination network address for filtering routes. They are useful if certain routes should be matched regardless of the prefix length, for instance to filter out routes to private address space:

```
!
router bgp 60055
 neighbor 192.0.254.17 distribute-list 10 in
!
access-list 10 deny    10.0.0.0 0.255.255.255
access-list 10 deny    172.16.0.0 0.15.255.255
access-list 10 deny    192.168.0.0 0.0.255.255
access-list 10 permit any
!
```

Note that the "wildcard bits" are the exact opposite of a regular netmask. Unlike standard access lists, *extended* access lists can also filter packets on source and destination address and on a range of protocol-specific items, such as port number. They are numbered from 100 to 199 or from 2000 to 2699. In route filtering, the source address part of the access list matches the destination address of the route, and the destination address part the network mask, with the bitmask of each indicating the range:

```
!
router bgp 60055
 neighbor 192.0.254.17 distribute-list 110 in
!
access-list 110 deny    ip 128.0.0.0 0.255.255.255 255.255.128.0 0.0.127.255
access-list 110 permit ip any any
!
```

This list filters out all announcements of /17 and longer prefixes in 128.0.0.0/8. The destination network address may be anything that starts with 128: the first byte of the mask is 0 (must match exactly); the three other bytes are 255 (wild). The mask part of the route matches all masks ranging from 255.255.128.0 (/17), 255.255.192.0 (/18), and so on, all the way to 255.255.255.254 (/31) and 255.255.255.255 (/32).

Prefix Lists

Prefix lists accomplish the same thing as distribute lists but in an easier to understand and more BGP-compatible manner. This prefix list allows only /20 and shorter prefixes in Class A and Class B space, and /24 and shorter prefixes in Class C space:

```
!
router bgp 60055
 neighbor 192.0.254.17 prefix-list infilter in
 !
 ip prefix-list infilter description inbound filter
 ip prefix-list infilter seq 5 permit 0.0.0.0/1 le 20
 ip prefix-list infilter seq 10 permit 128.0.0.0/2 le 20
 ip prefix-list infilter seq 15 permit 192.0.0.0/3 le 24
 !
```

The *le* keyword matches prefixes that are equal or shorter (less bits in the prefix, bigger blocks of address space). It's also possible to match equal or longer prefixes (more bits in the prefix, smaller blocks of address space) with the *ge* keyword or to specify a range by combining *ge* and *le*. The sequence numbers make it possible to delete individual lines or insert lines. You can't use distribute and filter lists at the same time for inbound or outbound filtering for a neighbor, but either can be combined with an AS path filter.

Internal BGP

Creating additional BGP sessions is straightforward: just adding the right *neighbor* statements to the BGP part of the configuration is enough. Don't forget to type *router bgp <as number>* to enter BGP configuration mode. As long as all BGP peers have similar properties (e.g., two peers are both ISPs), it's usually best to keep the filters for all BGP sessions the same. This keeps the number of access lists in the configuration limited to something manageable.

Having two connections to the Internet over different ISPs helps a lot to keep your network connected to the outside world in the presence of different kinds of external outages. But this means, the local network is now the weakest link. By removing single points of failure from the local network in addition to having multiple external links, you can at least make sure that any kind of failure won't affect connectivity to the *entire* network. This means a second BGP router, so two routers speak BGP with external ASes—and with each other. Adding another router for the second external connection is easily accomplished: you can pretty much copy the configuration of the first router and just change the Ethernet IP address and ISP-specific settings. Example 5-7 shows the BR2 configuration, with the security settings and access lists left out (these are the same as in the BR1 configuration).

Example 5-7. Second BGP router configuration

```
!
hostname BR2
!
interface Ethernet0
 ip address 192.0.2.66 255.255.255.192
!
interface Serial0
 description ISP B
 encapsulation ppp
 ip address 219.2.19.2 255.255.255.252
!
router bgp 60055
 network 192.0.2.0 mask 255.255.255.0
 neighbor 219.2.19.1 remote-as 50066
 neighbor 219.2.19.1 description BGP session to ISP B
 neighbor 219.2.19.1 filter-list 1 in
 neighbor 219.2.19.1 filter-list 2 out
 neighbor 219.2.19.1 distribute-list 3 out
!
ip route 0.0.0.0 0.0.0.0 Serial0
route 192.0.2.0 255.255.255.0 null0 250
!
```

With the second router in place and configured for BGP, there are now two announcements for the local network to the rest of the world. Both routers have the "network" statement and a matching route in their configuration, but the two are completely unaware of each other. There is no reason why this shouldn't work: if a packet happens to come in over ISP B, BR2 (the second router) will forward the packet to the host on the local network the packet is addressed to, just as BR1 would have done had the packet come in over ISP A. However, all outgoing traffic will end up on BR1, because that is the one the hosts have configured as their default gateway. And BR1 will always send the traffic to ISP A, because it has no way of knowing that a better route exists over BR2.

Enabling iBGP

By configuring the routers to talk internal BGP (iBGP) each can take advantage of the routes the other learns over external BGP (eBGP). This is accomplished in Example 5-8 by configuring iBGP over a dedicated Ethernet between the routers. This way, traffic doesn't have to traverse the same Ethernet twice and the second Ethernet can also provide a backup path when the Ethernet0 interface of either router is down.

Example 5-8. BR1 iBGP configuration

```
!
hostname BR1
!
```

Example 5-8. BR1 iBGP configuration (continued)

```
interface Ethernet1
 ip address 192.0.2.49 255.255.255.252
 description Connection to BR2
!
router bgp 60055
 no synchronization
 neighbor 192.0.2.50 remote-as 60055
 neighbor 192.0.2.50 description iBGP session to BR2
 neighbor 192.0.2.50 next-hop-self
!
ip route 0.0.0.0 0.0.0.0 192.0.2.50 250
ip route 192.0.2.64 255.255.255.192 192.0.2.50 250
!
```

The configuration changes for BR2 are identical to those for BR1, except that the IP addresses 192.0.2.49 and 192.0.2.50, and the names BR1 and BR2 are reversed.

 When running iBGP with more than two routers, the iBGP connections must be fully meshed. In other words: every iBGP router must have iBGP connections to all other iBGP routers. Under normal circumstances, iBGP sessions aren't configured with filters.

Default Routes

The *ip route 0.0.0.0 0.0.0.0 192.0.2.50 250* command in Example 5-8 creates a floating static route that lies dormant while the regular default route that points to Serial0 (*ip route 0.0.0.0 0.0.0.0 Serial0*) is active. But when the Serial0 goes down, the default route disappears, and the floating route is entered into the routing table. All traffic for which there's no route in BGP is then sent to the BR2 router, which uses its own default route to send it to ISP B. This route "floats" because it has an explicit higher administrative distance value of 250, while the regular default route with no explicit distance has the default administrative distance for static routes of 1.

The *ip route 192.0.2.64 255.255.255.192 192.0.2.50 250* command does the same thing for the Ethernet connecting the router to the rest of the internal network: as long as the Ethernet0 interface is up, the route to 192.0.2.64/26 is "directly connected" with a distance of 0, but when the interface is down, the floating static route makes sure packets for the internal network are routed over the other router.

If you get copies of the full global routing table from your transit ISPs, you don't need a default route in your BGP routers, but some ISPs send you a default route over BGP. This looks like any other route in the BGP table:

```
   Network    Next Hop       Metric LocPrf Weight Path
*> 0.0.0.0    192.0.254.17                     0 40077 i
```

You can filter out a default just like any other route. Example 5-9 shows a prefix list and a regular access list that both filter out just the default and let everything else through.

Example 5-9. Filtering out default routes in BGP

```
!
ip prefix-list nodefault description filter to remove default
ip prefix-list nodefault seq 5 deny 0.0.0.0/0
ip prefix-list nodefault seq 10 permit 0.0.0.0/0 le 32
!
access-list 130 remark route filter to remove default
access-list 130 deny    ip host 0.0.0.0 host 0.0.0.0
access-list 130 permit ip any any
!
```

The prefix list first denies exactly 0.0.0.0/0 (the entire IPv4 address space is the default route) and then allows all prefixes up to /32 in 0.0.0.0/0 (which is everything). The extended access list 130 does the same thing by denying address 0.0.0.0 with mask 0.0.0.0 and then allowing everything else.

Next Hop Processing

The *next-hop-self* command instructs the router to replace the next hop attribute in the route updates it sends to the peer with its own IP address. The next hop is the address where packets that match the route should be sent to. In eBGP, changing the next hop is handled automatically, but in iBGP the next hop isn't automatically changed. Without *next-hop-self*, the routes BR1 learns from BR2 contain the IP address of BR2's eBGP peer (219.2.19.1) as the next hop. But BR1 doesn't know this address, so it can't add the routes learned from BR2 to the routing table. In larger networks there are Interior Gateway Protocols so every router in the network knows how to reach all the eBGP peers for all its iBGP peers. In our test network it's easier to use the *next-hop-self* command. That way, routers running iBGP only have to know how to send packets to the right iBGP peer. Since they are obviously able to maintain a BGP session with that peer, this isn't a problem.

Synchronizing with the IGP

The *no synchronization* command is a bit tricky. By default, Cisco routers don't include routes they have learned through iBGP in the regular routing table until they see those routes present in an IGP. The theory behind this behavior is that if such a route isn't visible in the IGP, non-BGP-speaking routers between the iBGP peers won't know how to handle the traffic to the route's destination. Such an inconsistency between BGP and non-BGP speaking routers leads to black holes. So to avoid this, Cisco assumes you will be redistributing all routing information learned by BGP into your IGP. Nobody does this anymore, however, because it puts a lot of stress on

IGPs that weren't designed to handle 100,000 routes. Also, it's much easier to run just iBGP on all (core) routers. Routes that aren't used because synchronization is in effect usually (but not always!) show up as not synchronized in the output of the *show ip bgp <network address>* command, as shown in Example 5-10.

Example 5-10. An entry in the BGP table

```
BR1#show ip bgp 192.5.5.241
BGP routing table entry for 192.5.4.0/23, version 416923
Paths: (1 available, no best path)
  Not advertised to any peer
  40077 30099 3557
    192.0.2.50 from 192.0.2.50 (192.0.2.50)
      Origin IGP, localpref 100, valid, internal, not synchronized, ref 2
```

 Even, or rather especially, when running iBGP without an IGP, it's necessary to add the *no synchronization* command to your BGP configuration because otherwise, the router tries to synchronize. Even on a fast router, waiting for an IGP that isn't there takes a long time. Meanwhile, the iBGP routes just sit in the BGP table, but they won't be used to forward packets.

The Internal Network

Spending a lot of money to connect two BGP routers over diversely routed fibers to two different ISPs is still an exercise in futility if both routers are connected to the local network over a single switch, and the switch fails. Replacing the switch with a hub helps to some extent: hubs don't need any software to do their job so they are less likely to fail. However, even hubs sometimes stop functioning and have to be power-cycled. The solution is to use two switches (or hubs), as shown in Figure 5-2.

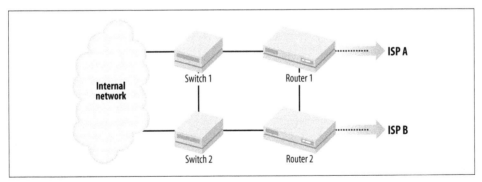

Figure 5-2. A simple fault-tolerant network design

During normal operation in this network design, each router looks at packets it receives from the internal network and sends those packets either directly to the ISP it's connected to or, if the path over the other ISP is shorter, to the other router (over the direct link between the routers). Incoming packets are transmitted to the internal network over the switch the router is connected to, and they travel over the link between the two switches if necessary. The routers handle failures of the external connection or the ISPs. When one router fails, the other detects this and handles all the traffic on its own. If a switch fails, the router connected to that switch is no longer reachable from the internal network, so systems on the internal network that run an IGP should detect this and start using the other router. If the switch is really down, the router no longer sees an active link on its Ethernet interface, the interface goes down, the floating static route appears, and incoming traffic flows over the link between the routers. However, switches often fail without it being visible to the routers and other systems connected them. In this case, the router continues to send traffic to the switch, and this traffic is lost.

Cisco's Hot Standby Routing Protocol

If the internal network consists of just a single Ethernet with a number of hosts such as web servers and PCs in it, the presence of an IGP is unlikely. Most servers support RIP as an IGP, but RIP has long time-outs, so this doesn't do much good. Alternatively, with Cisco's Hot Standby Routing Protocol (HSRP), two routers can each detect when the other fails without involvement from the rest of the network. With HSRP, two or more routers share an IP address. During normal operation, one router holds the address. Usually, other systems on the network will use the HSRP IP address as their default gateway. When the router holding the address goes down, another router takes over. Since all the hosts on our test network use the IP address of BR1 as their default gateway, it's easiest to give BR1 a new address and use its old address as the HSRP address. Example 5-11 shows the configuration changes to enable HSRP on BR1.

Example 5-11. Enabling HSRP

```
!
interface Ethernet0
 ip address 192.0.2.67 255.255.255.192
 standby 1 ip 192.0.2.65
 standby 1 timers 1 3
!
```

By default, HSRP sends hello messages every three seconds and times out after not seeing a hello message for 10 seconds. This means that if a router or switch goes down, it takes 10 seconds for another router to take over the shared address. In this example, the timers are changed to one second for the hello time and three seconds for the hold time, so there is only a three-second delay before another router takes over. The timers must be the same on all routers in an HSRP group. See the Cisco documentation for information on additional HSRP features. There's also a similar

Virtual Router Redundancy Protocol (VRRP), standardized in RFC 2338, but this isn't widely implemented throughout the Cisco product line.

Full BR2 Configuration

Example 5-12 shows the full BR2 configuration after incorporating all the changes discussed earlier in this chapter.

Example 5-12. Full BR2 configuration

```
!
version 12.0
!
hostname BR2
!
ip subnet-zero
no ip source-route
!
interface Ethernet0
 ip address 192.0.2.66 255.255.255.192
 standby 1 ip 192.0.2.65
 standby 1 timers 1 3
 no ip directed-broadcast
!
interface Ethernet1
 ip address 192.0.2.50 255.255.255.252
 description Connection to BR1
 no ip directed-broadcast
!
interface Serial0
 description ISP B
 encapsulation ppp
 ip address 219.2.19.2 255.255.255.252
 ip access-group 101 in
 ip access-group 102 out
 no ip directed-broadcast
!
router bgp 60055
 network 192.0.2.0
 no synchronization
 neighbor 192.0.2.49 remote-as 60055
 neighbor 192.0.2.49 description iBGP session to BR1
 neighbor 192.0.2.49 next-hop-self
 neighbor 219.2.19.1 remote-as 50066
 neighbor 219.2.19.1 description BGP session to ISP B
 neighbor 219.2.19.1 filter-list 1 in
 neighbor 219.2.19.1 filter-list 2 out
 neighbor 219.2.19.1 distribute-list 3 out
!
ip classless
ip route 0.0.0.0 0.0.0.0 Serial0
ip route 0.0.0.0 0.0.0.0 192.0.2.49 10
```

Example 5-12. Full BR2 configuration (continued)

```
ip route 192.0.2.0 255.255.255.0 null0 250
ip route 192.0.2.64 255.255.255.192 192.0.2.49 250
!
ip as-path access-list 1 deny .+_.+_.+_.+_.+_.+_.+
ip as-path access-list 1 permit .*
ip as-path access-list 2 permit ^$
!
access-list 3 permit host 192.0.2.0
access-list 101 deny   ip 192.0.2.0 0.0.0.255 any log
access-list 101 deny   ip host 192.0.254.18 any log
access-list 101 deny   ip host 219.2.19.2 any log
access-list 101 deny   icmp any any redirect log
access-list 101 permit ip any 192.0.2.0 0.0.0.255
access-list 101 permit ip any host 192.0.254.18
access-list 101 permit ip any host 219.2.19.2
access-list 101 deny   ip any any log
access-list 102 permit ip 192.0.2.0 0.0.0.255 any
access-list 102 permit ip host 192.0.254.18 any
access-list 102 permit ip host 219.2.19.2 any
access-list 102 deny   ip any any log
!
```

The configuration that the router shows with the *show configuration* or *show running-config* commands can be slightly different from the configuration you have entered. If a command enables the default behavior for a certain IOS version, it usually doesn't show up when listing the configuration. This can lead to problems when upgrading a router's IOS version or when copying a configuration to a router running another version of Cisco's IOS. For instance, the *ip directed-broadcast* command won't show in the configuration of a router running IOS Version 11.2, because forwarding directed broadcasts is the default behavior in this version. But after upgrading to 12.0, directed broadcasts are no longer forwarded because it doesn't say *ip directed-broadcast* in the configuration, and the default now is not to forward.

RPSL Routing Policy

Example 5-13 shows the routing policy in RPSL format for the example multihomed network discussed in this chapter. The sequence between the < and > characters is a regular expression for the AS paths that are accepted from each peer. These are full-blown POSIX regular expressions, so it's much easier to encode a sequence of fewer than seven AS numbers. Note that a dot equals an AS number here, not a single character in the AS path as with Cisco regular expressions, and {,6} means "repeat up to six times." Rather than disallowing AS paths with seven or more AS numbers, as in the router configuration, we allow six or fewer here. The ^ matches the beginning of the path, and the $ matches the end, so the expression matches six or fewer AS numbers only, and not any route that has a sequence of six or fewer AS numbers as a part of its AS path, which would be all possible paths.

Example 5-13. RPSL routing policy for multihoming with AS path filters

```
aut-num:      AS60055
import:       from AS40077 accept <^.{,6}$>
import:       from AS50066 accept <^.{,6}$>
export:       to AS40077 announce AS60055
export:       to AS50066 announce AS60055
default:      to AS40077
default:      to AS50066
```

Minimizing the Impact of Link Failures

When a remote router or the link connecting to this router goes down, it's important to recognize this situation as soon as possible so that traffic can be routed around the failure. To detect such failures, BGP uses keepalive messages and the hold timer. Whenever the router receives a keepalive message from a neighbor, the hold timer for that neighbor is reset to 0. When keepalive messages fail to appear, the hold timer eventually reaches the predefined limit, and the session is torn down. The default hold time is 180 seconds, so when a link or router goes down, it takes up to 3 minutes for the session to be terminated. In the meantime, packets are forwarded to the dead router or link, so they are lost.

In addition to the hold timer, Cisco routers also monitor the interface status and terminate the session as soon as the interface it runs over goes down. But with this *fast-external-fallover* feature enabled, even removing an Ethernet connector for a couple of seconds to untangle some cables means that the BGP session to a router on the other side of that Ethernet will be terminated. Thus, using the default *fast-external-fallover* behavior on interfaces that tend to go down for a few seconds once in a while isn't such a good idea, because it leads to route flapping. Most connections are stable, however, and most interface types don't declare themselves down at the drop of a hat. For instance, by default, PPP and Cisco HDLC use a keepalive mechanism of their own, with an interval of 10 seconds. The router sends out keepalives on the interface every 10 seconds, and only when it hasn't seen one return for three keepalive times (30 seconds) it puts the interface in the "down" state. The router also looks at physical indications to determine the interface status, but often those report only the status of the next device (such as a switch or the CSU/DSU unit for a leased line) rather than end-to-end connectivity. So depending on *fast-external-fallover* to detect link or interface failures doesn't help much, and there are circumstances in which it's actually harmful. Lowering the keepalive interval (in this case, to three seconds) helps:

```
!
interface Serial0
 keepalive 3
!
```

Short keepalive intervals can cause instability, and some line protocols (such as Cisco HDLC) don't react well to different keepalive intervals on each side of the connection.

If you prefer to disable *bgp fast-external-fallover*, or if the router can't detect whether
the connection to the other end is up or down (which is typically the case in
switched environments, such as Ethernet and ATM), you can minimize the time
between a link going down and the BGP session doing the same by drastically lowering the hold time and keepalive that govern the BGP session time-out. Cisco's default
of 60 seconds between keepalives is twice as high as the suggested value in RFC
1771, which is already conservative. The default hold time is three times the default
keepalive time, as recommended in the RFC: 180 seconds. So by default, it takes
three minutes for a BGP session to time out when there is no longer a link between
two peers.

Setting a lower hold time (and the related keepalive) is advisable. You may go all the
way down to one second for the keepalive timer, but be careful: if your connection is
of limited bandwidth, the keepalive packet may be in the output queues for a relatively long time, and your BGP sessions may time out because of queuing delays.
Cisco routers generally use a 40-packet output queue, so up to 60 KB of data may be
buffered. If this is the case, it takes nearly eight seconds for a BGP keepalive packet
to reach the router on the other side of a 64-Kbps line, and another eight seconds for
the response to travel back. Strictly speaking, there is no necessity for a keepalive to
have been answered before the next is sent, but setting the keepalive high enough to
have the keepalive come back before the next one is sent, and then using a the recommended hold time of three times the keepalive time, keeps the configuration easy
to understand. The hold time is the time after which the router will tear down the
session if no keepalives are seen from the other side. Table 5-1 lists minimum BGP
keepalive and hold times, assuming a maximum queue size of 40 1500-byte packets
and 4% PPP overhead.

Table 5-1. Minimum BGP keepalive times for lower-speed connections

Bandwidth (Kbps)	Queuing delay (sec.)	Minimum keepalive (sec.)	Minimum hold time (sec.)
64	7.8	20	60
128	3.9	10	30
256	2	5	15
512	1	3	9
1544	0.3	2	6

A good rule of thumb for lower keepalive and hold times for connections that are 1 Mbps or faster is a 5-second keepalive and a 15-second hold time.

Example 5-14 disables *fast-external-fallover*, sets the BGP keepalive to 5 seconds and the hold time to 15 seconds. Then the keepalive and hold time are set to 10 and 30, respectively, for a specific neighbor.

Example 5-14. Setting the timers and disabling fast-external-fallover

```
!
router bgp 60055
 no bgp fast-external-fallover
 timers bgp 5 15
 neighbor 192.0.254.17 timers 10 30
!
```

It isn't necessary for the timers to be configured the same on both peers, because they negotiate the hold time when the BGP session is established. The lower of the hold times the two routers want to use is selected, and if necessary, the keepalive time is lowered so that it's a third of the hold time. Setting a hold time below three seconds isn't allowed.

eBGP Multihop

It's required for eBGP neighbors to connect to a common subnet, such as an Ethernet segment (with or without a switch) or a point-to-point link. Sometimes it can be useful, however, to ignore this rule and configure an eBGP session between two routers that don't share a direct connection but need at least one other router in the middle to communicate, as illustrated in Figure 5-3.

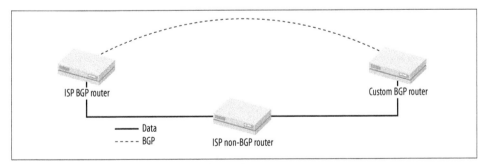

Figure 5-3. eBGP with a non-BGP router hop in between

The most common reason this is necessary is that a BGP customer connects to an ISP router that doesn't support BGP or doesn't have enough memory or CPU to handle full routing. The router will happily accept *neighbor* statements for a peer IP address that isn't directly connected, but under normal circumstances, the BGP session won't come up in such a setup. This is because the router checks whether the eBGP peer is directly reachable:

```
BR1#show ip bgp neighbors
[...]
    External BGP neighbor not directly connected.
    No active TCP connection
```

This behavior can be modified using the *ebgp-multihop* command, so eBGP over one or more extra hops is allowed for a neighbor. This is shown in Example 5-15.

Example 5-15. Configuring eBGP over multiple hops

```
!
router bgp 60055
 neighbor 192.0.252.93 remote-as 40077
 neighbor 192.0.252.93 ebgp-multihop 2
!
ip route 192.0.252.93 255.255.255.255 192.0.254.17
ip route 192.0.252.93 255.255.255.255 Null0 250
!
```

The first *ip route 192.0.252.93 ...* command makes sure the router always communicates with its BGP peer 192.0.252.93 over the ISP's non-BGP router 192.0.254.17 as long as this router is reachable; the second one makes sure this address isn't rerouted over another ISP by routing it to the null interface. This avoids loops and other strange behavior, such as the BGP session to ISP A running over ISP B. The command *neighbor ... ebgp-multihop 2* allows a single extra hop between the two eBGP peers:

```
BR1#show ip bgp neighbors
[...]
    External BGP neighbor may be up to 2 hops away.
```

A value of 1 for the *ebgp-multihop* command results in the default behavior in which the eBGP peers must be directly connected. Leaving out the number of hops is the same as configuring *ebgp-multihop 255*.

 The routing between both BGP peers must be compatible with what's in the routing table of the non-BGP router between them, or there will be routing loops.

CHAPTER 6

Traffic Engineering

Being multihomed means you have two (or more) routes to any destination connected to the Internet. In other words, you need a way to decide which route is better. When left to its own devices, a BGP router will try to send traffic over the route with the shortest AS path. Depending on the connectivity of your upstream ISPs and traffic patterns, this will suit the available bandwidth of the respective connections to varying degrees. Even though bandwidth is getting cheaper all the time, it's usually advantageous to try to balance the traffic so that it takes advantage of all the available bandwidth in a multihomed setup. Thus, if BGP decides that most of the outgoing traffic should go through the smallest pipe, you will have to tell it that this isn't what you want by tweaking one or more BGP attributes. Ideally, more traffic will then flow over the under-used connection. At the same time, you'll want the traffic to take the best route to a destination, if possible, whatever "best" may be. This type of activity is called *traffic engineering*.

Engineering outgoing traffic is the easy part, because you have control over what your own routers do. It's harder to get incoming traffic balanced properly over the available connections. At the end of the chapter, there is a discussion of queuing, traffic shaping, and traffic policing techniques that can be used to maximize network performance under low-bandwidth conditions.

The examples in this chapter all assume a network with Autonomous System number 60055 multihomed to two ISPs: ISP A (AS 40077) and ISP B (AS 50066). The way ISP A and ISP B interconnect with other ASes differs from example to example, however. See Figure 6-1.

Unlike in Chapter 5, the connections to both ISP A and ISP B terminate at the same router, so the settings for both ISPs can be shown side by side.

> The examples in this chapter show only the commands necessary to perform the function being discussed. You also need to configure filters and other features discussed in Chapter 5 to arrive at a working configuration.

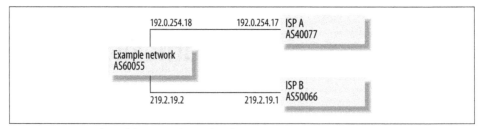

Figure 6-1. Network used for examples in this chapter

Knowing Which Route Is Best

Traditionally, there have been three figures that describe the quality of a connection: bandwidth, delay, and packet loss. A connection with high bandwidth, low delay, and low packet loss is obviously better than one with low bandwidth, high delay, and high packet loss. But which is better: a 45-Mbps satellite connection with a 300-millisecond delay,[*] or a 1544-Kbps terrestrial connection with a 3-ms delay? There is of course no easy answer: it depends. A protocol such as Telnet uses very little bandwidth, but when the user presses a key, he has to wait for the packet containing the input character to travel over the network and for the packet containing the response to travel back again before it shows up on his screen. So any delay of more than a few dozen milliseconds is immediately noticeable. With FTP, the time individual packets take to traverse the line is of little importance. What counts is the total time the file transfer takes, which depends mostly on the bandwidth of the connection. Both low-bandwidth, delay-sensitive applications such as Telnet and bandwidth-hungry, delay-tolerant ones such as FTP suffer from packet loss, because both typically use TCP. TCP uses complex algorithms to optimize performance (especially data throughput) for every possible combination of delay, bandwidth, and packet loss. TCP assumes packet loss indicates congestion in the network, so it slows down when packets are lost. (The TCP congestion management algorithms are discussed at the end of this chapter.)

Finding High- and Low-Quality Routes

There are no hard and fast rules about which quality makes a certain route better than another: application requirements are different, and the interaction between the bandwidth, delay, and packet loss parameters complicate matters further. But that doesn't mean there is nothing you can do. It may be hard to determine which of two good routes is best, but it isn't hard to determine that a route is bad. Some

---

[*] "Delay" usually means the time from the moment a bit enters a circuit on one end until the moment it appears at the other end, but it's used interchangeably with round trip time (RTT) here, as the time it takes to receive a reply for a packet sent.

experimentation with the *traceroute* program can bring interesting information to the surface you can use to base your route selection policy on.

---

traceroute

The *traceroute* program is available on almost every system that runs TCP/IP. Under Windows it's called *tracert*; on most other systems, it's simply *traceroute*.

traceroute manipulates the TTL field in the header of IP packets it transmits to the "traced" host. Every router is required to lower the TTL on packets it forwards and destroy packets when the TTL reaches 0. This way if there is a routing loop, packets won't circle the network forever.

In the first three probe packets, the TTL is set to 1. When the first router receives the packet, it decrements the TTL to 0. So the router throws away the packet and sends an ICMP "TTL exceeded in transit" error message back to the originating system. *traceroute* then prints the name and address of the router that sent the ICMP packet on the screen, along with the time the whole process took. When no ICMP message is received, the program prints an asterisk (*) on the screen.

After three probes with a TTL of one, *traceroute* sends out another three probes with a TTL of two. These packets are forwarded by the first router, but the TTL is decremented to 0 in the second router. So the next line on the screen has information about the second hop. The program continues to send probes with increasing TTLs until it finally receives packets from the destination host, at which time it stops.

The asterisks that indicate lost packets and the names (often containing a city or airport code) of routers along the way and the timing information can be informative. But because routers typically create the ICMP messages that are sent back to the *traceroute* program in a way that has little to do with actual packet forwarding, *traceroute* results offer only an indication of the network performance and not any definitive information.

Doing some traceroutes to destinations that are reachable over a certain path will often reveal some or all of the following information, which you may want to use to select the preferred route to certain destinations:

Congestion
  Congestion lowers the available bandwidth and increases delay and packet loss, so it's important to avoid routes over congested paths. Congestion shows up in a traceroute in two ways: there is usually packet loss, and the round-trip times are often inconsistent: most of the time high, but sometimes low.

Distance
  Two routes can have different paths. Some networks interconnect only at relatively few locations, so they may have to transport traffic over long distances to get it to its destination. Others have better interconnection, so the traffic doesn't

have to take a detour. There may be reasons not to prefer the more direct route, such as lower bandwidth or congestion, but generally a shorter geographic path is better. Every 100 kilometers or 60 miles of fiber adds about a millisecond to the round-trip time, because light travels at a speed of approximately 207,000 km or 129,000 miles per second in fiber. A trans-Atlantic or transcontinental detour can easily add up to more than 100-ms extra delay.

The distance of a path isn't directly visible in *traceroute* (apart from the higher delay), but many networks are helpful enough to give their router descriptive names, so it's possible to deduce the geographic path to some extent. Also, this information may be available in BGP itself in the form of communities that indicate where a route was learned.

Hops

In general, the number of hops that shows up on a traceroute isn't too important. But each hop potentially adds additional delay, because packets have to wait in a queue before they are transmitted, and the extra equipment in a path means that a failure somewhere along the way is more likely. So all else being equal, paths with fewer hops are slightly better. On the other hand, paths with few hops probably use some kind of layer 2 switching, such as frame relay or ATM, which adds another layer of complexity to the network.

It may be necessary to temporarily reroute outgoing traffic to observe the properties of alternative paths. See the section "Setting the Local Preference" for more details on how to do this. Example 6-1 is the output of a *traceroute* to a somewhat congested destination. (Parts of the domain names and IP addresses have been removed for brevity.)

Example 6-1. traceroute showing some congestion

```
traceroute to g.root-servers.net (192.112.36.4), 30 hops max, 40 byte packets
 1  208.100 (208.100)  0.602 ms  0.511 ms  0.498 ms
 2  63.1 (63.1)  0.306 ms  0.272 ms  0.415 ms
 3  pos3-2.gw2.dca8 (157.58)  0.982 ms  0.957 ms  0.967 ms
 4  0.so-3-0.XL2.DCA8 (46.94)  1.116 ms  1.104 ms  1.095 ms
 5  0.so-7-0.XL2.DCA6 (46.25)  2.456 ms  2.672 ms  2.444 ms
 6  POS7-0.BR4.DCA6 (52.233)  2.408 ms  2.356 ms  2.369 ms
 7  204.98 (204.98)  3.296 ms  3.395 ms  3.314 ms
 8  wdc-core-01.inet (205.37)  3.344 ms  3.320 ms  3.293 ms
 9  wdc-edge-05.inet (205.82)  3.465 ms  3.354 ms  3.295 ms
10  63.222 (63.222)  5.929 ms  226.962 ms  11.260 ms
11  198.50 (198.50)  52.694 ms  79.870 ms  33.990 ms
12  G.ROOT-SERVERS.NET (192.4)  23.892 ms  *  19.495 ms
```

Beginning at line 10, there is a sudden increase in delay, and the delay becomes inconsistent from one probe packet to another. If this was the result of distance, the increase in delay would be across the board; light always travels at the same speed. Also, both the source and destination of the trace are in Virginia in this example. A lot of interconnection takes place there, so a detour is unlikely. The delay stabilizes at the last hop, so the earlier delay figures are probably due to high CPU load for the two hops just before the last, and the ICMP processing took a relatively long time. But the 20-ms delay with a 4-ms (20%) difference between the two delay figures on the last line indicates either a rather slow connection or high queuing delays. There is no packet loss, however, other than the asterisk in the middle of the last line. A missing answer to the second probe on a line usually indicates that the responding host or router limits the number of responses to probe packets per unit of time. So the level of congestion seen here isn't high.

Is the Highest-Bandwidth Route Best?

As you may have noticed, bandwidth isn't on my list of route-selection criteria. Obviously, bandwidth can be a decisive factor. For instance, if you connect to the vBNS or another high bandwidth network, you'll want to take advantage of this connection. You should then probably prefer all routes over the high bandwidth link. But in most cases, you will connect to ISPs that have many times the bandwidth you require, even if one ISP has even more than another. And if one of your connections is faster than another, this doesn't mean you'll want to use the faster connection for all traffic. For instance, balancing traffic so three quarters of it flows over a 4.5-Mbps fractional T3 connection and a quarter flows over a T1 results in an effective bandwidth of 6 Mbps. Using the fractional T3 connection for all traffic means no individual stream or session is limited to the maximum bandwidth of the slower T1 line, but it limits the total available bandwidth to that of the 4.5-Mbps line.

If you know in advance the IP addresses that high bandwidth applications will connect to, you can prefer routes to those address ranges over the higher bandwidth connection. If these addresses are not known, or the list is too long, you'll have to look at other factors when configuring route selection parameters on the router.

Route Maps

Cisco IOS provides the network administrator with *route maps* to modify the Local Preference, AS path, and MED prior to inclusion of a route in the BGP table and the subsequent best route selection process, or before a route is propagated to a neighbor. A route map is much like an if-then construction in a programming language. First, a *match* line is applied. If the route matches, the *set* lines that follow are applied. The route is then passed to the BGP table or to the neighbor, depending on whether the route map is set for incoming or outgoing route updates. Route maps are grouped together using a tag or name, and each route map has a sequence number. The route map with the lowest sequence number is evaluated first. When all route maps that share the same tag have been evaluated but there is no match, or when there is an explicit *deny*, the route is rejected and not entered into the BGP table or announced to the neighbor. Here are the *match* criteria most relevant to BGP processing:

as-path
> Using an AS path access list

community
> Using a community list

ip address
> Using an access list or prefix list

ip next-hop
> Using an access list or prefix list

metric
> The Multi Exit Discriminator

Actions that can be taken using the *set* part of a route map include:

as-path
> Prepending extra AS numbers to the AS path

comm-list
> Deleting communities

community
> Adding or replacing communities

dampening
> Setting the flap-dampening parameters

ip next-hop
> Setting the next hop address

local-preference
> Setting the Local Preference

metric
> Setting or changing the MED metric

weight
> Setting the weight value

More information on route maps is available in the Cisco documentation, available over the Web at *http://www.cisco.com*.

Setting the Local Preference

The easiest and most effective way to influence the BGP path selection process is to adjust the Local Preference. This works well when certain routes are always better than others, for instance:

- Routes over the main connection are preferred over routes that use a slower backup connection.
- Routes from peering connections are preferred over routes from transit connections.
- Routes directly to customers are preferred over external routes.

Example 6-2 shows part of a BGP configuration where the routes received from both peers receive different Local Preference values.

Example 6-2. Setting the Local Preference for all routes received from a BGP neighbor

```
!
router bgp 60055
 neighbor 192.0.254.17 remote-as 40077
 neighbor 192.0.254.17 route-map ispa-in in
 neighbor 219.2.19.1 remote-as 50066
 neighbor 219.2.19.1 route-map ispb-in in
!
route-map ispa-in permit 10
 set local-preference 90
!
route-map ispb-in permit 10
 set local-preference 110
!
```

The *permit* keyword in the *route-map* statement means matched routes will be permitted to enter the BGP table or be propagated to the neighbor; a *deny* route map will filter out all routes matching the *match* clause. The number 10 is the sequence number, used to apply the different route maps with the same tag in the right sequence. In this case, there is only one route map for each tag (ispa-in and ispb-in), so the sequence number doesn't do anything.

Since we want to match all routes, there is no need to supply a *match* clause for the route maps. Both route maps just use a *set* clause to set the Local Preference for every route that is received from the respective neighbor. This has the effect that if ISP B has a route to a destination, this route will always be preferred over the route ISP A has to the same destination. Routes from ISP A will be used only if there is no matching route over ISP B. This would be a good routing policy if traffic over ISP B is a lot cheaper than traffic over ISP A. Example 6-3 shows the BGP table after applying the route maps.

Example 6-3. Partial BGP table with different Local Preferences

```
BR1#show ip bgp
BGP table version is 619734, local router ID is  192.0.254.18
Status codes: s suppressed, d damped, h history, * valid, > best, i - internal
Origin codes: i - IGP, e - EGP, ? - incomplete
   Network     Next Hop      Metric LocPrf Path
```

```
*  7.7.0.0/19  192.0.254.17       90 40077 397 i
*>            219.2.19.1         110 50066 5703 397 i
*  8.8.0.0/16  192.0.254.17       90 40077 30021 i
*>            219.2.19.1         110 50066 30021 i
*  9.9.0.0/20  192.0.254.17       90 40077 5930 1070 i
*>            219.2.19.1         110 50066 1070 i
```

Under normal circumstances, the router would choose the route over AS 40077 for network 7.7.0.0/19 because the path over AS 50066 is longer. The higher Local Preference has precedence over the AS path length, however, so the route over ISP B is selected, as indicated with a > character. For 8.8.0.0/16, the AS path is the same length, so under other circumstances the decision would have come down to the tie-breaking rules. And for 9.9.0.0/20, the higher Local Preference doesn't really make a difference, because the route over AS 50066 has a shorter path anyway.

This policy works well as long as ISP B provides good connectivity to all destinations on the Net. But maybe ISP B peers with AS 30088 over a heavily congested connection, as shown in Figure 6-2.

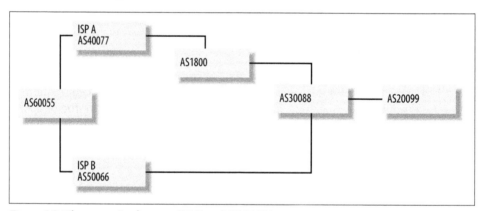

Figure 6-2. The congestion between ISP B and AS 30088

In this case, routes that traverse AS 30088 should be avoided. This is accomplished in Example 6-4.

Example 6-4. Setting the Local Preference depending on AS path

```
!
ip as-path access-list 4 permit _30088_
ip as-path access-list 4 deny .*
!
route-map ispa-in permit 10
 set local-preference 90
!
route-map ispb-in permit 10
 match as-path 4
```

Example 6-4. Setting the Local Preference depending on AS path (continued)

```
 set local-preference 80
!
route-map ispb-in permit 20
 set local-preference 110
!
```

The route map `ispb-in permit 10` uses a *match* clause pointing to AS path access list 4 to find all routes with AS number 30088 in their AS path. The underscore characters before and after the AS number match a space, and the beginning or the end of the path. For a five-digit AS number, this doesn't make a difference, but the regular expression "3008" not only matches paths with AS number 3008 in it, but also with AS numbers such as 13008, 30080, 30081 and so on.

The routes received from ISP B that match AS path access list 4 are assigned a Local Preference value of 80. Routes not matching AS path access list 4 will be evaluated by the `ispb-in permit 20` route map. There, they are always matched and assigned a Local Preference of 110.

Example 6-5 shows the result of applying these route maps for a route to a customer of AS 30088. Under normal circumstances, the second route would have been chosen because the path is shorter, but the modified Local Preference values make sure the first route is used.

Example 6-5. The result of Local Preference manipulation

```
BR1#show ip bgp 221.169.0.0
BGP routing table entry for 221.169.0.0/20, version 239188
Paths: (2 available, best #1)
  Not advertised to any peer
  40077 1800 30088 20099
    192.0.254.17 from 192.0.254.17 (192.0.254.17)
      Origin IGP, metric 20, localpref 90, valid, external, best, ref 2
  50066 30088 20099
    219.2.19.1 from 219.2.19.1 (219.2.13.237)
      Origin IGP, localpref 80, valid, external, ref 2
```

Manipulating Inbound AS Paths

Bypassing the AS path length comparison and the possible subsequent steps by setting the Local Preference isn't always the most appropriate way to influence the route-selection process. For instance, a route with twelve ASes in the path will be preferred over one with a single AS in the path if the Local Preference is higher, but it's hard to imagine a situation in which a path that's so much longer is still preferable. An alternative is to manipulate the way the router evaluates the AS path or to manipulate the AS path itself. Bay (now Nortel) routers allow a weight to be set for each AS, and the total weight of the path is calculated for each route. Cisco and most other vendors lack such an elegant and powerful mechanism, but they usually allow some sort of direct manipulation of the path. The usual way to do this is by prepending your own AS number to the end of the path one or more times. The path is then announced to external BGP peers in its modified state, which may not be desirable, so this technique is mostly suited for multihomed end-user networks and not for ISPs. Example 6-6 shows route maps to modify the AS path rather than the Local Preference as was done in Example 6-4. The ispb-in permit 10 route map prepends the path for paths that match AS path access list 4 because they contain AS 30088. Then the second ispb-in route map matches all remaining routes (without the need for either a *match* or a *set* clause), so they are included in the BGP table without modifications.

Example 6-6. Prepending the AS path

```
!
ip as-path access-list 4 permit _30088_
ip as-path access-list 4 deny .*
!
route-map ispa-in permit 10
 set as-path prepend 60055
!
route-map ispb-in permit 10
 match as-path 4
 set as-path prepend 60055 60055 60055
!
route-map ispb-in permit 20
!
```

As a result of these AS path manipulations, more traffic will flow over ISP B, since the path over ISP A is now longer. For some destinations, however, the longer path over ISP A may still be shorter, or the paths over A and B may be the same length, so that BGP has to employ the tie-breaking rules to select the best route. Example 6-7 shows the result for a route over AS 30088. Originally, the route over ISP B was shorter. But this route had its path prepended with the local AS number three times and the route over ISP A just once, so the route over ISP A is preferred.

Example 6-7. The result of AS path manipulation

```
BR1#show ip bgp 221.169.0.0
BGP routing table entry for 221.169.0.0/20, version 247873
Paths: (2 available, best #1)
  Not advertised to any peer
  60055 40077 1800 30088 20099
    192.0.254.17 from 192.0.254.17 (192.0.253.83)
      Origin IGP, metric 20, localpref 100, valid, external, best, ref 2
  60055 60055 60055 50066 30088 20099
    219.2.19.1 from 219.2.19.1 (219.2.13.237)
      Origin IGP, localpref 100, valid, external, ref 2
```

Note that the metric (MED) for the route over ISP A is 20, while the route over ISP B doesn't have a metric. Default IOS behavior is to treat a route without a MED metric as having a MED with the value 0. This may be changed to the opposite behavior (which conforms to IETF recommendations) using the *bgp bestpath med missing-as-worst* command in recent IOS versions. A missing MED then equals the highest (worst) possible value, as the command suggests. To me, the IETF behavior makes slightly more sense, but if you want to use MEDs, it's a good idea to make sure the routes actually have a MED set and do not depend on default behavior.

Inbound Communities

Depending on your upstream ISP, incoming routes may be "colored" with several communities. This can work both ways: later in this chapter, we'll see how setting communities for the routes you send to an ISP can trigger actions inside the ISP's network. Many ISPs use communities to convey information about the origin of routes. This information can include whether the route was received from a customer, a peer or an upstream ISP, or the location where the route was learned. The next example is based on the following:

- The AS 60055 network is located in Chicago.
- ISP A (AS 40077) is a national network connecting to MAE East but not to the Chicago NAP, and it doesn't use communities.
- ISP B (AS 50066) is a regional ISP that connects to the Ameritech (Chicago) NAP and to MAE East in Virginia.
- Routes ISP B learns at the Chicago NAP have the community 50066:3001.
- Routes ISP B learns at MAE East have the community 50066:3002.
- ISP B's connection to the Chicago NAP is excellent, but their connection to MAE East is somewhat congested.

This situation is depicted in Figure 6-3. The width of the lines connecting both ISPs to the interconnect locations indicates the available bandwidth.

Routes over the Chicago NAP through ISP B are most likely a lot better than routes to the same destinations over ISP A because of ISP A's lack of local or regional interconnection with other networks. It makes sense to assign a higher Local Preference to ISP B's Chicago NAP routes. If the paths for routes to destinations behind MAE East are the same, the path over ISP A should be preferred, because ISP A's connection to MAE East isn't congested. On the other hand, if ISP A's route to such a destination is much longer, it's probably better to suffer some congestion over ISP B than to take the scenic route over ISP A. This can be accomplished by assigning a default MED metric of 10 to all routes (overwriting the existing MED, if there was one), except routes from ISP B over MAE East; those get a metric of 20. Example 6-8 implements this routing policy.

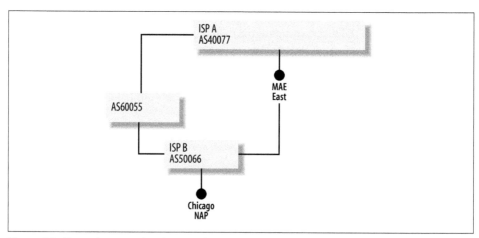

Figure 6-3. Example national and regional ISP connectivity

Example 6-8. Using communities to help select the best route

```
!
router bgp 60055
 bgp always-compare-med
!
ip bgp-community new-format
ip community-list 1 permit 50066:3001
ip community-list 1 deny
ip community-list 2 permit 50066:3002
ip community-list 2 deny
!
route-map ispa-in permit 10
 set metric 10
!
route-map ispb-in permit 10
 match community 1
 set metric 10
 set local-preference 120
!
route-map ispb-in permit 20
 match community 2
 set metric 20
!
route-map ispb-in permit 30
 set metric 10
!
```

The *bgp always-compare-med* command makes the router take the MED metric into account when comparing routes even when the two routes to a destination aren't received from the same AS. The *ip bgp-community new-format* command makes the router show all community-related information in the AS:nn format. Without it, communities are shown as single, very large numbers. Example 6-9 shows part of the

BGP table after the BGP sessions have been reset and the new route maps have been applied.

Example 6-9. Partial listing of the BGP table

```
BR1#show ip bgp
BGP table version is 620121, local router ID is  192.0.254.18
Status codes: s suppressed, d damped, h history, * valid, > best, i - internal
Origin codes: i - IGP, e - EGP, ? - incomplete
   Network        Next Hop       Metric LocPrf Path
*  7.7.0.0/19  192.0.254.17       10          40077 397 i
*>             219.2.19.1         10      120 50066 5703 397 i
*> 8.8.0.0/16  192.0.254.17       10          40077 30021 i
*              219.2.19.1         20          50066 30021 i
*  9.9.0.0/20  192.0.254.17       10          40077 5930 1070 i
*>             219.2.19.1         20          50066 1070 i
```

The first network in this example, 7.7.0.0/19, has a shorter path over ISP A (AS 40077), but it has the community 50066:3001 (not visible in this example) because ISP B (AS 50066) learned the route in Chicago, and the route map ispb-in has changed the Local Preference to 120. The route over ISP A has an empty Local Preference value, which is treated as a value of 100. Thus the route over ISP B is preferred.

ISPs A and B both peer with AS 30021 (network 8.8.0.0/16) at MAE East, so the route from ISP B contains the community 50066:3002, and the MED is changed to 20. The Local Preference and AS path length are the same for both ISP A and ISP B, so the MED is the deciding factor, and the router selects the route over ISP A.

The situation for network 9.9.0.0/20 is similar to that of network 8.8.0.0/16: ISP B also learns this route at MAE East. But ISP A doesn't directly peer with AS 1070, which explains the longer path. So the route over ISP B is selected because its path is shorter.

RPSL Routing Policy

Example 6-10 shows the Routing Policy Specification Language (RPSL) version of the routing policy for the configuration listed in Example 6-8 for inclusion in a Routing Registry.

Example 6-10. RPSL routing policy with communities

```
aut-num:    AS60055
import:     from AS40077
            action pref = 2; med = 10;
            accept ANY
import:     from AS50066
            action pref = 1; med = 10;
            accept community(50066:3001);
            action pref = 2; med = 20;
```

Example 6-10. RPSL routing policy with communities (continued)

```
              accept community(50066:3002);
              action pref = 2; med = 10;
              accept ANY;
export:       to AS40077 announce AS60055
export:       to AS50066 announce AS60055
default:      to AS40077
default:      to AS50066
```

The *import:* clauses are executed from top to bottom, so if a route has both communities 50066:3001 and 50066:3002 set, it matches the first clause and receive a *pref* of 1 and a *med* of 10. Note that the *pref* keyword in RPSL isn't the same as the Local Preference: a lower *pref* is more preferred, while for Local Preference, a higher value is more preferred. In this policy, Local Preference 100 is translated into *pref* 2, and Local Preference 120 becomes *pref* 1.

BGP Load Balancing

When a single router has two connections to the same AS, it's possible to load-balance outgoing traffic over those connections by instructing the router to insert more than one route with the same NLRI into the routing table. Depending on the switching mode the router uses, half the packets will flow over one connection and the other half over the other (per packet load balancing), or half the destination IP addresses will be routed over one connection and the other half over the other (per destination load balancing). Load balancing is enabled by setting *maximum-paths* to a value higher than one (the maximum is six):

```
!
router bgp 60055
 maximum-paths 4
!
```

With this setting in effect, up to four routes are entered into the routing table, as long as the routes are received from routers in the same AS, and the AS paths and MED metrics are identical. The *maximum-paths* keyword applies to all BGP peers: it isn't possible to enable load balancing for some peers and not for others. However, it's simple to prevent load balancing by giving each incoming route a different MED.

Load balancing can work in both directions only if there are multiple connections between one router at one end and one router at the other end. This means that *both* connections are unavailable if the router on either side fails, creating two single points of failure, unless there are other connections (terminating at other routers) in addition to the ones eligible for load balancing. There is no requirement that load balancing be enabled on both ends. For instance, if both connections terminate at different routers at your ISP, it isn't possible to load-balance your incoming traffic, but as long as both connections terminate on one router at your end, you can still configure load balancing for outgoing traffic.

Traffic Engineering for Incoming Traffic

Because the local router determines the route taken by outgoing packets, it isn't difficult to balance outbound traffic over multiple connections. The situation for inbound traffic is different. There are only a few routes you can influence to shift incoming traffic patterns: one for each address block for each ISP you connect to, instead of tens of thousands for outgoing traffic. In the typical multihoming case, with one address block and two ISPs, this leaves you with just two routes that can be manipulated to change inbound traffic distribution. This manipulation can take the form of:

- Setting the MED
- Prepending the AS path
- Setting outbound communities

You can also decide to "cheat" and break up a single address block that would normally be announced as a single route into several smaller blocks, so you can announce each separately, with different properties, for more fine-grained control.

Setting the MED

The MED metric is intended to be used only between two neighboring ASes. It isn't communicated to ASes beyond the neighboring AS. For this reason, the use of the MED in balancing incoming traffic is limited to the situation where there is more than one connection between two ASes: setting a higher MED for one route will make the traffic flow over the other. This is useful when one of the connections is of a much higher bandwidth, and the second one is a lower-bandwidth backup. Because you don't know whether the *bgp bestpath med missing-as-worst* command is in effect on the router terminating your connections at the other end, always set MEDs for the routes over both connections, as is shown in Example 6-11.

Example 6-11. Setting outbound MED values

```
!
router bgp 60055
 neighbor 192.0.254.17 remote-as 40077
 neighbor 192.0.254.17 route-map ispa-out out
 neighbor 219.2.19.1 remote-as 50066
 neighbor 219.2.19.1 route-map ispb-out out
!
route-map ispa-out permit 10
 set metric 10
!
route-map ispb-out permit 10
 set metric 20
!
```

We are now trying to influence *incoming* traffic, so we have to manipulate *outgoing* routing updates and apply the route maps to the neighbors using the *neighbor ... route-map ... out* command.

 The MED metric you see in the BGP table is *never* announced to eBGP neighbors. If you want a neighbor to receive a MED, you have to configure an outbound route map to set the MED for this neighbor.

Prepending Outbound AS Paths

When you bring up your second BGP session, you soon get to see how much traffic your routes attract over both ISPs. In many cases, the traffic will be distributed fairly equally over both connections, or one connection receives more traffic but there is enough spare capacity (for inbound traffic) so this isn't a problem. But maybe one connection attracts more traffic than it can handle, or you have one big pipe and a smaller one, and the traffic volumes are equal (or at least they try to be). Under these circumstances, you'll want to shift part of the incoming traffic load from one connection to the other. The most powerful option to change incoming traffic patters is making the AS path longer. This is effective, because the path is preserved between ASes, and BGP implementations use the path length early in the route selection algorithm. The biggest problem with making the AS path longer by prepending your own AS number to the path one or more extra times is that it may be *too* effective. Example 6-12 shows a configuration that prepends the path for the routes announced to an upstream ISP.

Example 6-12. Prepending the path for outbound routes

```
!
router bgp 60055
 neighbor 219.2.19.1 remote-as 50066
 neighbor 219.2.19.1 route-map ispb-out out
!
route-map ispb-out permit 10
 set as-path prepend 60055
!
```

The way the route map works should be familiar by now. Rather than applying the route map for incoming routes, the ispb-out permit 10 route map is used for outbound route updates. The number 10 is superfluous here, because there is only a single route map, but the router adds it to the configuration if you don't type it in yourself. The *set* clause adds 60055 to all routes.

Make sure all routes with prepended paths are accepted by your ISP and upstream networks. It isn't uncommon for the AS path filters that ISPs use to filter routes from customers not to allow path prepending. There usually isn't a good reason for this; it's just that allowing path prepending makes for more complex filters. If, after configuring path prepending, you use one or more looking glasses to see if they now receive your route in its prepended state, you may see only the unprepended route over your other ISP. It isn't always clear whether this means the route wasn't accepted, or routers further upstream just prefer the unprepended path over your other ISP because of the shorter AS path. The only way to make sure is to temporarily disable the BGP session to the nonprepended ISP:

```
!
router bgp 60055
 neighbor 192.0.254.17 shutdown
!
```

If the prepended route doesn't show up on remote looking glasses, or remote destinations on the Net become unreachable after shutting down your unprepended ISP, there must be a filter somewhere. Don't forget to let route propagation settle for a minute or two before drawing conclusions. You can determine where filtering takes place by tracerouting to an unreachable destination. The ASes that show up in the traceroute don't filter the prepended AS path. The filter must be between the last AS that shows up in the traceroute and the first one that doesn't. If your ISP is the one filtering out prepended routes, you can ask them to change their filters, but if the problem is further upstream, there is probably not a lot you can do. Don't forget to reenable the BGP session to your other ISP:

```
!
router bgp 60055
 no neighbor 192.0.254.17 shutdown
!
```

 The filter that prohibits routes with prepended paths from finding their way may be located inside your own router. It's best always to allow prepending your own AS, even if you don't plan on prepending in the near future:

```
ip as-path access-list 2 permit ^(60055_)*$
```

This regular expression matches all AS paths consisting of the beginning of the line (^), zero or more (()*) times the AS number, a space (_), and then the end of the line ($). In other words: an empty AS path or an AS path with just the AS number 60055.

The Effect of AS Path Prepending

Suppose you multihome to two ISPs that are similar: they interconnect at mostly the same NAPs and Internet Exchanges, and they peer with mostly the same networks. Under these circumstances, other networks see two similar paths for the routes you announce. Figure 6-4 shows an example of this.

If AS E (the example multihomed network, AS 60055) wants to receive more traffic over ISP A and thus makes the AS path longer over ISP B, the majority of traffic will

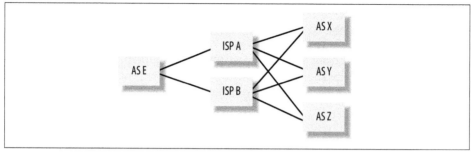

Figure 6-4. Multihoming to similar ISPs

flow over the ISP A, which now has the shorter path. In a situation with two similar ISPs, AS path prepending gives them only three choices:

- The default traffic distribution, which may or may not be balanced
- Longer path over ISP A: majority of traffic comes in over ISP B
- Longer path over ISP B: majority of traffic comes in over ISP A

Table 6-1 shows which route is preferred in the situation shown in Figure 6-4 without path prepending, with prepending the path to ISP A, and with prepending the path to ISP B.

Table 6-1. Prepended paths over similar ISPs

	AS X	AS Y	AS Z	Traffic distribution
Prepend to A	AEE	AEE	AEE	ISP A: 15%
	BE	BE	BE	ISP B: 85%
No prepending	AE	AE	AE	ISP A: 40%
	BE	BE	BE	ISP B: 60%
Prepend to B	AE	AE	AE	ISP A: 90%
	BEE	BEE	BEE	ISP B: 10%

For the purposes of calculating the traffic distribution, it's assumed that A always handles 15% of the traffic, B always 10%, and ASes X, Y, and Z are all the source of 25% of incoming traffic. ASes with "even" letters (X, Z) prefer to send traffic over ISP B when the paths are of equal length; "odd" ASes (Y) prefer ISP A in this example. The preferred path is listed in bold type in the table.

When the two ISPs are not as similar, increasing the length of the AS path has a more gradual effect, because the paths over ISPs A and B aren't the same for all networks. Figure 6-5 shows multihoming to dissimilar ISPs.

In this example, ISP B is a much smaller ISP that doesn't peer with networks X and Y, but rather buys transit service from AS C to reach those networks. Networks V and W don't peer directly with ISP A, so even if the path over ISP B becomes a lot

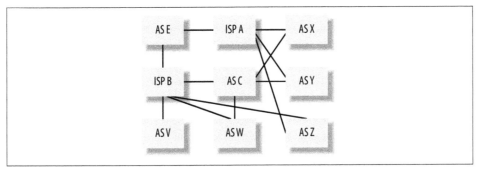

Figure 6-5. Multihoming to dissimilar ISPs

longer, they'll still prefer to send traffic to AS E over ISP B. Because this is a peering link, sending the traffic over this route is cheaper. Network Z, on the other hand, will immediately route traffic over ISP A when the path over ISP B is prepended, because the connections to both A and B are peering links. Table 6-2 shows the possible traffic distribution using prepending.

Table 6-2. Prepended paths over dissimilar ISPs

	AS C	AS V	AS W	AS X	AS Y	AS Z	Traffic distribution
2 to ISP A	BE	BE	BE	AEEE	AEEE	AEEE	A: 15%
			CBE	CBE	CBE	BE	B: 85%
1 to ISP A	BE	BE	BE	AEE	AEE	AEE	A: 35%
			CBE	CBE	CBE	BE	B: 65%
No prepending	BE	BE	BE	AE	AE	AE	A: 55%
			CBE	CBE	CBE	BE	B: 45%
1 to ISP B	BEE	BEE	BEE	AE	AE	AE	A: 75%
			CBEE	CBEE	CBEE	BEE	B: 25%

The traffic distribution in this example is 15% from ISP A, 5% from ISP B and ASes V and W, 10% from AS C, and 20% from ASes X, Y, and Z.

 All else being equal, it's a good idea to select dissimilar ISPs, for instance, one tier-1 ISP that peers with all the other large networks, and one tier-2 ISP that peers with many small networks. This way, you have a wide range of traffic engineering options.

Setting Outbound Communities

In many cases you'll want to prepend the path for certain upstream networks or peers of a transit ISP and not for others. For instance, if two of your ISPs have a transit network in common, you might want to have one ISP announce a prepended path to this transit network without changing the path that other transit networks and peers see over that ISP. To avoid spending a lot of time implementing this type of policy upon customer request, many ISPs provide their customers (and sometimes their peers) with a list of communities that trigger actions such as path prepending and setting the Local Preference. This can then be done for each route individually.

Well-known communities

Communities were introduced in BGP by RFC 1997. This RFC also defines the three well-known communities listed in Table 6-3.

Table 6-3. Well-known communities

Well-known community	Action
no-export (0xFFFFFF01)	Don't advertise this route to eBGP peers.
no-advertise (0xFFFFFF02)	Don't advertise this route to any peers, iBGP, or eBGP.
no-export-subconfed (0xFFFFFF03)	Advertise this route to iBGP peers with the same AS number, but not to other confederation members.

These communities can be useful under certain circumstances, for example, if an ISP wants to set the no-export community on routes it sends to a customer to make sure the customer doesn't accidentally announce the ISP's routes to another ISP. If the customer provides transit services to customers of his own, however, they won't receive the route unless the original customer of the ISP removes the no-advertise community.

> Setting the no-export, no-advertise, or no-export-subconfed communities can have the (possibly unwanted) side effect that *no* routes are announced, even if there are other routes that would otherwise be eligible for announcement.
>
> For instance, if you set the no-advertise community on routes announced to ISP B, other customers of ISP B won't see these routes because they aren't advertised. This is as intended. But routes with the same NLRI that ISP B has learned from ISP A will not be advertised either, because ISP B considers the directly received routes with the no-advertise community best, and only the best route is eligible for further announcement over BGP.

Common community actions

ISPs accepting communities provide their customers with a list of communities they use and what action is taken for each community. It's possible to set several communities for a single route, but the results may be unpredictable if your ISP doesn't expect this. Many networks list the communities they accept in their AUT-NUM object in the Routing Registry they use. Table 6-4 shows a fairly typical list of communities an ISP might accept.

Table 6-4. An example of communities an ISP accepts

Community	Action
50066:70	Set Local Preference to 70.
50066:90	Set Local Preference to 90.
50066:110	Set Local Preference to 110.
50066:5010	Announce this route for transit to ISP C.
50066:5020	Don't announce this route to transit ISP or peer C.
50066:5040	Prepend AS path to C once.
50066:5041	Prepend AS path to C twice.
50066:5042	Prepend AS path to C three times.
50066:10040	Prepend AS path once at interconnect point I.
50066:10041	Prepend AS path twice at interconnect point I.
50066:10042	Prepend AS path three times at interconnect point I.

Some ISPs require you to set a community indicating a route should be announced for transit, 50066:5010 in this example. This isn't common: most networks do the opposite and allow you to set a community indicating the route shouldn't be announced to transit networks. Be sure to notice the subtle difference between not announcing *for* transit and not announcing *to* transit networks: in the first case, the potential transit network still receives the announcement, but the route is treated as a peering route and not announced to peers and upstream networks of the transit network. In the latter case, the transit network doesn't get to hear the route at all.

Influencing the Local Preference in Upstream ASes

The MED is specifically intended to inform an upstream ISP that one connection should be preferred over another, but today this is often done with communities. Using communities instead of the MED may have benefits internal to the ISP network. For example, the ISP is then free to use the MED for another purpose, as we did for outbound traffic engineering in the beginning of this chapter. And, unlike the MED, using a community to set the Local Preference inside an ISP network also makes it possible to use a link to an ISP as a backup for a link to another ISP. When the Local Preference is set sufficiently low for the intended backup connection, the ISP it connects to will completely ignore the route and always send traffic over the other ISP as long as there is a route present over this ISP. This can't be accomplished with the MED; the AS path length overrides it, the MED isn't communicated from AS to AS, and by default, the MED is looked at only when two connections terminate at the same AS.

The impact of changing the Local Preference depends on the Local Preference values an ISP uses for routes learned from transit, peers, and customers. In this example, that would be 80 for transit, 100 for peers, and 120 for customers. If you have a fast main connection to this ISP along with a slower backup connection, you'll probably want to set community 50066:110 for routes announced over the backup connection. This makes sure all traffic flows over the main connection and the backup connection is used only when the main connection is unavailable. It's also possible to do this when you connect to two different ISPs: to ISP A with a main connection, and to ISP B with a backup connection. Then you'll want to set community 50066:90 or even 50066:70 so ISP B sends all traffic for you over a peering or transit connection to ISP A.

Example 6-13 shows a configuration for the router terminating the backup connection to ISP B. The main, high-bandwidth connection terminates at another router.

Example 6-13. Setting a community to indicate a backup route

```
!
router bgp 60055
 neighbor 219.2.19.1 remote-as 50066
 neighbor 219.2.19.1 route-map ispb-backup-out out
 neighbor 219.2.19.1 send-community
!
route-map ispb-backup-out permit 10
 set community 50066:5010 50066:70
!
```

The community 50066:5010 makes this route eligible for announcement as a transit route over AS C, but the community 50066:70 makes sure this route has the lowest possible Local Preference in ISP B's network. Thus, ISP B won't use it as long as there is any other route with the same NLRI (prefix), even if this means routing the traffic over ISP A.

 By default, Cisco routers accept incoming communities but don't transmit them over iBGP or eBGP. The *send-community* command enables sending communities to a neighbor.

Prepending the AS Path

Some smaller ISPs have path-prepending communities for each peer, but even medium-sized ISPs peer with many networks, so this soon gets out of hand. More often, an ISP has communities to prepend the path to each of its transit ISPs individually, as well as communities to prepend the path for an entire interconnect point. Our example ISP B (AS 50066) accepts path prepending communities for ISP X and interconnect point I.

AS W in Figure 6-5 (shown earlier this chapter) connects both directly to ISP B and also over transit AS C and then ISP B. Supposing the peering link between AS W and ISP B is congested, we'll want incoming traffic from AS W to flow over ISP C. This is accomplished by prepending the path ISP B announces to AS W twice, as is done in the configuration in Example 6-14.

Example 6-14. Setting a community to prepend the path

```
!
router bgp 60055
 neighbor 219.2.19.1 remote-as 50066
 neighbor 219.2.19.1 route-map ispb-out out
 neighbor 219.2.19.1 send-community
!
route-map ispb-out permit 10
 set community 50066:5010 50066:10041
!
```

Unfortunately, it's not possible to do something similar for outbound traffic: this will still flow over the congested connection between ISP B and AS C. This isn't the case if it's routed over ISP A and not over ISP B, of course, as is done in Example 6-4 earlier this chapter. Also, setting community 50066:10041 means the path is prepended twice towards all peers at this interconnect point. This may be undesirable, for instance if AS Z connects to ISP B over the same interconnect point as AS W. AS Z now sees the path C B B E over ISP B and the much shorter path A E over ISP A, so traffic from AS Z will now come in over the connection to ISP A.

Announcing More Specific Routes

When prepending the path and setting communities for outbound routes aren't enough to balance incoming traffic, there is a last resort: announcing more specific routes. This will inflate the global routing table, so announcing more specific routes should be done only when absolutely necessary. Because a more specific route always takes precedence over a less specific route, this technique always works, as long as the more specifics are accepted by your ISP and a reasonable number of their upstream (transit or peer) networks.

 Announcing more specifics is also useful when someone else announces your address block (by mistake, or by your request but no longer needed) and you don't want to wait for them to fix this.

Consider the situation outlined back in Figure 6-4. If the routers for ISP A consistently use a lower router ID (which defaults to the highest IP address in the box) than those of ISP B, it's possible that nearly all traffic comes in over ISP A. The AS paths are all the same length, and the tie-breaking rules favor the route from the neighbor with the lowest router ID. Prepending the path won't help: all traffic then comes in over ISP B. If neither A nor B allows selective prepending using communities, balancing the traffic is possible only by announcing more specific routes. For instance, if your address block is 220.37.0.0/20 (16 Class C's: 220.37.0 through 220.37.15), you could announce 220.37.0.0/21 to ISP A and 220.37.8.0/21 to ISP B. This way, all traffic to the Class C nets 220.37.0 through 220.37.7 comes in over ISP A, and all traffic to Class C nets 220.37.8 through 220.37.15 over ISP B. Example 6-15 shows a configuration that accomplishes this.

Example 6-15. Announcing more specific routes

```
!
router bgp 60055
 network 220.37.0.0 mask 255.255.240.0
 network 220.37.0.0 mask 255.255.248.0
 network 220.37.8.0 mask 255.255.248.0
 neighbor 192.0.254.17 remote-as 40077
 neighbor 192.0.254.17 description BGP session to ISP A
 neighbor 192.0.254.17 prefix-list ispa-ms out
 neighbor 219.2.19.1 remote-as 50066
 neighbor 219.2.19.1 description BGP session to ISP B
 neighbor 219.2.19.1 prefix-list ispb-ms out
!
ip route 220.37.0.0 255.255.240.0 Null0
ip route 220.37.0.0 255.255.248.0 Null0
ip route 220.37.8.0 255.255.248.0 Null0
!
ip prefix-list ispa-ms description outbound filter for ISP A
ip prefix-list ispa-ms seq 5 permit 220.37.0.0/20
ip prefix-list ispa-ms seq 10 permit 220.37.0.0/21
ip prefix-list ispa-ms seq 15 deny    220.37.8.0/21
ip prefix-list ispb-ms description outbound filter for ISP B
ip prefix-list ispb-ms seq 5 permit 220.37.0.0/20
ip prefix-list ispb-ms seq 10 deny    220.37.0.0/21
ip prefix-list ispb-ms seq 15 permit 220.37.8.0/21
!
```

To announce the two more specific routes in addition to the original /20 route (as a fallback in case the more specifics are filtered), each route must be listed in the BGP configuration with a *network* statement, and there must be matching local (pull up) routes, as provided by the *ip route ... Null0* statements. The prefix lists limit the routes announced to ISP A to 220.37.0.0/20 and 220.37.0.0/21, and those announced to ISP B to 220.37.0.0/20 and 220.37.8.0/21. Having two routes with the same address part isn't a problem: the NLRI consists of both the address and the prefix parts of a route. Two routes are considered different if either differs.

Figure 6-6 shows the propagation of routes, and Example 6-16 shows how these routes might show up in the BGP table of a remote AS. (Don't forget to register ROUTE objects in the Routing Registry of your choice for the more specific routes.)

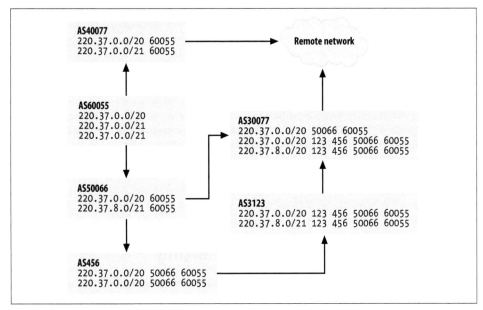

Figure 6-6. Propagation of more specific routes

Example 6-16. More specific routes as seen by a remote AS

```
BR1#show ip bgp
BGP table version is 933017, local router ID is  195.30.2.198
Status codes: s suppressed, d damped, h history, * valid, > best, i - internal
Origin codes: i - IGP, e - EGP, ? - incomplete
   Network         Next Hop      [...] Path
*> 220.37.0.0/21  192.0.254.17  [...] 40077 60055 i
*> 220.37.0.0/20  192.0.254.17  [...] 40077 60055 i
*                 219.2.19.1    [...] 50066 30077 60055 i
*> 220.37.8.0/21  219.2.19.1    [...] 50066 123 456 60055 i
```

As you can see, there are two routes for the /20, but only a single route for each of
the more specifics. Also, the path over ISP B (AS 50066) for the /20 is shorter than
the path of the /21: apparently, AS 30077 filters out the more specific route and
allows only the /20 from AS 50066. But ASes 123 and 456 don't filter, so there is still
a route for the /21. And since it's the most specific route, this is the one that is actually used, as the routing table for this remote network shows in Example 6-17.

Example 6-17. More specific routes in the routing table

```
BR1#show ip route 220.37.0.0
Routing entry for 220.37.0.0, 3 known subnets
  Variably subnetted with 2 masks
B       220.37.0.0/20 [20/0] via 192.0.254.17, 1d12h
B       220.37.0.0/21 [20/0] via 192.0.254.17, 1d12h
B       220.37.8.0/21 [20/0] via 219.2.19.1, 1d16h
```

Note that the 220.37.0.0/20 route is actually in the routing table, although it will never be used for forwarding as long as both 220.37.0.0/21 and 220.37.8.0/21 are available, because those cover the exact same address range. The "B" indicates that the route was learned from BGP, and 20/0 is the administrative distance (20, the default for eBGP) and metric (0, a missing MED).

 When deploying IP addresses, try to avoid putting all high-bandwidth hosts in the same or nearby subnets. Putting half the high-bandwidth hosts in the first /24 and the rest in the second is a better idea. If you ever need to announce more specifics to balance incoming traffic, it's a lot easier to announce two /21s out of a /20 or announce just a /24 separately in addition to what's normally announced, rather than having to announce very specific routes (prefixes longer than /24) or do some renumbering within your own address range in a hurry.

Queuing, Traffic Shaping, and Policing

Traffic engineering works only if you have bandwidth to spare on one of your connections. Even the most sophisticated traffic balancing techniques won't help you when there is just too much traffic. When the output queues for interfaces start filling up, interactive protocols start noticing delays, and bulk protocols start noticing lower throughput. The best way to handle this would be to get more bandwidth, but with some smart queuing techniques, it's possible to increase performance for some protocols or sessions without hurting others very much. Or just give way to "important" packets and let less important traffic suffer. There are three ways to accomplish this: special queuing strategies, traffic shaping, and rate limiting. Before choosing one, you should know how each interacts with TCP.

Nearly all applications that run over the Internet use the TCP (RFC 793) "on top of" IP. IP can only transmit packets of a limited size, and the packets may arrive corrupted by bit errors on the communications medium, in the wrong order, or not at all. Also, IP provides no way for applications to address a specific program running on the destination host. All this missing functionality is implemented in TCP. The characteristics of TCP are:

"Stream" interface
Any and all bytes the application writes to the stream come out in the same order at the application running on the remote host. There is no packet size limit: TCP breaks up the communication into packets as needed.

Integrity and reliability
TCP performs a checksum calculation over every segment (packet) and throws away the segment if the checksum fails. It keeps resending packets until the data is received (and acknowledged) successfully by the other end, or until it becomes apparent that the communications channel is unusable, and the connection times out.

Multiplexing

TCP implements "ports" to multiplex different communication streams between two hosts, so applications can address a specific application running on the remote host. For instance, web servers usually live on port 80. When a web browser contacts a server, it also selects a source port number so that the web page can be sent back to this port, and the page will end up with the right browser process. Well-known server ports are usually (but not always) below 1024; client source ports are semirandomly selected from a range starting at 1024 or higher.

Congestion control

Finally, TCP provides congestion control: it makes sure it doesn't waste resources by sending more traffic than the network can successfully carry to the remote host.

Most of what TCP does falls outside the scope of this book, so it won't be discussed here.* It's good to know about the congestion control mechanisms TCP employs, however, because they have a strong impact on the traffic patterns on the network.

TCP Congestion Control

Apart from the basic self-timing that happens because TCP uses a windowing system where only a limited amount of data may be in transit at any time, there are four additional congestion-related mechanisms in TCP: slow start, congestion avoidance, fast retransmit, and fast recovery. These algorithms are documented in RFC 2001.

Slow start

When a TCP connection is initiated, the other side tells the local TCP how much data it's prepared to buffer. This is the "advertised window." Setting up a connection takes three packets: an initial packet with the SYN control bit set (a "SYN packet"), a reply from the target host with both the SYN and ACK bits set, and a final packet from the initiating host back to the target acknowledging the SYN/ACK packet. This is the *three-way handshake*.

After the three-way handshake, the local (and remote) TCP may transmit data until the advertised window is full. Then it has to wait for an acknowledgment (ACK) for some of this data before it can continue transmitting. When the remote TCP advertises a large window, the local TCP doesn't send a full window's worth of data at once: there may be a low-bandwidth connection somewhere in the path between the two hosts, and the router that terminates this connection may be unable to buffer such a large amount of data until it can traverse the slow connection. Thus, the

---

* W. Richard Stevens' book *TCP/IP Illustrated, Volume 1: The Protocols* (Addison-Wesley) has an excellent description of TCP internals.

sending TCP uses a *congestion window* in addition to the advertised window. The congestion window is initialized as one maximum segment size, and it doubles each time an ACK is received. If the segment size is 1460 bytes (which corresponds to a 1500-byte Ethernet packet minus IP and TCP headers), and the receiver advertises a 8192-byte window, the sending TCP initializes the congestion window to 1460 bytes, transmits the first packet, and waits for an ACK. When the first ACK is received, the congestion window is increased to 2920 bytes, and two packets are transmitted. When the first one of these is ACKed, the congestion window becomes 5840 bytes, so four packets may now be in transit. One packet is still unacknowledged, so three new packets are transmitted. After receiving the next ACK, the congestion window increases beyond the advertised window, so now it's the advertised window that limits the amount of unacknowledged data allowed to be underway.

Congestion avoidance

Congestion avoidance introduces another variable: the *slow start threshold size* (*ssthresh*). When a connection is initialized, the *ssthresh* is set to 65,535 bytes (the maximum possible advertised window). As long as no data is lost, the slow start algorithm is used until the congestion window reaches its full size. If TCP receives an out-of-order ACK, however, congestion avoidance comes into play. An out-of-order ACK is an acknowledgment for data that was already acknowledged before. This happens when a packet gets lost: the receiving TCP sends an ACK for the data up to the lost packet, indicating, "I'm still waiting for the data following what I'm ACKing now." TCP ACKs are cumulative: it isn't possible to say "I got bytes 1000–1499, but I'm missing 500–999."

Upon receiving a duplicate ACK, the sending TCP assumes the unacknowledged data has been lost because of congestion, and the *ssthresh* and also the congestion window are set to half of the current window size, as long as this is at least two times the maximum segment size. After this, the congestion window is allowed to grow only very slowly, to avoid immediate return of the congestion. If the sending TCP doesn't see any ACKs at all for some period of time, it assumes massive congestion and triggers slow start, in addition to lowering the *ssthresh*. So as long as the congestion window is smaller than or equal to the *ssthresh*, slow start is executed (congestion window doubles after each ACK), and after that congestion avoidance (congestion window grows slowly).

Fast retransmit and fast recovery

When TCP receives three out-of-order ACKs in a row, it assumes that just a single packet was lost. (One or two out-or-order ACKs are likely to be the result of packet reordering on the network.) It then retransmits the packet it thinks has been lost, without waiting for the regular retransmit timer to expire. The *ssthresh* is set as per congestion avoidance, but the congestion window is set to the *ssthresh* plus three maximum segments: this is the amount of data that was successfully received by the other end, as indicated by the out-of-order ACKs. The result is that TCP slows down a bit, but not too much, because there is obviously still a reasonable amount of data coming through.

TCP Under Packet Loss and Delay Conditions

The result of these four mechanisms is that TCP slows down a lot when multiple packets are lost. The problem is even worse when the round-trip times are long, because the use of windows limits TCP's throughput to a window size per round-trip-time. This means that even with the maximum window size of just under 64 KB (without the TCP high-performance extensions enabled), TCP performance over a transcontinental circuit with a round trip delay of 70 ms will not exceed 900 Kbps. When a packet is lost, this speed is nearly halved, and it takes hundreds of successfully acknowledged packets to get back up to the original window size. So even sporadic packet loss can bring down the effectively used bandwidth for a single TCP session over a high-delay path. This means that packet loss can be tolerated only on low-delay connections, and only as long as those connections are not part of a high-delay path.

The behavior of the two main categories of non-TCP applications under packet loss conditions is different. These categories are multimedia (streaming audio and video) and applications based on small transactions that don't need a lot of overhead, such as DNS. Streaming audio and video are generally not too sensitive to packet loss, although the audio/video quality will suffer slightly. For things like DNS lookups, packet loss slows down individual transactions a lot (they time out and have to be repeated), but the performance penalty doesn't carry over to transactions that didn't lose packets themselves. Because non-TCP applications don't really react to packet loss, they often exacerbate the congestion by continuing to send more traffic than the connection can handle.

Although some lost packets are the result of bit errors on the physical medium or temporary routing inconsistencies, the typical reason packets are lost is congestion: too much traffic. If a router has a single OC-3 (155 Mbps) connection to a popular destination, and 200 Mbps of traffic comes in for this destination, something has to give. The first thing the router will do is to put packets that can't be transmitted immediately in a queue. IP traffic tends to have a lot of bursts: traffic can get high for short periods of time ranging from a fraction of a second to a few seconds. The queue helps smooth out these bursts, at the expense of some additional delay for the queued packets, but at least they're not lost. If the excessive traffic volume persists, the queue fills up. The router has no other choice than to discard any additional packets that come in when the queue is full. This is called a "tail drop." The TCP anti-congestion measures are designed to avoid exactly this situation, so in most cases, all the TCP sessions will slow down so the congestion clears up for the most part. If the congestion is bad, however, this may not be enough. If a connection is used for many short-lived TCP sessions (such as web or email traffic), the sheer number of initial packets (when TCP is still in slow start) may be enough to cause congestion. Non-TCP applications can also easily cause congestion because they lack TCP's sophisticated congestion-avoidance techniques.

Queuing

Queuing happens only when the interface is busy. As long as the interface is idle, packets will be transmitted without special treatment. Regular queues invariably employ the first in, first out (FIFO) principle: the packet that has been waiting the longest is transmitted first. When the queue is full, and additional packets come in, tail drops happen. More sophisticated queuing mechanisms usually employ several queues. Packets are classified by user-configurable means and then placed in the appropriate queue. Then, when the interface is ready to transmit, a queue from which the next packet will be transmitted is selected as per the queuing algorithm. Cisco routers support several queuing strategies: FIFO, WFQ, RED, priority, and custom queuing. Note that special queuing mechanisms have effect only when it's not possible immediately to transmit a packet over the output interface. If the interface is idle and there are no queued packets, the new packet is transmitted immediately.

First in, first out

FIFO queuing is the most basic queuing strategy: packets are transmitted in the same order they come in. This is the default for fast interfaces. FIFO queuing is enabled by removing all other queuing mechanisms:

```
!
interface Serial0
 no fair-queue
!
```

Weighted fair queuing

WFQ tries to allocate bandwidth fairly to different conversations (typically TCP sessions) so high-bandwidth sessions don't get to monopolize the connection. WFQ is the default for lower-bandwidth interfaces. It can be enabled with:

```
!
interface Serial0
 fair-queue
!
```

Random early detect

RED starts to drop packets as the output queue fills up, in order to trigger congestion-avoidance in TCP. The sessions with the most traffic are most likely to experience a dropped packet, so those are the ones that slow down the most. Weighted random early detect (WRED) takes the priority value in the IP header into account and starts dropping low-priority packets earlier than their higher-priority counterparts. Unlike WFQ, priority, and custom queuing, RED doesn't need much processing time and can be used on high-speed interfaces. It needs a transmit queue bigger than the default 40-packet queue to be able to start dropping packets early and avoid tail drops.

```
!
interface Ethernet0
 random-detect
 hold-queue 200 out
!
```

 In RFC 2309, the IETF recommends using RED for Internet routers.

Priority queuing

This queuing strategy allows traffic to be classified as high, normal, medium, or low priority. If there is any high-priority traffic, it's transmitted first, then medium-priority traffic, and so on. This can slow down lower-priority traffic a lot or even completely block it if there is enough higher-priority traffic to fill the entire bandwidth capacity. Example 6-18 enables priority queuing and assigns a medium (higher than normal) priority to DNS traffic and a low priority to FTP.

Example 6-18. Enabling priority queuing

```
!
interface Serial0
 priority-group 1
!
priority-list 1 protocol ip medium udp domain
priority-list 1 protocol ip low tcp ftp
priority-list 1 protocol ip low tcp ftp-data
!
```

Custom queuing

Custom queuing has a large number of queues and transmits a configurable amount of data from a queue before proceeding to the next. This queuing strategy makes it possible to guarantee a minimum amount of bandwidth for certain traffic types, while at the same time making the bandwidth that is left unused available to other traffic types. Example 6-19 assigns 75% of the bandwidth to WWW traffic, 5% to the DNS, and 20% to all other traffic.

Example 6-19. Enabling custom queuing

```
!
interface Serial0
 custom-queue-list 1
!
queue-list 1 protocol ip 1 tcp www
queue-list 1 protocol ip 2 udp domain
queue-list 1 default 3
queue-list 1 queue 1 byte-count 7500
queue-list 1 queue 2 byte-count 500
queue-list 1 queue 3 byte-count 2000
!
```

If there is more WWW traffic than can fit in 75% of the interface bandwidth, and the non-WWW/non-DNS traffic requires only 5%, the unused 15% is reallocated to WWW traffic so that no bandwidth is wasted.

Traffic Shaping and Rate Limiting

With traffic shaping, all the traffic for an interface, or just that matching a certain access list, is counted. This happens regardless of whether the interface is idle or packets are queued for transmission. When the traffic reaches a user-configurable bandwidth threshold, additional packets are put in a queue and delayed, so bandwidth use is limited to the configured amount.

Rate limiting, sometimes referred to as traffic policing or CAR, is similar to traffic shaping, but instead of being delayed, the excess traffic is treated differently from regular traffic in a user-configurable way. A common way to handle the excess traffic is simply to drop it, but it's also possible to do other things, such as lowering the priority field in the IP header. Example 6-20 enables traffic shaping for one interface and rate limiting for another.

Example 6-20. Enabling traffic shaping and rate limiting

```
!
interface Serial0
 traffic-shape rate 128000 8000 8000 1000
!
interface Serial1
 rate-limit output 128000 8000 8000 conform-action transmit exceed-action drop
!
```

Both the *traffic-shape rate* and the *rate-limit output* commands take bandwidth limit as their next argument. The other figures are burst and buffer sizes. For most applications, having those isn't desirable (TCP performance is even a bit worse when there is room for bursts), so for traffic shaping, you can leave them out; for rate limiting, you can set them to the minimum of 8000.

Traffic shaping and rate limiting are often used to limit a customer's available bandwidth when a customer buys a certain amount of bandwidth that is lower than that of the interface that connects them. This isn't a good use of rate limiting, however, because it drops a lot of packets, which makes TCP think there is congestion. So it slows down, but after a while it tries to pick up the pace again, and then there is more packet loss, and so on. Traffic shaping, on the other hand, just slows the packets down so TCP adapts to the available bandwidth. Example 6-21 shows the FTP performance over a connection that is rate-limited to 128 Kbps.

Example 6-21. FTP over a 128-Kbps rate-limited connection

```
ftp> put testfile
local: testfile remote: testfile
150 Opening BINARY mode data connection for 'testfile'.
100% |*******************************| 373 KB  00:00 ETA
226 Transfer complete.
382332 bytes sent in 35.61 seconds (10.48 KB/s)
```

The TCP performance is only 84 Kbps, about two thirds of the available bandwidth. Example 6-22 is the same transfer over the same connection, but now with traffic shaping to 128 Kbps in effect.

Example 6-22. FTP a 128-Kbps traffic-shaped connection

```
ftp> put testfile
local: testfile remote: testfile
150 Opening BINARY mode data connection for 'testfile'.
100% |*******************************| 373 KB  00:00 ETA
226 Transfer complete.
382332 bytes sent in 24.73 seconds (15.10 KB/s)
```

The performance is now 121 Kbps, which is just a few percent under the maximum possible bandwidth, considering TCP, IP, and datalink overhead.

Apart from combating denial-of-service attacks, as discussed in Chapter 11, rate limiting has another potential use, because unlike traffic shaping and the different queuing mechanisms, it can also be applied to *incoming* traffic. When an ISP and a customer agree on a certain bandwidth use, the ISP can easily use traffic shaping to make sure the customer doesn't receive more incoming traffic than the agreed upon bandwidth with traffic shaping. But since it's impossible to traffic shape packets coming in on an interface, the customer is responsible for traffic shaping their outgoing traffic. To make sure they don't send out more traffic than agreed, the ISP can implement additional rate limiting for incoming traffic.

CHAPTER 7

Security and Integrity of the Network

"The only thing necessary for the triumph of evil is for good men to do nothing."
—Edmund Burke

Because your network depends on connections to other networks in order to function, it's also potentially vulnerable to problems inside remote networks, or even to malicious actions carried out from elsewhere on the Net. This is in addition to the integrity and security threats stemming from within your own network. As soon as you connect your network to the Internet, if not before, you can expect a number of different people to try to gain access to it for a number of different reasons:

Spammers

Spammers are just looking for mail servers they can use to bombard others with their unwanted advertisements. Make sure you have no "open relays" (mail servers that will relay mail from someone outside your network to someone else outside your network), and they'll go away.

Script kiddies

There are many small programs or scripts floating around the Net that exploit known vulnerabilities in all kinds of hardware, software, and protocols. Some people must love to see what happens if they turn these loose on your network. Script kiddies can be dangerous, because there are a lot of them, and they usually don't understand the programs they're using. Make sure you are aware of all the potential vulnerabilities for every piece of hardware that is connected to the network and all the software that runs on it. Script kiddies are often easily provoked by derogatory remarks and will then attack the offender with everything they've got.

Hackers

Hackers are the people who find and publicize new ways to break into systems. In many cases, they do so with the intention to improve security and inform you and/or the vendor before they go public. Hackers are ingenious and not easily deterred. If they want to get into your systems and can't get access using known or even unknown vulnerabilities or guessing passwords, they may resort to "social engineering": trying to trick people into telling passwords or other privileged information, usually over the phone. Don't assume you can completely protect yourself from a determined hacker. Up-to-date systems, strong passwords, and a good level of security awareness does help, but the main thing is to detect successful and unsuccessful hacking attempts, so look out for unusual log messages and strange network usage patterns.

Corporate spies and thieves
If there is anything of value to be found on your network, you may also be targeted by criminals or corporate spies with hacker-like skills. If they can't get access over the network, they may use conventional tactics such as breaking in, bribery, and extortion. Keep the part of your network that is connected to the Net as separate as you possibly can from the sensitive part. Monitor everything closely, especially the systems that are connected to both parts of the network.

 Even if you are theoretically immune to all threats, you still can't be sure the software in your network equipment or hosts is doing what it should be doing. Software bugs and design deficiencies may directly cause problems, or they can make it possible for attackers to gain access to your network.

When in doubt, hire someone to evaluate the security risks. Don't let an outsider make all the decisions about how everything should be protected, however, because if she goes overboard, the security procedures might be too strict for the employees who have to follow them. If people can't do their jobs because security procedures get in the way, they'll find a way around them, wasting your time and theirs and leaving the network insecure as before. The only good security procedures are those actually being followed!

Not to increase your paranoia (there is enough of that going around in network security), but here's a final word of warning: a large percentage (some say most) of all security breaches come from employees or ex-employees. Employees should not be suspects in a totalitarian regime, "guilty until proven innocent," but on the other hand, it's also possible to be too trusting. When asked why they committed their crime, many embezzlers answer, "It was so easy." Don't let this happen to you.

Passwords and Security

Managing access to routers becomes a complicated matter as networks grow. It might be tempting to use some sort of centralized access control, such as a RADIUS authentication server, to more easily manage access to the routers. But this is a mistake. Authentication servers have the nasty habit of being unreachable whenever you need to access your routers the most: when there is a network outage. It's possible to use central authentication and still have local authentication if the former fails, but it's hard to get (and especially keep) this method working as intended. It's a better idea to create locally administered accounts for everyone who may need to access the router and have different enable passwords for different sets of routers. This way, everyone logs on to all routers with their username and a password. There is no reason this password can't be the same for all routers. Then, if someone is authorized for enable access on a router, he will know the enable password for this group of routers. People who just connect customers to gateway routers should have the enable password only for the set gateway routers. Core routers and border routers should probably also have different enable passwords, although it's likely they will be managed by the same people. The enable passwords are shared by a large group of people, so changing them is a bit of a hassle. It's best to put a single person in charge of this task. Everyone has to get the new enable password directly from her, so she knows who has it. This prevents the password from slowly seeping through the organization over time. It's best to change enable passwords each month, so doing it becomes routine. Keep copies of the enable passwords and a set of regular login passwords in envelopes in a safe, so the network is accessible when none of the regular network staff is available. (Or when no one can remember the password!)

Telnet Versus SSH

More and more equipment supports SSH access in addition to Telnet. The Secure Shell protocol supports strong encryption and public-key-based authentication. SSH is certainly the protocol of choice over connections that may be subject to packet sniffing. Traditionally, this is unswitched Ethernet, where everyone connected to the same hub can listen in on all conversations. This makes it easy for intruders to capture passwords and log in to your routers and switches. Ethernet switches often have some kind of support for monitoring ports or can be fooled to have traffic pass through an unintended host, so they aren't completely impervious to sniffing, but it's not as easy to intercept traffic flowing through a switch as with a hub. Packets traveling over serial lines, ATM, and Packet over SONET are hard to intercept because they require special hardware. If someone goes to the trouble of connecting enough equipment to your network to capture data at will, they're probably in it for more than just your passwords. So use SSH if you can, but if you can't, don't worry too much about being sniffed, unless you use shared (unswitched) Ethernet in your network.

 If someone can connect something to the console port of your router, they can execute the password recovery procedure, which overrides the enable password, and then copy or change the configuration and decode all user account passwords that use weak encryption.

Some people are so distraught by the potential security problems inherent in Telnet that they disable the protocol. This is a mistake, in my opinion. Telnet clients are available everywhere: routers have them built in, and even Windows comes with one. SSH, on the other hand, needs a much more sophisticated software infrastructure. There are many things that can go wrong: you can lose a private key that is necessary for authentication, or at some point you may not have access to a machine with an SSH client on it. Because the security problems Telnet imposes are only related to actually *using* the protocol, and not just to having it *enabled*, it's a good idea to leave it enabled so you have a fallback when SSH fails. However, there's something to be said for disabling all network services and access mechanisms that are not actually used. That way, you don't have to worry about vulnerabilities in those protocols. Carefully weigh the risks.

The Telnet or SNMP management interfaces make routers and switches susceptible to security problems, so it's a good idea to restrict access to trusted IP addresses. On the other hand, if there is a network problem, you might want to access a router from outside your own network. Very strict access control can lead to a frustrating vicious circle: you can't access a router because the trusted hosts are unreachable, and you can't bring the network up because you can't access the router. Therefore, it's a good idea to have another "trusted" host somewhere on the Net from which you can Telnet to your routers. Note that in this context, trusted means only that it's not too likely that your network will be attacked from there. You should still use passwords to restrict access to authorized personnel.

 Telnet and most SNMP implementations don't use any encryption, so if traffic between your workstation and a router or switch is intercepted, others can see the passwords. Typically, everybody who has full (root) access to the host you are on or onto a host connected to a shared Ethernet somewhere along way can intercept management (and other) traffic. When available, use SNMPv3 and SSH instead of Telnet, so your session is encrypted. Cisco supports SSH in some IOS software images on their high-end routers.

Software

Vendors do their best to test software, so it's pretty rare that problems are immediately visible. Usually, there is a specific set of circumstances that triggers the problem. For instance, a router might reboot after running for a certain period, after forwarding a certain number of packets, and so on. Our first impulse when confronted with a software problem is to upgrade to a newer version. This isn't always the best approach. The problem may well be present in the newer version as well, and installing new software disrupts network services. So the first step should be to find out whether this is a known problem and whether there is a fix or a workaround. If the workaround is something that can be easily implemented, you can avoid the risks of upgrading to a new version of the software: bug fixes sometimes introduce new bugs, and new features nearly always introduce new bugs, sometimes in areas that seem completely unrelated. So when you upgrade, use a version that doesn't introduce new features but just fixes bugs.

Software Lifecycle

Understanding the software lifecycle will help you determine when to upgrade and how big the risks are. This is a general description of the overall software lifecycle for products for which new versions with new features are released from time to time. It isn't intended to be an accurate description of any one vendor's procedures.

New general release (new version): small bugs are found
> The lifecycle of software starts with the release of a new version with new features. In the first few days or weeks, customers find a lot of small bugs that were overlooked during testing and are the result of the software being deployed in real networks with real users. Depending on the vendor, there can be a rapid succession of new bug-fix releases, or most of the bugs are fixed in a single release a bit later.

Fundamental problems surface
> After a few weeks, the software is widely used, and more fundamental problems surface: some features don't always work as intended, under certain conditions the performance isn't what it should be, there are security problems, and so on. The number of small bugs that warrant bug-fix releases decreases.

Interim release
> A few (or many) months later, the more fundamental problems are addressed in an interim release. This introduces some new smaller bugs, so there will be a number of bug-fix releases after that. This is the point at which the software is mature, and the vendor starts to focus his efforts on a new version with new features. There may be several interim releases as important problems are discovered over time.

New version
> When new versions are released, some customers keep using the older one. So if bugs are found, there are still bug-fix releases for the older version.

Falling behind
> The number of bugs that are found in the old version starts to rise again: the software has to interact with an environment that is different from the one it was built for: higher speeds, new protocols, and new versions of old protocols that aren't always as backward-compatible as they should be.

End of lifecycle
> The vendor keeps fixing the new bugs for a while, but at some point the version is declared to have reached the end of its lifecycle, and it's no longer supported.

Loading new software into networking equipment is rather awkward: you need to run a TFTP server or special management software to do it over the network, or you can use a directly connected cable. Go over the procedure ahead of time, so you'll be able to perform an emergency software upgrade without delay when the need arises. Always keep a copy of the old software.

Cisco IOS Versions

Major IOS versions are numbered 11.2, 11.3, 12.0, 12.1, and so on. In theory, there should be a bigger difference between 11.3 and 12.0 than between 12.0 and 12.1, but I'll leave that to the connoisseurs. After the version number, there is a release number in parentheses. As a simple rule of thumb, the best way to select a stable release is to stay at least one major version behind and use the highest available release number.

The number of different software images for any one Cisco IOS version is huge. Obviously there are different images for different router platforms, but within an IOS version and a platform, there are still numerous images. The most important are the *IP only* and the *service provider* images. IP only is the cheapest, because it contains the fewest extra protocols, but it still does IP and IP routing, which is sufficient for our purposes. The service provider images can't be ordered, but if you have a Cisco Connection Online (CCO) account, you should be able to download them. The service provider images are intended for ISPs. If you need extra features, such as non-IP protocols or support for protocols using cryptography (such as IPSec), give your neighborhood Cisco reseller a call. Since this costs extra, they'll be happy to tell you all about these versions.

 In the past, there have been security vulnerabilities found in Cisco IOS. Some were Cisco-specific; others were common to implementations from several vendors. It's likely other such vulnerabilities will be found in the future.

Protecting BGP

Attackers have two ways to do bad things to your BGP sessions. The first is to take over a peer's IP address and present themselves as your peer. The routers will then set up a BGP session, and the attacker can inject disruptive information in your routing tables, unless the filters for this peer are strict. The attacker may even route some of your address space to himself and present himself to the outside world as a host on your network, so he can receive your email and web requests.

It isn't unheard of for a telco to make a mistake so that a leased line doesn't connect to the intended endpoint, but to someone else's equipment. But this doesn't happen often. A more likely source of such attacks is an Internet Exchange. In many cases, it's possible for anyone connected to an IX switch to take over any IP and/or MAC address. Obviously, when someone takes over your peer's IP address, this will soon be noticed, but the damage may have already been done. For more information on connecting to an IX, see Chapter 12.

Even if an attacker can't take over a suitable IP address to make a BGP connection to your router, he can still use a second method to disrupt your network: by getting you or your peer to reset the BGP session. TCP incorporates a RST feature to reset sessions when one end of the connection no longer recognizes them. This usually happens when one system reboots during a TCP session. The other system continues to send packets until the first system is back online again. When this system receives a packet belonging to a TCP session it doesn't recognize, it sends back a RST packet to terminate the session. An attacker can falsify a RST packet to disconnect the BGP session between two routers. For private interconnects, this isn't such a big problem, because the falsified source addresses are easily filtered out. But a router can't tell if a packet coming in from the IX switch really came from the peer indicated by the source address or if it came from some other system that is also connected to the IX. The attacker would also have to know a valid 32-bit TCP sequence number, so this attack still isn't easy. An attacker who has intimate knowledge of the hardware and software involved, however, may be able to guess the sequence number within much fewer than the full 2^{32} tries.

The solution to prevent these attacks from succeeding is to use a password for BGP sessions. Since the TCP RST attack happens at the TCP level, BGP authentication also operates at the TCP level. Every TCP packet that is part of a password-protected BGP session carries a TCP option containing an MD5 hash value over the TCP payload and the password. When a router receives such a packet, it recomputes the MD5 hash and checks whether it matches the one in the TCP option. If it does, the TCP packet is allowed through for further processing. If not, the packet is ignored. This way, only someone in possession of the password can create packets that will be processed successfully. Then even an attacker who can intercept and change packets at will can't inject false information in BGP. If it isn't possible to use passwords (or if you don't trust your peer 100%), it's a good idea to explicitly reject incoming routes to your own address space. Example 7-1 both filters and sets a password.

Example 7-1. Protecting BGP

```
!
router bgp 60055
 neighbor 192.0.254.17 password abc def ghi
 neighbor 192.0.254.17 prefix-list infilter in
!
ip prefix-list infilter description inbound filter
ip prefix-list infilter seq 5 deny 192.0.2.0/24 le 32
ip prefix-list infilter seq 10 permit 0.0.0.0/0 le 32
!
```

The password is case-sensitive ("secret" is a different password from "Secret" or "SECRET"). The password can include spaces, and it may be up to 80 characters long. The only limitation is that it may not begin with a number. Make sure you have the password written down somewhere, because some versions of IOS immediately encrypt it. After entering ... *password abc def ghi*, typing *show running-config* will reveal something like ... *password 7 00051105445F0E004F264447*. However, this isn't true for all IOS versions. The number 7 immediately following *password* indicates the password has been encrypted, so the router knows not to encrypt it again. A number 0 indicates the password has not (yet) been encrypted. If the other side hasn't configured the password/MD5 protection option, or the MD5 doesn't match, you'll see %TCP-6-BADAUTH error messages on the router's console, the log buffer and other places the router is configured to send logging information to. Note that you may even see these messages for BGP sessions that aren't active because the *neighbor ... shutdown* command is in effect: the TCP MD5 option processing is done before the configured state of the neighbor is considered.

The prefix list in this example denies routes for 192.0.2.0/24 and any subsets (longer prefixes), including single IP addresses. The second line allows all other routes, from the default route 0.0.0.0/0 all the way down to every possible /32.

The router may also accept the syntax *permit 0/0 le 32* instead of *permit 0.0.0.0/0 le 32*, but it takes this to mean the entire IPv6 address space, rather than the entire IPv4 address space.

Alternatively, you may want to explicitly configure which prefixes to accept from a peer and reject everything else. Doing this manually requires a lot of maintenance, however, because this information changes often. Using a tool to generate filters from a Routing Registry is problematic because not every network registers everything properly. Also, larger networks may announce hundreds of prefixes, so the filters can become long.

Avoiding Black Holes

The default behavior of BGP is to announce all routes to all peers. So if someone forgets to configure the appropriate filters, excess routes leak out. Then, when peers start to send their traffic for these destinations, the incorrectly filtered network becomes overloaded, and the black hole is firmly in place. An even worse type of black hole is the one resulting from improperly redistributing BGP into an IGP and then the IGP into BGP, as discussed in Chapter 10. One way to avoid black holes is to apply inbound filters and allow only a predefined list of prefixes for every peer. This approach works well, and many networks use it. The downside is the amount of maintenance needed to keep the filters up to date. Many networks inform their peers about new address ranges only shortly before they are put into use, so you must be prepared to perform daily filter updates if you choose this approach. If this is unfeasible or undesirable, an alternative isn't to filter the actual announcements for each peer but just limit their number. Because black holes are typically the result of a network announcing either the entire global routing table or a sizable subset, a sudden increase in the number of routes received is a good indication of trouble. Example 7-2 shows a configuration that will allow only 25 routes from a peer.

Example 7-2. Setting the maximum allowed routes for a peer

```
!
router bgp 60055
 neighbor 192.0.254.17 maximum-prefix 25 50
!
```

The second value (50) makes the router generate a %BGP-4-MAXPFX warning message when 50% of the maximum allowed prefixes has been reached. This message is repeated as the number of prefixes increases. The warning threshold value may be omitted; the default is 75%. When the actual configured prefix limit (25 in this example) is exceeded, the router sends a %BGP-3-MAXPFXEXCEED message to all its logging outputs, such as the console, the logging buffer in memory, and any configured syslog servers; and the BGP session is torn down. The session will remain inactive and not be reestablished, showing the state Idle (PfxCt) in *show ip bgp summary*. You can reinitialize the session with *clear ip bgp <peer address>* when the peer router no longer announces an excessive amount of routes or when you have increased the prefix limit. If the *warning-only* keyword is present, the session remains active, and the router just generates a warning the first time the limit is exceeded.

When the Internet is in turmoil because of large-scale outages, it isn't uncommon for networks to help each other out by providing temporary (partial) transit service. You'll then see a larger number of prefixes from some peers. Under these circumstances, it's best to change to *warning-only* prefix limits and carefully monitor the situation for as long as the unusual circumstances persist.

Prefix filtering and *maximum-prefix* protect you only against black holes that are the result of a network announcing routes it has no business announcing. There is no way to protect yourself against another kind of black hole, where a network announces legitimate routes but fails to transport the traffic. When this happens, the routes are the way they should be. The difference from problem-free operation is that packets somehow can't reach their destination. The design of the TCP/IP family of protocols is such that routers can't detect this problem. It's rare for this kind of black hole to persist for more than a few minutes; the usual reason they appear is because a physical connection fails, but the associated BGP session doesn't immediately disappear. This situation usually corrects itself as soon as the BGP session times out. Also, the problem impacts only traffic going through the network with the black hole. This kind of black hole doesn't "attract" traffic from peers, so it affects mainly the customers of the network itself. This includes multihomed customers. However, unlike single-homed customers, they can just shut down the link to the black hole network and still enjoy connectivity to the rest of the world over their other connection.

Denial-of-Service Attacks

If your network or the services hosted on it have a high profile, or you did something to provoke the wrong people, you can easily end up on the receiving end of some kind of attack. Attackers are lazy, so they'll go for the easy targets. If your hardware or software or the protocols you use have known vulnerabilities, they'll try to exploit those. Even worse, attackers are continually scanning networks they have no beef with to find vulnerable systems they can abuse to attack people they don't like. With software and protocols becoming more complex every day, it isn't easy to keep all the systems on your network secure so they can withstand known attacks. But even if they can, you're not out of the woods: attackers can still swamp your hosts or the entire network with random traffic or seemingly legitimate requests, thereby using up all resources so that requests from real users can't be handled, denying them service. When an attack originates from a (large) number sources, it's called a *distributed* denial-of-service (DDoS) attack. The four most popular DoS attacks are, in no particular order:

Packet flood
   This attack works by simply sending so much traffic that it completely saturates the incoming connections of the attacked network. The traffic can be anything, but ICMP echo requests are particularly effective because many hosts answer with an echo reply, introducing even more traffic into the network. Also, ICMP messages can be small (as little as 28 bytes), so the number of packets per second is as high as possible for a given amount of bandwidth, increasing the CPU time needed to process the packet stream. Finally, lower-layer overhead is as large as possible: a 28-byte IP packet takes up 672 bits on the wire for Ethernet, three times the original size. The source addresses are often falsified in packet-flooding attacks.

Smurf directed broadcast amplification
   "Smurf" attacks use misconfigured intermediate networks to multiply traffic, allowing attackers to easily muster up large amounts of traffic without the need to hack any systems. The attacker sends ICMP echo request packets with the source address set to that of the intended victim to a directed broadcast address of an amplifier network. The router at this network turns the packet into a broadcast, so all hosts connected to the subnet receive it. Many of these hosts will reply with an echo reply message, which will be sent to the apparent source of the echo request message. As a result, the network under attack will see large amounts of incoming ICMP echo reply messages from many different hosts. In this case, the source addresses are those of the amplifying network, not of the attacker. Some attackers use other amplification mechanisms, such as UDP echo

packets or short DNS queries that generate large reply packets. These are less common.

SYN flood

A SYN flood doesn't depend on saturating the full bandwidth of the network (although it may succeed at this), but tries to open more TCP sessions than the attacked host can handle. The attacker just sends TCP packets with the SYN bit set and the ACK bit cleared, which look like regular TCP session establishment requests. The host under attack then reserves some resources for this session and sends back an acknowledgment. When there is no answer, the incomplete session times out after a while, but in the meantime, it occupies resources that can't be used for legitimate sessions. The source addresses in SYN flood attacks are almost always falsified. Because the host sends back packets to these addresses, routers that use some kind of route cache (such as Cisco's fast or optimum switching) will experience a higher CPU load than usual and may even run out of memory.

Worm scanning

Strictly speaking, this isn't a DoS attack, but the results are often similar. More and more people run web servers on their PCs. The vulnerabilities that exist in many of these servers have always been explored by people with questionable intentions, but the proliferation of "always on" Internet access technologies, such as cable and ADSL, has made it possible to create worms that automatically spread from vulnerable system to vulnerable system with unprecedented virulence. Some of these worms infect so many systems and scan for new targets so aggressively that the traffic from their scans effectively becomes a denial-of-service attack. Unlike other attacks, worms scan using legitimate source addresses, but the large number of infected systems makes manually installing filters against the sources of the scans unfeasible. The worms scan large blocks of IP address space, so they are especially harmful for networks with a lot of address space. When a significant amount of address space is directly routed to an Ethernet, even just the large number of ARP requests triggered by the scan can create problems.

The first thing you need to do is identify the type of attack and the destination and source addresses in the packets. Then you can decide on a course of action: tracking down and stopping the source, filtering or rate-limiting the packet stream (either on your own routers or on those of one or more of your ISPs), or deflecting the attack using BGP.

Identifying Attacking Packets

Scanning by worms is easily detected on any system that runs an HTTP server: there will be requests for long and unusual URLs, often with the name of an executable (*.exe*) in it. A remote host will fire off a quick succession of similar requests, after a while another host will do the same, and so on. SYN floods result in huge numbers of TCP sessions in the state SYN_RECEIVED in the *netstat* output on an affected host. Packet floods are a bit harder to recognize, because they can take several forms. Having a look at incoming traffic with a program such as *tcpdump* usually reveals the nature of the attack quickly, however, and it provides a lot of additional information. The *tcpdump* program intercepts traffic from an Ethernet (and some other networks) and dumps the packet contents on the screen or in a file, so you can examine what's happening on the network. It's available for Unix and Unix-like systems, and also for Windows under the name *WinDump*. More information on *tcpdump* is available at *http://www.tcpdump.org*.

Just look for many similar packets that are either very small or very large, and try to find out what they have in common: are they TCP, UDP, or ICMP? What are the source and destination addresses, the UDP or TCP source and destination ports, and ICMP type? Are the packets fragmented or not? Is the TCP SYN bit set? If it's impossible to run *tcpdump* or a similar program, you can use a router to collect most of this information by creating an access list that matches the type of packet you're looking for and then examining the access list counters using the *show access-list ...* command. Example 7-3 shows an access list that will help identify several DoS attack types.

Example 7-3. Access list for detecting DoS attack type

```
!
access-list 100 deny    ip 192.0.2.0 0.0.0.255 any log-input
access-list 100 deny    icmp any any redirect log-input
access-list 100 permit icmp any any echo log-input
access-list 100 permit icmp any any echo-reply log-input
access-list 100 permit icmp any any
access-list 100 permit tcp any host 192.0.2.174 eq www established
access-list 100 permit tcp any host 192.0.2.174 eq www
access-list 100 permit tcp any any eq www established
access-list 100 permit tcp any any eq www log-input
access-list 100 permit tcp any any established
access-list 100 permit tcp any any
access-list 100 permit udp any any
access-list 100 permit ip any any log-input
!
```

The first two lines are standard antispoofing fare to reject incoming packets with internal source addresses and ICMP redirects, but with the *log-input* keyword added so that details about the packet will be logged by the router. Note that the router doesn't log all individual packets that match the access list, but rather a more or less representative sample. The logging of packets matching lines with *log-input* looks like this:

```
%SEC-6-IPACCESSLOGP: list 100 permitted tcp 192.168.208.27(1384) (FastEthernet0 00ed.
78bf.8890) -> 192.0.2.83(80), 33 packets
```

The log message includes the input interface, along with the MAC address if applicable, even if the access list is applied to another interface for output. This is useful to find out what the source (or at least the previous hop) of the attacking traffic is. The *ip source-track address* feature accomplishes the same thing without the need to install an access list. Unfortunately, this feature is only available on the Cisco 12000 platform. See the Cisco documentation for more information.

 At this time I want to once again stress the importance of antispoofing filters for outgoing interfaces. If everyone would allow only valid source addresses in outgoing IP addresses, half the battle against DoS attacks would be won. See Appendix A for an example.

The next three lines in Example 7-3 match ICMP echo request and echo reply messages and all remaining ICMP packets. A high number of echo requests indicates a packet flood using ICMP; a high number of echo replies is usually the result of a Smurf attack. The two lines after that match all HTTP packets from established TCP sessions to the WWW server, and then the remaining HTTP packets. Because packets from established sessions were matched in the previous line, this line will match only the first (SYN) packet of each new session. When the number of SYN packets is larger than the number of established packets, this indicates a SYN flood. The line matching established packets from HTTP sessions for the rest of the network isn't very interesting, but the line after that is: it matches connection attempts to the HTTP service on systems that aren't web servers. This usually indicates worm-scanning activity, so it's logged for further inspection. Finally, all remaining TCP and UDP packets are matched. In most cases, the number of UDP packets should be a good deal smaller than the total number of TCP packets, because most applications use TCP. A relatively high number of UDP packets can be the result of a packet flood, but there are also legitimate applications that generate a lot of UDP traffic, such as multimedia and online gaming. The last line of the access list matches all remaining IP packets. IP packets that carry something other than TCP, UDP, or ICMP are suspect, since they obviously don't transport regular applications. A high number of them is probably the result of a packet flood. Lower numbers may be caused by legitimate traffic from routing protocols or IP tunnels.

It's hard to see in *tcpdump* whether the source and/or destination addresses are more or less random, or there is a large but finite set of them. A better way to find out source and destination addresses is to use the IP accounting facility on the router. When enabled, IP accounting counts the number of packets and bytes for each pair of source and destination addresses. This condenses the information so that it's much easier to pinpoint the addresses. IP accounting must be enabled per interface, and will count only packets transmitted out of those interfaces. To see traffic in both directions, you need to enable IP accounting on two interfaces. Example 7-4 shows how to do this.

Example 7-4. Enabling IP accounting

```
!
interface Ethernet0
 ip accounting output-packets
!
interface Serial0
 ip accounting output-packets
!
```

 IP accounting makes packet forwarding a little slower. If you enabled
IP accounting for diagnostic purposes during a DoS attack, disable it
as soon as you don't need it anymore to avoid unnecessarily using up
CPU time.

You can then use the *show ip accounting* command to display the statistics gathered
by the router. This is what IP accounting statistics for regular traffic look like:

```
BR1#show ip accounting
     Source          Destination       Packets      Bytes
   192.0.2.174      16.28.98.5            10         5532
   16.28.98.5       192.0.2.174           14          809
   222.36.78.101    192.0.2.173          367       215860
   192.0.2.73       222.36.78.101        212        11636
```

When the network is under attack, you will see either a seemingly endless list of
source IP addresses with a limited (and often equal) number of packets per address,
or a list of source addresses that may still be quite long but with higher packet counts
per source address, and the number of packets keeps increasing each time you repeat
the *show ip accounting* command. In the former case, it's likely you are seeing falsified source addresses; in the latter case, the source addresses are probably real. Use
clear ip accounting to remove the current IP accounting statistics from memory and
start a new set.

I once encountered an unusual DoS traffic pattern: huge amounts of incoming TCP
data *from* port 80 to random ports on two hosts in our network, along with a great
deal of ICMP port unreachable messages. This didn't seem like a DoS attack at all,
except that traffic to the two hosts consumed nearly all available bandwidth. Eventually I realized the two hosts weren't the targets of an attack, but rather the *source*:
both were infected with the Nimda worm and were aggressively scanning for vulnerable systems elsewhere on the Net. As soon as I installed filters to prevent both hosts
from sending packets to the rest of the world, incoming traffic quickly returned to
normal.

Tracking Down and Stopping the Source

Ideally, you would look up the contact information for the network where the attack
originates in the appropriate registry (APNIC, ARIN, or RIPE), get the right person

on the phone, explain the situation, and get immediate resolution. However, this approach isn't always successful, for a variety of reasons:

- The source addresses are falsified.
- The attacks often stop before they can be positively identified (when the addresses are falsified), so they are hard to track down.
- Communication problems, such as lack of (good) contact information in the appropriate registries and on their web site, prevent contacting the source, or you can't get the right person on the phone.
- The other side is unable to help. Don't forget that most systems used for attacking others are compromised, so the owners clearly were unable to properly secure them in the first place.
- The other side is unwilling to help because of legal or policy reasons or because they just can't be bothered.

So don't rely on identifying and informing the source network as the most important means to stop the attack. On the other hand, the originating network might be helpful, so contact them if this doesn't take too much time away from your other efforts to stop the attack. As a general rule, non-ISP organizations are more inclined to act on DoS complaints than ISPs, and small ISPs more than large ones.

Filtering DoS Traffic

If you were successful in determining the common characteristics of the packets used in the attack, you can now design a filter to get rid of them. You can filter on source address, protocol and port, or destination address. Each has benefits and drawbacks:

Source-address filtering
> This type of filter has the least amount of impact on legitimate users, because only addresses participating in the attack are blocked. Unfortunately, filtering on source addresses is often impossible because either they are falsified and continuously change, or the list is too long.

Protocol and port filtering
> Sometimes attackers are helpful enough to address their packets only at unused or unimportant services, such as a random UDP port or the ICMP echo service. These can easily be filtered out without any impact on real traffic. Obviously, this won't work for attacks on important services, such as most SYN floods or worm scans; in this case, blocking the port will do exactly what the attacker wants: disrupt service for legitimate users.

Destination-address filtering
> When the attack is directed at a single IP address, a range of addresses, or a small number of individual IP addresses, it can make sense to sacrifice those for the greater good of the network and filter them out so the rest of the network

can function properly. However, this isn't a great solution, since the attackers have now reached their goal: wiping the attacked addresses off the face of the Net.

The best place to install a filter would be as close to the source of the attack as possible. In practice, this means on the other side of your connection to your ISPs, or possibly somewhere else in your ISP's network. That way, your connections don't get congested with traffic you have no use for. But if your ISPs are uncooperative, or while you're waiting for them to install the filter, it can still be beneficial to apply the same filter to your ISP connections. Routers often have limited CPUs compared to hosts. Under normal conditions, this may not be a problem, but as soon as the network gets flooded, routers sometimes completely lock up. You can give the router more breathing room by filtering out the traffic as soon as it enters the router: on the first line of the access list for the incoming interface. This saves the router from investing CPU time in the abusive packets by trying to forward them. You may also want to disable CPU-intensive features, such as complex filters and sophisticated queuing mechanisms, for as long as the attack lasts.

Rate-Limiting DoS Traffic

When completely filtering out the DoS traffic isn't an option (or at least not an attractive option) because it would also hurt regular users and applications, it can be useful to at least limit the DoS traffic. The rate-limiting mechanism discussed in Chapter 6 is well suited to do this. However, applying rate limits will also hurt legitimate users, if their traffic can't be separated from the DoS traffic. But compared to the problems the DoS attack already creates, the extra impact should be fairly negligible, and this way there will at least be a reasonable amount of bandwidth for sessions that can be successfully separated from the DoS traffic. The way rate limiting is applied depends on the type of attack. The ICMP or UDP packets that typically result from packet floods and Smurf attacks can usually be filtered, so there is subsequently no need to rate-limit them, but rate limiting can be useful in the event of a SYN flood. SYN floods are routinely directed at hosts and ports used for important services, so completely filtering them out isn't an attractive proposition, because it effectively disables the targeted service.

Different operating systems react differently to SYN floods, but even if a host can handle the SYN overload, it still can't do anything useful if the SYNs preempt all other traffic. There is a point between blocking all SYNs and letting them all through where the remaining useful performance of the server is at its highest. If you have a very fast server, you may want to start limiting the SYN rate to a level that must certainly be higher than the optimum level, for instance, 25% to 50% of available bandwidth. Then you work your way down, seeing improved performance, until the performance gets worse again. On the other hand, if your server is slow, start at the lowest possible rate, 8 Kbps (about 25 SYNs per second), and work your way up from there until the server gets in trouble. In both cases, go back a little, and you've found the optimum rate limit. If the attack targets more than one host or service, you may want to rate-limit individually to be able to better fine-tune the individual rate limits for the best possible performance.

In a network with many web servers, there isn't much you can do about scanning by worms.* However, many networks have large numbers of workstation PCs or other hosts that don't run any service on TCP port 80, enabling you to rate-limit incoming SYNs to slow worms down. This limits the amount of bandwidth worms can use and also slows down the rate at which vulnerable hosts are infected. But this also throws away some of the incoming SYNs for legitimate services, which your users won't like. Another way to go is to keep a tight lid on outgoing TCP resets. When a worm tries to contact port 80 at a certain IP address to see if it can infect this host, and there is no HTTP server running, the TCP/IP stack sends back a "reset" message to inform the worm it's unable to accept the request ("connection refused"). It's not possible to simply filter all TCP resets, since they are also used to terminate orphaned TCP sessions, which is necessary when a host reboots in the middle of a session. Some lost reset messages due to rate limiting shouldn't be a problem when this happens, because the host generates a new one for each packet it receives belonging to an unknown TCP session. Rate-limiting TCP resets also slows down aggressive port scans, because these generate even more TCP resets in a short period of time than worms do. Rate-limiting outgoing ICMP port unreachables has the same effect for UDP port scans. Example 7-5 implements several rate limits.

Example 7-5. Rate limiting against DoS attacks and scans

```
!
interface Serial0
 bandwidth 1544
 rate-limit input access-group 131 152000 8000 8000
   conform-action transmit exceed-action drop
 rate-limit input access-group 132 72000 8000 8000
   conform-action transmit exceed-action drop
 rate-limit output access-group 133 8000 8000 8000
   conform-action transmit exceed-action drop
 rate-limit output access-group 134 8000 8000 8000
   conform-action transmit exceed-action drop
!
access-list 131 permit tcp any host 192.0.2.174 established
access-list 131 permit tcp any host 192.0.2.174 eq www
access-list 132 permit icmp any any
access-list 133 permit tcp any any rst
access-list 134 permit icmp any any port-unreachable
!
```

---

* Some routers are able to look "deeper" inside packets than just the IP and TCP headers and can filter on application-layer information, such as the requested URL in HTTP packets. This makes it possible to stop worms at the edge of the network.

The first *rate-limit input* command applies access list 131 to input traffic. This list matches only incoming SYNs to port 80 of a specific web server (192.0.2.174). If this traffic stays below 10% of the link bandwidth, it's allowed through. All matched traffic exceeding this limit is dropped. The rate-limit bandwidth settings work in increments of 8 Kbps, so the router adjusts the 154,400 bps (10% of a T1) figure to the closest 8-Kbps value. The additional two "8000" values are the burst and maximum burst values, which can accommodate temporary bandwidth spikes. Since this isn't needed here, both are set to their lowest possible value.

The second *rate-limit input* command limits all incoming ICMP packets (matched by access list 132) to 5% of the T1 bandwidth. Because the packets have already traversed the link, dropping them as they are received doesn't really help to keep legitimate traffic flowing over the T1 link, but at least the rest of the network is protected to some degree. It would be more effective to perform this rate limiting for output on the ISP's side of the connection. The two *rate-limit output* commands limit outgoing TCP resets (access list 133) and ICMP port unreachables (access list 134) to the minimum of 8 Kbps each. That's about 25 resets and a slightly higher number of port unreachables per second. Note that all these values, especially the limit on the number of SYNs, may affect legitimate traffic to some degree. Make sure they are appropriate for the available bandwidth, traffic type, and number of addresses in your network, and don't leave these limits in place when the attack is over.

Deflecting DoS Traffic Using BGP

When an attack gets really bad, and cooperation from upstream ISPs isn't forthcoming, there is one last thing you can try before just giving up and no longer announcing the address block under attack: you can try to receive the attacking packets over one line so the other is free for regular traffic.

The easiest way to do this is to stop announcing the affected address block over all ISP connections but one, and stop announcing all other address blocks over the ISP that now has the privilege of supplying you with the attacking traffic. This of course assumes you have at least two address blocks, and it has the disadvantage that an entire address block remains affected by the attack. Networks have been known to request special address blocks for the purpose of being able to isolate DoS-sensitive hosts (such as IRC servers) from the rest of the network when the need arises. There's another way to do this, however, which leads to better-targeted results and also works for networks with a single address block. First, stop announcing anything to one ISP, and then start announcing the individual address or addresses affected or as small a range of addresses as this ISP and/or important upstream transit ISPs and peers will accept. Example 7-6 shows a BGP configuration implementing this.

Example 7-6. Changing announcements to deflect a DoS attack

```
!
router bgp 60055
 network 192.0.2.0
 network 220.37.0.0 mask 255.255.240.0
 network 220.37.3.245 mask 255.255.255.255
 neighbor 192.0.254.17 remote-as 40077
 neighbor 192.0.254.17 description BGP session to ISP A
 neighbor 192.0.254.17 prefix-list ispa-out out
 neighbor 219.2.19.1 remote-as 50066
 neighbor 219.2.19.1 description BGP session to ISP B
 neighbor 219.2.19.1 prefix-list ispb-dos-out out
!
ip route 192.0.2.0 255.255.255.0 Null0
ip route 220.37.0.0 255.255.240.0 Null0
ip route 220.37.3.245 255.255.255.255 Null0
!
ip prefix-list ispa-out description outbound filter for ISP A
ip prefix-list ispa-out seq 5 permit 192.0.2.0/24
ip prefix-list ispa-out seq 10 permit 220.37.0.0/20
ip prefix-list ispb-dos-out description DoS filter for ISP B
ip prefix-list ispb-dos-out seq 5 permit 220.37.3.245/32
!
```

The configuration changes compared to the regular configuration are small: an extra
network statement in the BGP configuration, a pull-up route for this "network," and
a new prefix list, which allows just the address under attack and nothing else, for the
session to ISP B.

> Because DoS attacks can be so devastating, when you are selecting
> ISPs, discuss what level of cooperation you can expect when you find
> yourself being attacked. See Chapter 11 for ideas about what ISPs can
> do to help customers in the event of DoS attacks.

CHAPTER 8

Day-to-Day Operation of the Network

Finally! All the connections are in place, all the routers have been configured, all the BGP sessions are up, and lots of traffic is flowing. So now you can go back to doing your regular work, right? Don't count on it. Few users of the network are familiar with the details of interdomain routing, so they'll come to you whenever they can't reach their favorite web site or when an email bounces. It's possible to deter them by adopting a brusque demeanor, of course, but this will give you only temporary relief until the users counter this with unpleasant attitudes of their own. A better solution is to make sure you can quickly separate the problems you should deal with from the perceived problems that don't exist, must be fixed by someone else, or just can't be fixed and must be endured. Unfortunately, in all but the smallest organizations, even taking a quick look at all the potential problems users drop at your feet takes a serious amount of time. This is one of the three main reasons why it's a good idea to create a *Network Operations Center* (NOC).

Another reason is the fact that you are now participating in the worldwide interdomain routing system. This means you should be reachable in case others want to notify you when there are problems that affect your network or, worse, originate there. The third reason may seem a bit silly, but it's just as important: the fact that there is a dedicated part of the organization dealing with interdomain routing issues gives people (both within the organization and elsewhere) confidence that keeping the network running is a priority, so they feel safe depending on it for important work.

The Network Operations Center

When they hear the words "Network Operations Center," most people immediately think of "mission control"-style rooms with huge screens on the walls and rows of consoles with industrious technicians behind them. Some NOCs really look like this, but others are nothing more than a phone extension and an email box. Just running BGP doesn't warrant a huge NOC: a single engineer keeping an eye on one or two management consoles while doing other work is enough, as long as this other work may be interrupted when the network needs attention. When the NOC is larger, this is either because the organization is (or acts as) an ISP so there are many connections to external networks, or because of additional responsibilities apart from monitoring and troubleshooting interdomain routing (IDR). There are basically three types of NOC relevant to IDR:

- NOCs where managing interdomain routing is handled alongside managing the physical part of the network. This type of NOC is common with ISPs and ISP-like organizations that have many BGP-speaking customers. In this case, it makes little sense for all NOC engineers to be familiar with IDR, because most NOC engineers will be doing other things most of the time.

- NOCs that use a broad interpretation of the word "network" and are responsible for extra equipment and services in addition to managing the actual network. These NOCs are mostly found within organizations in which operating a large number of servers is an important activity, such as web hosting or e-commerce businesses. However, most people have an inclination towards administering servers and a dislike for routers, or the other way around. Only a few people develop both skills to the same degree over time. So in many cases this situation grows towards the third type of NOC.

- NOCs that focus just on managing the network at the physical level, and a separate IDR group that handles the interdomain routing issues. This kind of NOC is found mostly in large organizations. Rather than having to train each NOC engineer in interdomain routing troubleshooting, the IDR issues are handled by a small group of specialists. The IDR specialists are then called in when the NOC engineers detect a problem in the network they can't fix.

The NOC and the Help Desk

Every network has users, and all users need some level of support. Usually, there is a help desk of some sort to provide this support. It makes life a lot easier if everyone can identify the responsibilities of the NOC and those of the help desk. Users are likely to prefer calling or emailing the NOC rather than the help desk, because the NOC staff is more knowledgeable, and the response times are better. Or at least they should be. When a user calls the help desk and has to wait, this wastes time for just a single person. But if someone with information that could restore the network has to wait before he can talk to a NOC engineer, all users of the network (which may include customers trying to do business over the Net) have to wait.

The essential difference between the NOC and the help desk is that the help desk is there to help *people*, while the NOC looks after the *network*. If someone can't read his email, and he calls the help desk, the support engineer may spend a good deal of time on the phone, trying to figure out what the problem is and how to fix it and possibly explaining the whole process to the user. A NOC engineer, on the other hand, is likely to say, "Thank you for bringing this potential network problem to our attention. Good-bye." There is probably some room for politeness, but one thing has to be absolutely clear: the NOC isn't a help desk. Even seemingly harmless things, such as forwarding email messages to the help desk or transferring calls, can lead to major problems down the road. Imagine a situation in which a user calls the NOC when she can't send email. The NOC engineer quickly checks the status of the network and says, "The network is OK. It's probably your PC, so I'll transfer you to the help desk." When this happens once or twice a day, there is really no problem.

But there will come a day when the problem actually is the network. And then everybody will be calling the NOC, and the NOC staff will be constantly interrupted by the phone while trying to fix the problem. On the other hand, if users were "trained" to call the help desk, they'd be informed that there is a problem and it's being worked on. This assumes the NOC keeps the help desk informed about what's going on, of course. But this is in the interest of the NOC too, since it helps limit the number of calls to the NOC number. To avoid excessive phone calls when there are problems, some NOCs don't even accept calls from regular users, but only from registered "NOC callers." This is appropriate when the network has a huge user base, such as that in a regional educational network. But this can also be counterproductive, because it can delay important information in reaching the NOC. So you should establish rules on who can call the NOC for what issues, depending on the size and experience level of your user base.

Contacting the NOC

There are two main ways for the NOC to be contacted by people who feel they have something to share: email and the phone. Email is important for day-to-day things, such as peers letting you know they are announcing some new prefixes or users complaining the network is too slow. The most appropriate email address for the NOC is probably *noc@domain*, but anything conveying "this is the email address of the people managing the network" is fine, for instance, *netops@domain*, *info@operations. domain*, or *network@domain*. Don't use an email address that isn't recognizable as a NOC email address, because people may assume it won't be read at regular intervals or by the right people. For a not-too-big NOC, a good way to handle incoming email is to have NOC email forwarded to the full NOC staff. When someone replies, she copies the reply to the NOC email address so everyone knows this particular email has been answered. This is also an excellent way to transfer knowledge between NOC staffers: everyone reads the answer to all problems. One person should be in charge of regularly making sure all emails have been answered. Larger NOCs should probably use a ticket system for the NOC email address: each incoming email is assigned a ticket number, and someone assigns tickets to specific NOC engineers. An engineer then notes the progress made in the ticket before closing it (when the problem is solved) or reassigning it to someone else, if necessary. Working with a ticket system isn't a whole lot of fun, but it's the only way to keep track of unsolved problems in a larger organization. A ticket system also facilitates cooperation between the help desk and the NOC: the help desk can open tickets, enter all available information, and assign them to the NOC if they can't solve the problem themselves.

People elsewhere on the Net tend to expect certain email addresses to exist, such as *peering@domain*, *abuse@domain*, *webmaster@domain*, *postmaster@domain*, and *root@domain*. None of these addresses should go to the NOC mailbox, but if they don't exist or email to them isn't replied to, you may eventually find messages concerning all kinds of non-NOC issues in the NOC mailbox, because that one is listed in RIR and RR databases. There is really not much you can do about this except try to get the people who receive those emails to answer them and clearly list an abuse email address in the remarks sections of your objects in the Routing Registry. Email to the abuse address concerns mainly things like spam or worms emanating from IP addresses (or domains) inside your network and questionable IP packets, such as port scans.

While it's a good idea to encourage people to use only email for contacting the NOC, they'll pick up the phone anyway when something really bad happens. Trying to hide your phone number doesn't work: when a user can't get any work done because the network is down, he has plenty of time to track down your number, and he will be that much more annoyed when he finally gets you on the phone. So if you can, have a dedicated NOC number that you can list in all the right places, such as:

- ARIN, APNIC, and RIPE databases, and Routing Registries
- On the NOC web page
- At the bottom of NOC-related emails

Obviously, the level of frustration will reach unprecedented heights when people call this number and can't get an actual human being on the phone. Have this number answered by a person, not a machine, if at all possible. Even someone who doesn't know anything about the network is a lot better than a voicemail box: that way, the person answering the phone can be asked to go find you or someone else who can handle things if the severity of the problem warrants it. If the NOC phone is answered by a NOC engineer (which is the best way to go), you might want to implement some rules to make sure the phone lines and NOC staff aren't unnecessarily tied up by incoming calls. These rules might include:

- No support. The NOC isn't a help desk.
- "Can you send us an email instead?" The NOC phone isn't there to save users from typing email.
- A time limit for calls to the NOC number. When a call reaches the limit, the NOC engineer ends the conversation, promising to look into the matter and call back. This gives the NOC staff some time to actually look at the problem rather than getting an earful.
- No transfers. The NOC staffer who picks up the phone is competent to handle the problem or to at least get a detailed enough description. If the caller wishes

to speak to a particular NOC staffer, he has to dial the right number himself if these numbers are given out, or he will be called back.

Even if it makes your job a bit harder, you should enforce any rules you adopt enough to make sure that callers take them seriously, as long as the network is up and running. This will make your life a lot easier when crunch time arrives.

It can be useful to have a few web pages with NOC information, but only if they are up to date. Incorrect information is worse than no information at all. So if you have any NOC web pages, you must be able to modify them yourself at any time. "I asked the webmaster to change the phone number on the web page two months ago" isn't good enough. Also, put information up on the web only if you know you will be able to keep it current.

NOC Hardware Facilities

NOC staffers need to be able to read their email, look at web pages, edit documents, and draw pictures just like everyone else. They may use poor judgment in downloading questionable software or opening email attachments, just like everyone else, so they should have office computers behind a firewall just like everyone else. But the office network, and especially the firewall that separates it from the rest of the world, are likely to be big single points of failure. You don't want to have to explain to your customers that you couldn't stop a DoS attack because the office firewall broke down as a result of the same attack. So you need another way to access the network, and if you don't allow office PCs to access the networking equipment, you need *two* other ways to access the network.

The alternative way to access the network can be anything from a simple VT100 terminal connected to the console port of a router to a dedicated NOC network with workstations, one or more servers, and possibly a firewall. The main thing is diversity: the regular office systems and the NOC systems shouldn't be susceptible to the same problems, so the hardware, network connections, operating system (or at least the OS version), and essential tools should be different. Essential management (Telnet or console access) should also be possible from the equipment room, so managing the network can be done when there are power, network, or physical problems at the NOC office location.

There are people who swear by out-of-band access for network management. With out-of-band access, you can still access your network if the connections that carry actual traffic are down. In practice, I've never needed out-of-band access for a network with a reasonable level of redundancy. Modem access to locations that are connected to the rest of the network over a single circuit can be useful on occasion, but as a general rule, save yourself the extra work and expense and just use in-band access.

Good things to have at the NOC include:

- VT100-compatible terminals and/or old MS-DOS laptops to use for console access (the laptops may be new, but they must have a serial port)
- Shell access to remote Unix or similar systems to evaluate the reachability of your network by looking in from the outside
- A modem, dial-up accounts at different ISPs, and a system with a flexible PPP implementation for dial-up access if your network can't reach the Internet
- A Unix or Linux box that can perform reachability and statistics measurements and where routers and switches can store their software images and configurations using TFTP
- A printer for printing emails and configurations, preferably directly from the Unix box
- A dedicated NOC mail server
- A safe for keeping passwords, backups, original software, and licenses

And don't forget a plentiful supply of screwdrivers, wire strippers, UTP crimpers, serial cables, gender changers, null modems, and all permutations of UTP cabling: regular Ethernet, crossed Ethernet, straight and flipped UTP console cables, and their connectors. When you encounter broken cables or connectors, throw them out. I'm always amazed to see people get frustrated wasting a good deal of time before they find out that a cable or connector doesn't work, only to put it back in a drawer so the whole process can repeat itself a few weeks or months later.

SNMP Management

The Internet Architecture Board (IAB, formerly the Internet *Activities* Board) is a technical advisory group that oversees the architecture of protocols developed for use over the Internet. The actual development of new protocols is done in the IETF working groups. Since anyone can participate in the IETF by joining working group mailing lists or visiting IETF meetings, some oversight is necessary from time to time. In the late 1980s, the IAB made the following recommendation, if we are to believe RFC 1157:

> The Internet Activities Board recommends that all IP and TCP implementations be network manageable. This implies implementation of the Internet MIB (RFC-1156) and at least one of the two recommended management protocols SNMP (RFC-1157) or CMOT (RFC-1095).

This recommendation has been taken to heart by vendors of networking equipment: they implemented the Simple Network Management Protocol (SNMP) in pretty much all their networking products. SNMP isn't simple in all regards, but basic operation does the name justice, because the range of supported operations is limited:

Get
> The managing system reads an object from the system being managed.

Get next
> The managing system can discover the next object in the hierarchy of available objects in the managed system.

Set
> The managing system writes a new value to an object on the managed system.

Trap
> The managed system sends an unsolicited message to the managing system.

Monitoring a system is done by periodically polling objects describing the system's status and by listening for trap messages that are sent after significant events occur, such as the system rebooting or a link going down. Actively managing a system is then done by writing new values into objects that determine how the system operates. For instance, when the management station wants a router to stop forwarding packets, it would write a value with the meaning "NOT acting as a gateway" into the ipForwarding object.

The main complexity of SNMP is defining the objects. This is done in one or more Management Information Bases (MIBs). A MIB defines a place in the hierarchy of managed objects for each object, along with information about the object: whether it's a read-only, read-write, or write-only object; the syntax of the object's values; and more. For instance, the sysUpTime object lives in the object group "system" of the MIB-II (a more recent version of the standard Internet MIB). The object is identified by the number 1.3.6.1.2.1.1.3, or iso.org.dod.internet.mgmt.mib-2.system. sysUpTime in human-readable form. It contains the time since the last system reboot in hundredths of a second. Describing all objects in such detail makes it possible for management software to manage all systems for which there is a MIB, without any need to have specific prior knowledge about such a system. A good example of this extensibility is the Remote Management (RMON) MIB. Systems implementing RMON collect statistics about the different systems on a network. A management station can then retrieve this information from the remote monitoring agent and display it, thereby monitoring the network behavior of a range of systems without the need for these systems to implement SNMP themselves.

It's important to note that SNMP isn't a secure protocol. SNMPv2 and SNMPv3 address this weakness, but the original SNMP is still in wide use. SNMPv1 access control is based on the idea of "communities." Several communities with different authorization levels can coexist. By default, the community "public" allows read access, and the community "private" allows read and write access. Cisco equipment doesn't have these default communities, but many vendors still build them into their products. There are many helpful individuals on the Net who are eager to help you out by dedicating time and effort to manage your network. Unfortunately, their idea of the best way to run a network might be slightly different from yours, so you may want to at least change the names of the communities to something that is hard to guess (you should think of the community name as a password). Preferably, you shouldn't enable SNMP write access and you should implement IP-based access controls for read access. Example 8-1 shows how to enable read-only SNMP access with IP-based access restrictions and a hard-to-guess community string. The only SMNP requests the router answers are read-only requests coming from IP addresses permitted by access lists 99 (213.16.43.19 and 213.16.43.168 through 213.16.43.175) with the community string set to "mysecretcommunitystring". The chassis ID, location, and contact are purely informational and will show up in appropriate places on a management station.

Example 8-1. Enabling and securing SNMP

```
!
access-list 99 permit 213.16.43.19
access-list 99 permit 213.16.43.168 0.0.0.7
!
snmp-server community mysecretcommunitystring RO 99
snmp-server location Chicago office, room 318, rack 6
snmp-server contact Example Corp. NOC: noc@example
snmp-server chassis-id BR2
!
```

There are several ways to put SNMP to use in your network, ranging from all-encompassing integrated network-management suites to tools that perform only a single, simple function.

Network-Management Suites

At the high end, there are integrated network-management suites such as HP Open-View or Sun Net Manager. Their impressive features come with a matching impressive price tag. The network-management suite also adds a layer of complexity of its own on top of the complexity of the underlying network infrastructure. I suppose I'm a bit unfair in saying this, but I always feel that systems like this make things that were simple in the first place even easier but complicate the already complex things even further as well. Network-management suites are especially suited for large networks, where it's easy to lose sight of the forest because there are so many trees. They make it easier to delegate routine tasks to junior staff. Network-management suites can typically be expanded by adding new MIBs.

Product-Specific Management Software

The second category consists of product-specific software packages. Web-based management is more in vogue now, but some vendors offer (or even bundle with products) management software written specifically for one product or product range. These are often SNMP-based. The main problem with these systems is lack of integration: each manages only a small part of the network infrastructure. They are sometimes useful when you need to perform certain tasks that would otherwise be complex, such as upgrading the software image in a router or switch. This type of management software has the same MIBs built in as the products it manages, so there is no need to support importing new MIBs.

Generic SNMP Tools

Next, there are SNMP tools that perform a specific function: they receive and log traps, monitor system or link status, or keep track of statistics. These tools often implement only the standard MIBs but can interact with objects from other MIBs to some degree by manually configuring the desired object identifier. Popular tools for network management include the CMU SNMP tools, NOCOL (now SNIPS) for monitoring the status of the network, and the MRTG for gathering and displaying bandwidth usage and other statistics. They all run on most Unix and Unix-like systems.

MRTG

Multi Router Traffic Grapher (MRTG) is an excellent network management tool consisting of a set of Perl and C programs that periodically perform SNMP polls on routers and other equipment and produce web pages with graphs showing statistics. MRTG runs on pretty much everything that has Perl, such as Unix and Linux, but also Windows NT. It was originally written to monitor bandwidth use, but it can be used to monitor just about every value that changes over time, from interface error counters to CPU usage. The default configuration (which the supplied *cfgmaker* tool will create for you when you point it at some SNMP-manageable piece of equipment) creates web pages with graphics displaying the input and output bandwidth of an interface over the last day, week, month, and year. It does this by periodically reading the interface's input and output byte-counters and reworking these values into bandwidth numbers. MRTG also understands objects of type "gauge," such as processor load and temperature, and it can call external scripts. This is useful for monitoring values that aren't available in SNMP, such as the number of prefixes received from a BGP peer. The program uses a special log file format that keeps the log file size constant over time. The MRTG home page can be found at *http://ee-staff. ethz.ch/~oetiker/webtools/mrtg/*. Installation can be a bit complicated, because you need several libraries. The installation document tells you which versions you need and where to get them. Don't download newer versions than those listed, because these sometimes require even more libraries.

BGP-4 Management Information Base

There is also a BGP-4 MIB, specified in RFC 1657. Using this MIB, it's possible to query a router for lots of information about individual peers and individual routes (referred to as "paths" here) in the BGP table. However, the BGP-4 MIB lacks objects that would provide a good insight into the overall health of the BGP routing process. For instance, you might want to have NOCOL/SNIPS check whether the bgpPeerState stays in the "established" state or use MRTG to track bgpPeerInUpdates to stay aware of routing instabilities, but the MIB doesn't allow you to determine the number of routes received from a peer or the total size of the BGP table without querying all individual entries. To keep track of these, you'll have to use cruder methods, such as executing one or more *show ip bgp ...* commands using the *remote command (rcmd)* facility on the router. Example 8-2 shows part of an MRTG configuration file that uses both SNMP and external commands to gather statistics. The global options are left out; the *cfgmaker* program will create these for you.

Example 8-2. Using MRTG to graph BGP statistics

```
LoadMIBs: /usr/local/mrtg-2/BGP4-MIB.my
Target[br1as40077]: bgpPeerInUpdates.192.0.254.17&bgpPeerOutUpdates.192.0.254.17:
mysecretcommunitystring@br1 * 300
MaxBytes[br1as40077]: 1000000
Options[br1as40077]: growright, nopercent
YLegend[br1as40077]: Updates per 5 min
ShortLegend[br1as40077]: upd/5min
Legend1[br1as40077]: Incoming BGP Updates per 5 min
Legend2[br1as40077]: Outgoing BGP Updates per 5 min
Legend3[br1as40077]: Max. 5 min. Incoming BGP Updates
Legend4[br1as40077]: Max. 5 min. Outgoing BGP Updates
Title[br1as40077]: BGP updates for AS40077
PageTop[br1as40077]: <hr><H3>BGP updates for AS40077</H3>
Target[tblas40077]: `rsh br1 show ip bgp summary | awk -f /usr/local/mrtg-2/awkprogram`
MaxBytes[tblas40077]: 150000
Title[tblas40077]: BR1 BGP Table Size
PageTop[tblas40077]: <H1>BR1 BGP Table Size</H1>
Options[tblas40077]: gauge, noinfo, nopercent, growright
YLegend[tblas40077]: prefixes received
ShortLegend[tblas40077]: prefixes
Legend1[tblas40077]: Prefixes received from AS40077
Legend2[tblas40077]: Prefixes preferred over internal BGP
LegendI[tblas40077]: AS40077
LegendO[tblas40077]: iBGP
```

The first thing this MRTG configuration file does (after processing the global options, which have been left out) is load the BGP-4 MIB file. You need the MIB definitions file *BGP4-MIB.my* for this, which is available on the Cisco FTP server *ftp. cisco.com* in the */pub/mibs/v2/* directory. The definition of the br1as40077 target follows. This target uses SNMP to read the bgpPeerInUpdates and bgpPeerOutUpdates information from the BR1 router with the "mysecretcommunitystring" community string. The results are multiplied by 300 to get a number of updates per five-minute period. Without this, MRTG would calculate the number of updates per second from the BGP update-counter values. The number of updates per second is typically so low it won't produce good graphics. The tblas40077 target uses the remote shell command and the *awk* program shown in Example 8-3 to create statistics for the number of routes received from a peer. Example 8-4 enables the remote command (*rcmd*) facility on the router. This makes it easy to execute commands on the router from a remote system that supports the *rsh* command.

Example 8-3. Accompanying awk program

```
BEGIN {}
/192.0.254.17  / { print $10 }
/213.156.4.177 / { print $10 }
END { print "a long time" ; print "the bgp router" }
```

Example 8-4. Enabling remote command access on the router

```
!
ip rcmd rsh-enable
ip rcmd remote-host root 192.0.2.98 root
ip rcmd remote-host nobody 192.0.2.98 nobody
!
```

The *awk* program processes the output of the *show ip bgp summary* command one line at a time. When it encounters a line matching the string 192.0.254.17 (the peer IP address), it prints out the 10th item on this line, which is the number of prefixes received from this peer. The same is done for the other IP address, and when the program ends, it prints two extra lines. This completes the output MRTG expects: two numeric values, an uptime, and a system name. The noinfo option keeps the uptime and system name information from being displayed, however. Because the number of routes received from a peer is in the form of an absolute value and not that of an ever-increasing counter, like the number of bytes received on an interface, the gauge option is also set. growright makes MRTG add new information on the right of the graphic, rather than at the left side.

Router Names

For some reason, people just love to use a mythological or astronomical theme when naming their hosts. It can be fun to show off your knowledge in either of these areas by coming up with clever naming schemes with obscure references for your routers, but there will come a day when you can't remember whether you named the routers connecting the financial department after the moons of Mars, or after two of the three Fates.* These naming schemes also lack flexibility and extensibility. The best way to name routers and switches is by function, if all your routers have distinct functions (border, core, customer/gateway) and by location. Include numbers so you

---

* Mars is orbited by Phobos (panic) and Deimos (fear). The three Fates are Clotho, who weaves life, Lachesis, who measures it, and Atropos, who cuts the thread. They laugh at our feeble attempts to cheat them because they always prevail.

can have several routers performing the same function in the same location, and so it's possible to have several points of presence in the same city. I prefer to use the full names for cities, but this can make the names a bit long. Others use their own abbreviations or use airport codes. You might also want to use the exchange point name for Internet Exchange locations. Table 8-1 shows some example router names.

Table 8-1. Example router names

Name	Location	Function/number
br1-paloalto1	Palo Alto location 1	Border router 1
border1.paix	Palo Alto Internet Exchange	Border router 1
newyork3-2	New York location 3	Router 2
cust1.newyork1	New York location 1	Customer connect router 1
cr2.mae-east2	MAE East location 2	Core router 2

But it doesn't end there. Routers have more than one interface, so if you want to be able to ping individual interfaces, it's a good idea to assign individual names to those. If the interface is down, it won't be reachable by pinging. This means you can't Telnet to this IP address either, by the way. Giving the router an IP address on a loopback interface (which is always up) makes sure the router has an address that is always up for Telnet and SNMP access. This is also the address you put in the DNS. See the section "Using Loopback Addresses for iBGP" in Chapter 10 for an example that shows how to configure a loopback address and how to use it for iBGP processing.

Some people prefer to use the interface names in the DNS reverse zone files, so they show up in traceroutes. This can be useful if you make use of redundant paths (either physical through multiple interfaces, or virtual through multiple ATM or frame relay PVCs) between two routers: a traceroute will show you exactly which interfaces and/or PVCs packets travel through:

```
# traceroute www
  1  dallas1-3 (172.16.1.3) 0.783 0.841 0.732
  2  fa0.dallas1-2 (172.16.3.8) 1.25 1.103 1.392
  3  117.atm3.chicago2-1 (172.18.45.117) 35.183 121.atm4.chicago2-1 (172.18.46.121)
37.108 117.atm3.chicago2-1 (172.18.45.117) 38.19
  4  www (172.19.3.1) 40.133 39.783 40.388
```

In this example, the packets are load-balanced over two ATM interfaces on the chicago2-1 router. They show up on alternate turns on line 3. I lean slightly towards recommending against putting interface names in the reverse DNS as a general practice, because it gives potential attackers a lot of insight into your network, and it clutters up the traceroute output.

General IP Network Management

This is a book about BGP, so there is no room to go into every detail of managing your network. But there are four subjects that warrant a few words here. Look them up in a book on IP networking if you need more information.

Logging

Routers generate log information with potentially important information. There are several ways to view these log entries:

- On a terminal connected to the console port
- In the syslog of a syslog host
- Over a telnet session using the *show log* command (to review old log entries) or with *terminal monitor* (to receive live logging information during the rest of a telnet session; *terminal no monitor* to turn it off)

If there is any chance the router may generate a lot of logging information, it's best to disable logging to the console port, because this port is relatively slow and may slow down the system under log-heavy situations. Example 8-5 does this, along with increasing the size of the logging buffer in memory and specifying a syslog host. It also enables logging of BGP neighbor changes (peer going up or down).

Example 8-5. Customizing logging

```
!
service timestamps log datetime
!
logging buffered 32768 debugging
no logging console
!
router bgp 60055
 bgp log-neighbor-changes
!
logging trap warnings
logging  192.0.2.98
!
```

The *service timestamps* command adds time information to the log entries. This is, of course, redundant for logging to a syslog server, because the syslog daemon does this as well. The memory-logging buffer is set to 32 KB here, and the level is set to debugging, which means all possible logging. The console doesn't receive any log messages. The *logging trap* command sets the log level for syslog logging. It has nothing to do with sending SNMP trap messages. Warnings (severity 4) is a good choice here, because "configured from console" messages won't end up in the syslog. The *bgp log-neighbor-changes* command makes the router generate the following log messages when a BGP session comes up or goes down:

```
May 28 05:43:13 MET: %BGP-5-ADJCHANGE: neighbor 192.0.254.17 Down User reset
May 28 05:43:29 MET: %BGP-5-ADJCHANGE: neighbor 192.0.254.17 Up
```

Cisco routers can also be managed using HTTP, but just say no and don't enable the HTTP server in the router. It's basically a dumbed-down and harder to use version of the Telnet interface.

Version Control

If you have many routers and many people entering configurations changes, it's a good idea to do some kind of version control on the configurations. The configurations are regular text files, you can easily store them in generic version control systems such as SCCS, RCS, or CVS. Version control systems are extensively used in software engineering, because they make it possible for a group of people all to work on the same set of source files at the same time. The system keeps track of who is making changes to which file and keeps copies of all versions of all files. If someone wants to compile the software, she can request read-only copies of the latest versions of all files and compile them. Thus, one programmer can work on version 1.7 of file A, while another programmer works on version 2.3 of file B. When the first programmer compiles the software, he uses the A version 1.7 that he's working on and requests the latest version of B present in the system, which is version 2.2. When the other programmer compiles the program, she uses B version 2.3 and the system gives her A version 1.6.

This principle can be applied to router configurations by splitting them up into several different files, for instance, files for the general configuration, the interface configurations, and BGP, and files for all the filters that regularly change. A script then combines the different files to create the full configuration and uploads it to the router. A less ambitious use of a version control system is to have a script periodically retrieve the configurations and check them in. However, in both cases a remote system is allowed to perform potentially dangerous operations on the router, and there is no easy way to do this securely. It's possible to configure the *rcmd* facility on the router to allow remote execution of privileged (enable) commands, but this isn't safe enough.

See the RCS home page at *http://www.cs.purdue.edu/homes/trinkle/RCS/* for more information about RCS and links to other version control systems.

The Network Time Protocol

Many routers and switches don't have a battery-backed-up clock, so when they boot they are unaware of the time. Routers don't need to know the time to function, but correct time information can be useful in recreating a sequence of events when a problem occurs. Use the Network Time Protocol (NTP) to synchronize their clocks with a master NTP server, as shown in Example 8-6.

Example 8-6. Synchronizing a router's clock using NTP

```
!
ntp clock-period 17179676
ntp server 10.67.79.202
ntp server 192.168.6.65
!
```

You can configure several NTP servers using the *ntp server* command. The router will synchronize with the one it considers best. The *ntp clock-period* command will be generated by the router after running NTP for a while. It's used to adjust the clock speed to achieve higher clock accuracy when synchronization with the NTP servers is lost.

Scheduled Reloads

Always first save the router configuration to NVRAM before making "dangerous" changes. This way, when something goes wrong in a bad way, and you're unable to get the router functioning properly again, you can simply reboot it, and it will be back running under the original configuration in less than a minute. In the old days, it was necessary to powercycle the router if it became unreachable, but IOS can now do it automatically with a "scheduled reload." Simply type *reload in 10*, and the router schedules a reload for 10 minutes later. You can then make your configuration changes, and if everything goes well, you simply cancel the scheduled reload with *reload cancel*. If things go awry, you have to wait until the router reboots and then try again.

Don't forget the *reload cancel* command. Use an egg timer or an alarm clock if necessary.

CHAPTER 9

When Things Start to Go Down: Troubleshooting

Your network now has enough built-in redundancy to survive the most common causes of network outages: failing connections, failing hardware, and failing ISPs. It's rare for two routers, connections, or ISPs to fail at the same time (but don't think it never happens), so the most common source of problems in a multihomed network is the BGP configuration itself. This chapter tells you how to diagnose and correct BGP problems quickly. Read this chapter carefully, imagine the impact on your network of each of the problems mentioned, and take action to minimize the damage that would result. But first a few paragraphs about handling the stress of troubleshooting network problems when an outage occurs.

Keeping a Clear Head

Remember the time when you weren't multihomed? When the network went down, this created a fair amount of stress. In a multihomed situation, the network survives most of the problems that are fatal for a single-homed network, so outages are far less frequent. As a result, the amount of stress you experience when there is such an outage—and you know you're the one who has to fix the problem—reaches unprecedented heights. Clammy hands and a sinking feeling in your stomach may not make you feel better, but your body's stress response can actually be an advantage. It's also perfectly natural. Even experienced performers get stage fright, so don't worry about "staying cool." If you do a good job, nobody will complain. Your body is equipped to handle stressful situations regularly, as long as you allow it to fully restore in between.

The *fight or flight* response uses stress hormones to clear up fatigue and hunger, dull pain, and prime your brain for optimum performance for either battle or flight. You can use this state to your advantage by focusing on the job at hand, but be careful not to give in to any feelings of fear or anger that may present themselves. The stress hormones are just as happy to intensify anger- or fear-induced bouts of self-destructive behavior as to improve your concentration. It pays to muster up some self-control, because the negative feelings may appear quickly, but they disappear just as fast if you concentrate on something else.

Managing the Troubleshooting Process

To be able to troubleshoot effectively, you must do three things at once: apply deductive reason to analyze the problem in a structured way, apply creativity to arrive at a solution intuitively, and manage the troubleshooting process. If you had all the time in the world, you could choose to either completely analyze every aspect of the problem or wait until you have an epiphany. But you don't, so you'll have to put both brain hemispheres to work at the same time. This is done by eliminating possible sources of the problem one by one. Rather than starting at potential problem source number one and working your way up until you've eliminated them all, you allow your intuition and experience to select the most likely candidates. When the creative side of your brain draws a blank, you just continue down the systematic path until inspiration strikes again. Don't cut any corners by immediately jumping to something else as soon as you see your hunch was wrong or because you suddenly get a new hunch. If your hunch was "maybe it's the collisions on the Ethernet interface," you should take a few moments to look at the other interface statistics while they're on the screen, so you don't have to waste time later by coming back and checking something that was right under your nose.

Balancing rational and intuitive thinking is hard. Regularly take a step back to check whether you're getting anywhere with your current approach, and ask yourself if there is something else you could be doing with better results. A good example of this, from personal experience, is the time a border router kept rebooting for obscure reasons. There was obviously a problem with the software, but since this hadn't occurred before, there had to be something new that triggered the problem. I first upgraded to a newer version of the IOS software, and then downgraded to an older one, but this didn't help. I tried to figure out which configuration option triggered the problem, but I couldn't find it. Rather than continuing my fruitless efforts while customer traffic was being interrupted by regular reboots, I eventually convinced myself I wouldn't solve the problem in the next five minutes, so I moved the connection to one of our ISPs that terminated on the ill router to the other border router. Fortunately, the other router had a spare interface of the required type. Thus, both ISP connections were available and stable again. This sounds like a perfectly logical and easy-to-make decision, but at the time it seemed like admitting failure, so it was hard to do. The cause of the continuous reboots turned out to be a hardware problem, and the router had to be sent away for repair. During this time, the other border router handled both ISP connections, so there was no customer impact.

The most important thing to remember during troubleshooting (except everything there is to know about BGP, of course) is that it invariably takes either more or less time than expected for the problem to be corrected, so be prepared for both. A reasonable timeline to follow is:

When the problem presents itself

When you first start investigating the problem, note the time, then work on the problem for five minutes. If one or two people call, tell them you'll call them back unless they have important information about the problem at hand. If more people call, proceed to the five-minute point, because you're not going to solve the problem in a few minutes if you're on the phone the entire time.

After five minutes

If after five minutes you don't have specific enough information to assume the problem will be corrected in another few minutes, you should take a few moments to get some things organized before resuming your troubleshooting efforts. This is the moment you mobilize help. If you're working together with other network administrators, it's a good idea to tell them about the problem and ask them if they reconfigured the network earlier. If you're the only network administrator, it's even more important to get help at this point. It's likely that users of the network will start calling you soon, and you can't effectively troubleshoot while you're on the phone, so get someone to answer the phone who can tell people that you know about the problem and are working on it. Draft someone if you have to. Your helper should be in the same room if possible, so when something interesting comes up during a phone conversation, he can easily relay it to you. Get a notepad and a pen to write things down.

Depending on how critical the network is for the organization, you may also want to inform the most important representative of the user community at this time.

After 15 minutes

If the problem isn't (nearly) fixed after 15 minutes, you're past the point where you can fix the problem before most of the users notice something is wrong. So now is the time to inform everyone about what's going on and how long you expect it will take to fix the problem. This is also the time to switch to a more structured approach if you were just following hunches until now and to start writing things down in more detail. It's especially useful to keep track of the changes you make to router configurations, because it's likely you'll have to reverse them later.

After an hour

If you don't know what the problem is and how to fix it after an hour, you should seriously consider the possibility that you will not be able to fix it within a reasonable time frame. It's still entirely possible that you'll find the problem and fix it within the next five minutes, but after trying for an hour, it would be extremely optimistic to expect results soon. Now is the time to solicit assistance from an expert.

If you have backup or disaster recovery plans, you should start preparing to put them in action. For instance, if your backup plan includes taking an important server to a backup location, you should call ahead so the people there can prepare, and you should have someone prepare the server for transport without actually disconnecting it yet. This is also a good time to make a backup tape or copy important information to another system if this can be done in one or two hours, so that you have an up-to-date copy of the most important information, which can then be transported to another location if necessary.

Stand up from behind your computer for a minute or two, get a glass of water or a cup of coffee, and see how everybody is doing before continuing your search for a solution to the problem at hand.

After three hours

If a problem isn't fixed after three hours, this is usually because you are waiting for the telco, upstream ISP, or the power company to fix an outage. You should now be focusing on your backup plans unless you have specific information that the problem will be solved in less time than you need to execute the backup plan. On the other hand, realize that the problem can still be repaired at any moment, especially if it's a telco, ISP, or power outage. Make sure you are prepared if this happens. It isn't unheard of for power cables to be unplugged when the power comes back on, or for router interfaces to be in loopback mode when a circuit is restored, so there is an additional delay before everything is working again. Don't let this happen to you.

As the end of the working day approaches, some practical things need attention. Until what time will you and your staff stay? Is there a place you can take a nap if you stay all night? What about food and clean clothes?

Dealing with Service Providers

When you experience a telco or ISP outage, your mission, should you choose to accept it, is to call them and get them to fix the problem as soon as possible. This sounds simple enough, and often it is. However, there are many things that can go wrong: someone could lose their temper, and there is lots of room for miscommunication. It's also important to know what really happened and when, who was responsible, and how long it took to fix the problem, because these factors determine who gets to send the other a bill and for what amount. Dealing with people effectively over the phone is a complex skill, that takes a serious amount of psychological insight or years of experience to develop. But you can probably shave off a year or so by observing some guidelines:

- The key thing here is to control your temper and be polite. If you annoy the people you talk to on the phone (which is sometimes necessary), they'll try to find a reason to no longer have to deal with you, so they can hang up or put you on hold. Don't give them that reason: stay polite, but be as firm as necessary.

- Don't talk down. Always show respect for the person you're talking to, however simple you may think their job is. (Would you be able to stay polite talking to disgruntled customers on the phone all day?)

- When discussing something important (or, even better, always) write down the time, the name of the person you spoke with, and any promises made. This is especially important for the first call: make sure you have documentation that shows when you first reported the problem.

- Ask for a ticket number. Telcos and ISPs invariably use incident-tracking systems. If they have such a system but don't open a ticket, you can be pretty sure nothing is going to happen.

  Having a ticket number will also help tremendously if there's any disagreement over whether the service levels agreed upon in a Service Level Agreement (SLA) were met.

- Make sure you're understanding each other. Some people like to engage in all kinds of theoretical discussions about what they *could* do, without the implied promise they actually *will* perform any of the mentioned actions. Others don't like to admit they don't understand or can't do something. At the end of the conversation, it should be extremely clear what is going to happen, who is going to make it happen, when it will be done, and who gets a status update afterwards.

- Be reasonable. This isn't the time to act on past (or present) grievances: it's the result that counts. But don't feel obliged to accept the unacceptable. Some people are experts at making you feel like a fool when making perfectly reasonable requests. Just continue the conversation. The worst thing that can happen is that you waste a little more time. Often persistence is rewarded.

Quite often, the person answering your call doesn't really know much about the specific service you're using. For instance, a large ISP I worked for has a single customer support number for both dial-up users and leased-line customers. So a 155-Mbps customer gets to talk to customer support people who spend most of their time explaining Microsoft Outlook to 56K customers. This is frustrating for everyone involved. When this happens, it's best first to go after a ticket number and then see if you can be transferred to someone who knows more. The ticket number is important, because if you get put on hold for too long or if you are disconnected, you can cite the ticket number and immediately ask to be transferred to someone knowledgeable, rather than explain the problem again. If you know the right person or group that can help you, it's usually still best to go through the "proper channels" to get a ticket number and then get the right person on the phone. This way, you're not putting anyone in the position of having to work outside the official system.

If there isn't enough progress in solving the problem, you should escalate it higher up the organizational ladder. If your service provider has an escalation procedure, follow it closely, but don't be afraid to jump ahead if you feel the situation really warrants it (not just because you're impatient). Before escalating, you may want to contact an account manager or a sales person you've dealt with in the past. Often, they can bypass congested parts of the organization and get you in touch with the person that can actually do something for you.

Physical and Datalink Layer Problems

To be able to diagnose a problem, the first thing you should know is which people, systems, protocols, and destinations are affected by the problem. When a lot of people can't reach many destinations, this will obviously be a more serious problem then when only a few people can't reach a small number of destinations (unless these people or destinations are especially important for some reason). More importantly, this information will help you isolate the problem. Performance problems usually show in "heavy" protocols, such as FTP or multimedia applications. Internal problems tend to affect only a subset of the network; BGP problems affect all systems equally. When you know what *is* happening, you should ask yourself what *should* be happening. Sometimes a user complains about an apparent problem situation, but later it turns out this is just the way things normally are.

It's not always immediately apparent if a problem has something to do with BGP or if there is something wrong with a lower-layer protocol or even something physical, such as a wire or a piece of equipment. BGP makes use of the physical infrastructure and lower layer protocols, so these must function properly in order for BGP to do its job.

Broken Cable or Circuit

It's almost impossible to distinguish a cable break from equipment or power failure at the remote end. The thing to do is make contact with the router or switch at the other end to see whether it's still functioning. If you manage the system on the other end yourself, telnetting to it makes sense. If the system on the other end is a router that isn't under your management, it's easiest to do a traceroute. A router will respond to a traceroute (but not to a ping) to an address of an interface that is down: you'll see replies from a different address, but the fact that the traceroute stops shows you've reached the right router. If the traceroute starts showing lines with only three asterisks at some point, something must be broken (or filtered) at the router that is supposed to be next after the router that supplied the last good line, or somewhere between those routers. This is the time when you'll be glad you have documentation of how everything connects together.

Sometimes the ICMP and UDP packets used for *ping* and *traceroute* are filtered, so don't attach too much significance to not being able to ping a system, or not seeing a good last line in *traceroute*, unless you know this normally works. Running *traceroute* on a router may also fail because it uses an unfortunate source address, so run *traceroute* with options if necessary.

Link status and keepalives

The router will usually detect a broken circuit by one of two methods:

- Carrier or link status
- Keepalives

Most interface types have some kind of hardware support for telling the router whether the interface is up or down, but this usually means only that the device on the other end of the connection is alive. For instance, on serial connections, the DCD (carrier detect) line means only that the leased line is connected to the telco equipment at the central office. It doesn't mean there is any end-to-end connectivity. SONET is more advanced and may be able to tell you if it's a line or path (end-to-end) problem. For switched Ethernet, the link indication tells you the connection to the Ethernet switch is operational. Note that the Ethernet link indication tells you only that your router, switch, or hub can receive information from the device on the other end of the cable; it doesn't mean the connection is operational in both directions. Point-to-point links use keepalives to monitor end-to-end connectivity in addition to physical status indications. The router periodically sends keepalive packets to the other side, and as long as responses keep coming back, the line is considered "up."

Last input and loops

If you're not sure an interface is really functioning, you might want to look at the "last input" time in the *show interface ...* output. If no packets entered the interface for several minutes, it's likely there is something wrong with the connection. If the routers at both ends of a telco circuit both show outgoing data but no incoming data, this indicates a problem in the telco SONET network (even if your connection is non-SONET). You may want to put the interface at one end in loopback mode to make sure there isn't a local hardware or wiring problem:

```
!
interface Serial0
 loopback
!
```

If the interface is in loopback, the input and output time and packet counters should increase in tandem after executing the *clear counters interface ...* command. If the problem is really in the telco circuit, the looped side should see its own maintenance traffic (such as keepalives or PPP link negotiation) return over the looped interface, but there shouldn't be any change for the remote side. Don't forget to remove the loop:

```
!
interface Serial0
 no loopback
!
```

Line encoding and framing

Most interface types support only one way for packets to be put in a "frame" using additional control bits (framing) and one way the for the bits to be converted to electrical signals (line encoding). For instance, 10-Mbps Ethernet always uses Ethernet frames with Manchester encoding. Other interface types have been enhanced over the years, so several variations exist in parallel, and both sides of the connection must agree on what they will use. This is especially common for telco connections such as T1, E1, T3, E3, and SONET/SDH. Make sure you use the correct line encoding and framing type; otherwise, you'll see huge numbers of errors, and communication may be impossible. Note that some line encodings require a specific framing type. It's best to accept the telco defaults for line encoding and framing, unless there are important reasons why you need something else. By using less common settings, you run the risk that the settings for your connection will revert to the defaults when the telco performs maintenance.

Power and Equipment Failure

By looking at a box, it's hard to tell whether it has completely died or is just not getting any power. Neighboring systems can provide a good indication: one dead router is a dead router; five dead routers is probably a power problem. But even if it's a single box, it never hurts to switch the power cables around to make sure. Even when the lights are still on in the equipment room, your routers may not be receiving power: it's likely they are on a different fuse from the light fixtures, and there are also power distributors and probably uninterruptable power supplies and/or surge protectors between the utility power and the routers and switches, each of which can fail and leave your equipment powerless. You need to be on site to be able to really make sure whether it's an individual piece of equipment or the power that has failed. Obviously, more widespread power failures are much easier to detect, because they affect more than just your equipment.

Poor Network Performance

Sometimes interfaces are up but performing poorly. The usual reasons for this are either too much traffic (congestion) or too many errors, but don't discount the possibility you have broken hardware on your hands.

Too much traffic

When there is more traffic for an interface than the available bandwidth can accommodate, there will be delays and possibly packet loss. Congestion will normally show as bandwidth use close to the full line capacity. But even if the *show interface* command shows bits-per-second figures that aren't close to the available bandwidth, there will be intermittent delays due to the bursty nature of network traffic. You can see this happening for outgoing traffic when there are packets waiting in the output queue:

```
BR1#show interface ethernet 0
[...]
  Output queue 8/40, 351 drops; input queue 1/75, 0 drops
[...]
```

In this example, there is an output queue with room for 40 packets, and there are now 8 packets waiting to be transmitted. The congestion was even worse earlier, because 351 packets were dropped. This happens when a packet arrives, and the output queue is full. The input queue holds packets that must be process-switched, so high numbers there don't indicate lack of bandwidth, but rather that the CPU is busy and/or too many packets are process-switched. Possible solutions to bandwidth problems are:

- Upgrade the connection to a faster one.
- Balance traffic better over the available connections.
- Deploy a more sophisticated queuing strategy to allocate the available bandwidth more fairly, such as Weighted Fair Queuing or Random Early Detect.
- Manually allocate more bandwidth to important protocols with traffic shaping, priority queuing, or custom queuing.

High CPU load

On systems in which the CPU performs packet forwarding, sluggishness may also be the result of high CPU loads. You can check this with the *show processes cpu* command:

```
BR1#show processes cpu
CPU utilization for five seconds: 18%/16%; one minute: 10%; five minutes: 5%
```

The router relates the average CPU utilization for the last five-second (18%), one-minute (10%), and five-minute (5%) periods. The second number in the five-second output (16%) is the amount of time (as a percentage of all available CPU time) the CPU spends in interrupt mode, in which most packet forwarding takes place. The first number is the total CPU utilization; this is also what the one- and five-minute figures are. The CPU load figures are followed by a list of processes running on the router. Under normal circumstances, no process should be using more than a few percent of the CPU, but during BGP session establishment, the BGP process will take all available CPU time. This is normal, because the router tries to synchronize its

---

BGP table with that of the neighbor as fast as possible. If the CPU spends a lot of time in interrupt mode or in the IP Input process, you may be able to free it up to some degree by taking the following actions for all interfaces:

- Simplifying or removing input and output filters
- Removing complex queuing mechanisms and using FIFO instead

If the router doesn't have enough memory to store all the BGP routes, it may disable CEF in order to free up memory. When this happens, packet-forwarding performance suffers.

Ethernet collisions, broadcasts, and loops

On Ethernets, performance may be lower than expected because of collisions, broadcast storms, or loops in the topology. Collisions are *not* an error condition, but a normal part of half-duplex Ethernet operation. On large Ethernets with long wires, and when using small packets, collisions can eat up a significant percentage of the available bandwidth as traffic increases. For Ethernets with shorter cables and bigger packets, the performance penalty is largely inconsequential. But even if the number of collisions isn't high, sharing the Ethernet may slow everyone down, simply because there isn't enough bandwidth available. When this happens, you'll see a high "deferred" counter in the *show interface* output: the router wanted to send a packet, but the Ethernet was already occupied. It never hurts to upgrade to switched Ethernet, preferably full duplex, to avoid this problem. It can be beneficial to use one Ethernet interface exclusively for output and another only for input on a router that connects to a switch but doesn't support full-duplex operation. This gets rid of collisions and improves performance somewhat.

Switches are useful to get rid of collisions and improve bandwidth by forwarding packets only to where they are actually needed, but they still copy broadcast packets to all ports. So if a broadcast packet that makes the receiving system reply with another broadcast enters the network, the resulting *broadcast storm* will take out the entire Ethernet. You'll probably have to power-cycle most of the switches at the same time to get rid of the disruptive packets. Even if the number of broadcast packets doesn't reach storm levels, they still do harm because all systems connected to the network must process them. Thus, you may want to segment your Ethernet network using VLANs. Packets that need to go from one VLAN to another must pass a router. Routers forward only specific types of broadcasts, and only if configured to do so.

Ethernet loops are pretty spectacular to watch: the switches keep forwarding the same packets to each other, so the network soon becomes completely congested. When you remove the loop, the network returns to normal. You should enable the spanning tree protocol or keep tight control over the Ethernet topology so there are no loops.

Too many errors

When a signal travels down a cable, it gets weaker with distance. At the same time, the cable picks up noise. So if the cable is too long, runs along too many sources of noise, or is just not of the right quality, the receiver can't recognize the original bits in what is left of the signal. Then a bit that should have been 0 is received as a 1, or the other way around. Most datalink protocols will detect this by means of the CRC check and throw away the packet. When lost packets are the result of bad or too-long wires or too much noise, larger packets run a greater risk of having a flipped bit and being discarded as a result of a CRC error, because they have more bits in them. So if you're unable to check the error counters for an interface, for instance, because the problem occurs somewhere in the network of your ISP, it's a good idea to perform two pings: one with small packets and one with large packets. If the packet loss rates are much higher for the large packets, check the wiring. Example 9-1 shows how to do a ping with larger packet sizes on a Cisco router. You must be in privileged (enable) mode to perform a ping with options.

Example 9-1. ping with options

```
BR1#ping
Protocol [ip]:
Target IP address: 192.0.2.3
Repeat count [5]: 50
Datagram size [100]: 1000
Timeout in seconds [2]:
Extended commands [n]:
Sweep range of sizes [n]:
Type escape sequence to abort.
Sending 50, 1000-byte ICMP Echos to 192.0.2.3, timeout is 2 seconds:
!!!!!.!.!!!!!!!.!!!!!!!!.!!.!!!!!!!!..!!!!!!.!!!!!
Success rate is 84 percent (42/50), round-trip min/avg/max = 116/117/120 ms
```

The router will send a new packet as soon as the previous one has been received or timed out, unlike host-based pings, which send packets at regular intervals. A ! means the packet came back; a . means that it was lost. Also, when the router says it sends ICMP echo packets of a certain size, this is the actual size of the packet, including IP and ICMP headers. Host-based pings generally add 28 bytes to the requested packet size, so a *ping -s 100 <address>* will use 128-byte packets.

CRC errors on ATM

Apart from bit errors on the wire, there are two sources of CRC errors: cell loss on ATM connections or Ethernet duplex mismatches. Congestion in ATM has much worse effects than congestion in packet-oriented networks. When there is congestion in an ATM network, the ATM switches start to drop cells, because they don't have any mechanism to slow down incoming cells. If an Ethernet switch receives 10 packets when it can transmit only 9, it drops a single packet. With ATM it works slightly differently. If these packets are all 20 cells long in an ATM network (for a total of 200 cells for 10 packets), the ATM switch throws away 20 cells, but those can easily belong to 4 different packets. When one or more cells making up an IP packet have been lost, it's no longer possible to reconstruct the original IP packet successfully. The AAL5 tries anyway, with a CRC error because of the missing cells as a result. So the same amount of congestion leads to a much higher packet loss rate in an ATM network. There isn't much you can do about this, except to make sure there is no congestion in the ATM network. Many ATM router interfaces have hardware that can limit the number of cells entering the ATM network, and Cisco routers also support traffic shaping in software. Both can be used to keep the ATM network congestion-free.

Ethernet errors because of duplex or speed mismatch

Ethernet supports autonegotiation for several options, including speed and duplex. However, not all implementations support autonegotiation, and sometimes it fails. In this case, or when full and half duplex are configured manually on opposite ends, it's possible that one system thinks the connection is full duplex, and the other thinks it's half duplex. When this happens, the full-duplex side will see CRC errors whenever both sides start to send at the same time, because the half-duplex side will send an incomplete packet. The half-duplex side will send its packet again, but the full-duplex side won't, so that packet will be lost. The number of CRC errors and lost packets increases as the line gets busier and both sides start transmitting at the same time more often. To avoid this problem, try to avoid manually setting full or half duplex, and if you do, make sure it's done on both ends. The same goes for the Ethernet speed: if you connect a device configured for 100-Mbps Ethernet to a simple 10-Mbps hub, the entire hub stops functioning.

There are a few other error conditions that may lead to packet loss:

No buffer, so packets are ignored
Packets are coming in faster than the hardware or software can handle, so they are simply ignored.

Late collisions
A collision is detected after the minimum packet length was already transmitted. Collisions must be detected within the time it takes to transmit a minimum-length packet. When late collisions occur, small packets may be lost in undetected collisions. This happens when the wires get too long or there are too many repeaters (hubs) in an Ethernet.

Excessive collisions
This is when the same packet encountered collisions on each of 16 successive transmit attempts. The packet has been dropped. When this keeps happening, there is probably a wiring problem somewhere.

Routing and Reachability Problems

If you can't reach anything on the Internet at all, in most cases there is either a problem with all your BGP peers, or the announcements for your address blocks aren't making it to the rest of the world. But always remember to make sure you don't have some sort of local problem on your hands first!

BGP Session Is Down

BGP sessions with peers need to be up in order for BGP to send traffic over a connection. However, you may be using a default route, so there can still be outgoing traffic, and the peer may use an internal routing protocol to deliver incoming traffic when there is no BGP session. There may be other valid reasons why traffic is low; the amount of traffic isn't a good indication of whether a session is up. But lower than usual traffic is a solid indication that there is a problem, so it warrants further investigation. The number of routes received from a peer is a more reliable indication, but it's best to look at the actual session state using SNMP or the *show ip bgp summary* command. Usually, the summary command will list the state of the current session or the reason why there is no session, such as the maximum prefixes reached. If the state is "idle" (and stays that way for more than a few moments), this means the router has decided that there is no point in trying to set up a BGP session, so the first thing you should do is run *traceroute* to the peer address. If the address is unreachable, or if it needs more than a single hop when you didn't configure the peer for multihop operation, the router won't be able to set up a session. If the address is reachable, or if you can't tell because there is ICMP filtering in place, you can type *telnet <peer address> 179* on the router. The router will then try to initiate a Telnet connection to the BGP port of the remote router. The Telnet and BGP protocols won't interact in any meaningful way, of course, but this is a good way to see if everything works at the TCP level. If the session is established, the remote router is configured to speak BGP with your router. If the connection is refused, either there is already a BGP session or there is a filter that doesn't allow the BGP session. The third possibility, of course, is that the remote router isn't configured to talk BGP with yours. You can also issue the *show ip bgp neighbors <peer address>* command to learn why a session wasn't established. For instance:

```
BR1#show ip bgp neighbors  192.0.254.17
[...]
   External BGP neighbor not directly connected.
```

If the neighbor is, in fact, directly connected, the interface state may be "down."

BGP Session Is Unstable

Sometimes BGP sessions become unstable and keep going down and coming back up again. There are three ways this can happen:

- Inadequate memory in the router
- Recursive routing
- Denial-of-service attack

When the router runs out of memory during BGP processing, which can easily happen due to the large number of routes in the global routing table, it terminates the BGP session. This clears up a lot of memory, because all information received from the disconnected peer is removed. After a while, the session will be reestablished, but presumably, the situation has not changed, so the session will be terminated again as soon as the router runs out of memory once more. This can continue for a long time. Eventually the router's memory will be so fragmented that processes will start to fail, and the processes that fail may be completely unrelated to BGP. Running out of memory often happens when there is a sudden increase in the size of the global BGP table. This happens from time to time when a large network doesn't aggregate its routes for a while. If you implement prefix limits, you'll still experience problems, because the session will be terminated. But at least the router will remain stable because the session stays down until it's cleared manually and there is no memory fragmentation. You can determine the router's memory situation with the *show memory* command:

```
BR1#show memory
              Head     Total      Used      Free  Lowest  Largest
Processor [...] 23634752  21662692  1972060  1121452  919500
      I/O [...]  8388608   1185356  7203252  7202132 7202420
```

This router has two types of memory: processor and I/O. The processor memory is what usually runs out; this is where processes running on the router get their memory. The I/O memory is for packet data. The total of the two types of memory is less than the amount of memory the router has on board. The difference accounts for the IOS image that is copied to RAM during boot time. In this case, the free processor memory is less than 2 MB, which is cutting it close. There was even a time when the router had only 1095 KB free. However, the largest block is still nearly a megabyte, so fragmentation isn't too bad.

Recursion is another possible cause for BGP instability. When a peer announces a prefix that includes its own address (for instance, 192.0.2.67 announces 192.0.2.64/26), the peer is reachable over a route received from that peer, and a recursive route is born (unless there is a more specific route). The router regularly checks for recursive routes and removes them when found. Then the BGP session goes down, only to come back up again a little later. The route is then added to the routing table again, and the cycle restarts. Recursive routing can only happen for iBGP and eBGP with multihop, or when there are IP tunnels where the tunnel endpoint is routed through the tunnel.

During denial-of-service attacks, slower routers with relatively complex configurations can get so swamped with traffic that they don't have time to do anything other than process incoming packets. As a result, the remote router doesn't get an answer for its keepalive messages and tears down the BGP session after a while. There is then no longer any traffic, so the BGP process has the CPU all to itself, and the session is reestablished. The DoS traffic starts flowing again, and the cycle is complete. Countermeasures against DoS attacks are discussed in Chapter 7.

Address Blocks Aren't Announced

A quick and easy check to see if your address announcements make it to the rest of the world is trying two traceroutes: one with a source address that falls within your own address block and another with a source address from one of your ISPs. You can do this on a system that has both types of address, such as a border router, which usually has an ISP-assigned address on the interface that connects to this ISP. If you just type *traceroute* on a Cisco router in enable mode, the router asks you for several options, including the source address it should use. Alternatively, you can just type *traceroute <address>* on the border router, and it automatically uses the address of the output interface where the traceroute packets leave. If you repeat the same command on a system that has addresses only from your own range, you'll have two sets of *traceroute* output to compare. If there is a problem with your address announcements, running *traceroute* with your own source address will fail, but the one with the ISP-assigned source address should make it to the other end just fine. To make absolutely sure, you should check a looking glass to see if there is a route to your network in the routing tables of remote networks. If the route is visible as a valid route in the looking glass (not as a history or flap-dampened entry) several minutes after the problems started, there is a black hole somewhere. If the route isn't there, it's filtered somewhere along the way, or it isn't properly announced in the first place. Obviously, when you can't reach any remote destinations, you may have to dial in to be able to use the looking glass.

If it looks like there is a problem with your announcements, the first thing to check is whether your own routers have the route in their BGP tables. Example 9-2 shows a route that is both received from another local router over iBGP and sourced by the router itself.

Example 9-2. Locally sourced BGP announcement

```
BR1#show ip bgp 192.0.2.0/24
BGP routing table entry for 192.0.2.0/24, version 324
Paths: (2 available, best #2)
  Advertised to non peer-group peers:
    192.0.254.17 219.2.19.1
  Local
    192.0.2.66 from 192.0.2.66 (192.0.2.66)
      Origin IGP, metric 0, localpref 100, valid, internal, ref 2
  Local
    192.0.2.67 from 0.0.0.0 (192.0.2.67)
      Origin IGP, metric 0, localpref 100, weight 32768, valid, sourced, local, best, ref 2
```

In this example, the route is announced to both peers, so if there is a problem, it must be at the remote side. If there is a route in the BGP table, but it isn't advertised to the right peers, there is probably a problem with a filter or route map. If you are unable to pinpoint the problem because of complex filter setups, you'll have to debug the filters and route maps. But this should be a last resort, and make absolutely sure first to disable BGP sessions so there are no nonlocal routes in the BGP table, otherwise you could be creating a black hole. You can use the *show ip bgp* command to check whether you were successful in removing all routes except the ones you want to announce to your peer from the BGP table. When you're sure there is nothing you shouldn't be announcing in your BGP table, you can remove the filters one by one and reset the BGP session after removing each filter to see which one gets in the way of your announcement.

 If you depend on communities to trigger actions at upstream ISPs, verify that the route maps for setting these communities are working properly, and make sure *neighbor ... send-community* has been configured.

If the *show ip bgp <address range>* command comes up empty for your address blocks, you should check the routing table for a matching route. Remember, the router will generate an announcement only if the network is mentioned in the BGP configuration or distributed from another routing protocol, but in both cases, a matching route must be present in the routing table, where "matching" means the exact same prefix length. Example 9-3 shows a pull-up route for locally sourced BGP route in the routing table.

Example 9-3. Pull-up route for a locally sourced BGP announcement

```
gw#show ip route 192.0.2.0 255.255.255.0
Routing entry for 192.0.2.0/24
  Known via "static", distance 250, metric 0 (connected)
  Routing Descriptor Blocks:
  * directly connected, via Null0
      Route metric is 0, traffic share count is 1
```

If everything is the way it should be at your end, the problem must be at the remote side. Fortunately, it's rare for two ISPs both to have problems at the same time. It's also rare for an announcement suddenly to get lost without any prior event triggering this. A lost announcement is almost always associated with a BGP session reset (but this may be between two distant ASes) or with the route being withdrawn and then announced again. These are the times your routes are checked against filters in the ISP's network. When the filters are changed (which will happen if the ISP connects a new BGP customer), these changes will normally not be applied to existing sessions. Thus, if there is a mistake, and your routes or AS number aren't allowed through anymore, you won't know this until your BGP session is reset or until you first revoke and then reannounce your routes. Resetting BGP sessions always carries some risk with it. Doing it several times will also trigger route flap-dampening further upstream. All flap-dampening information is removed from memory when the BGP session the information pertains to is reset. This makes it impossible to be flap-dampened by a network you directly connect to. However, resetting BGP sessions triggers flap dampening in the next network if it's enabled there. Unfortunately, there's no good way to detect whether you are flap-dampened or your route isn't allowed at all. You can wait 20 minutes to an hour to see if the situation clears up or contact the network where your traceroutes start hitting the wall and ask them what's going on.

If you're doing path prepending, you may want to turn it off when your routes seem to disappear. Many ISPs allow only routes from their customers with the customer's AS and nothing else as the AS path to avoid black holes. Even if they allowed prepending before, it's possible they made their filters more restrictive without fully realizing the consequences.

Make sure the information for your address blocks and AS in the Routing Registry is always current; some networks use it to generate filters automatically.

Filters Further Upstream

If you pay someone for transit, it's reasonable to expect him to accept your routes. But most networks connected to the Internet don't receive any payment from you or your transit ISPs, and some of them may choose not to accept your routes from their peering partners, making it impossible for you to communicate with anyone connected to their network. Unfortunately, there isn't much you can do about this except making sure your address blocks aren't likely to be filtered.

A special case is when you're shooting a hole in someone else's address block. This happened to me when I had a customer with a Class B net out of a large block of Class B's announced by a large ISP. The customer needed only a fairly small address range, but they insisted on using the Class B net for this, which they hadn't really used until now. It took a bit of time to get the cooperation of the ISP from which the addresses came (and our upstream ISPs), but since the customer had a lot of clout and the assignment was done in pre-CIDR times, everyone involved eventually agreed. The addresses were deployed just fine, but every six months or so we would get a complaint from the customer that they were unable to reach any customers of the ISP the addresses came from. Every one of those times, the large ISP had just performed maintenance and no longer allowed incoming routes for addresses that fell within their larger aggregate. The moral of this story: don't shoot holes in an address block of an ISP you're not connected to. This will cost you and them a lot of time. The second moral: when you configure your network to cope with some specific situation, and the existence of this situation isn't immediately obvious, document the situation well so that the reasons for it don't get lost over time.

Outgoing Traffic Not Going Out

A router needs a route to be able to send outgoing traffic in the right direction. If you have a default route, this won't be a problem unless the interface the default points to is down. If you run defaultless, you'll receive host-unreachable messages from your border router if you try to communicate with a network that isn't in your routing table. You can check whether this is the case with *show ip bgp <address>*.* This shows the most specific route available for this address in the BGP table. If the network isn't in the BGP table, this is usually because of a problem close to the source, such as a circuit being down. Even large, well-known sites experience problems from time to time. On the other hand, this may be the symptom of a more widespread problem, so you should check your BGP sessions to be sure they are up and that you are receiving the regular number of routes. This is why it's a good idea to make MRTG stats of the number of routes received from each peer, as discussed in Chapter 8.

If you aren't receiving any routes at all, but the session is up, there must be a problem with a filter somewhere: you should always see at least the routes sourced by your peer. (The exception to this would be when your ISP's router or PoP has been isolated from the rest of their network.) If you're receiving fewer routes than usual, your ISP may be experiencing an outage. Another possibility is that they are purposely limiting the number of routes they're sending to you, either because they think you can't handle a full table or because the router you connect to at their end can't.

If the route is present but marked as "suppressed due to dampening," local flap dampening has suppressed the route, as shown in Example 9-4.

Example 9-4. A route suppressed due to flap dampening

```
BR1#show ip bgp 192.5.5.241
BGP routing table entry for 192.5.4.0/23, version 416923
Paths: (1 available, no best path)
  Not advertised to any peer
  40077 30099 3557, (suppressed due to dampening)
    192.0.2.50 from 192.0.2.50 (192.0.2.50)
      Origin IGP, localpref 100, valid, external
      Dampinfo: penalty 2929, flapped 3 times in 00:01:14, reuse in 00:29:30
```

---

* You may need to supply a network mask in prefix or subnet format if the router tells you your command is "ambiguous."

You can wait for the route to be used again when the reuse time arrives, or you can clear all flap dampening with the *clear ip bgp dampening* command. If the route shows up as "history entry," as in Example 9-5, the peer isn't currently announcing the route, so it can't be used. It's kept in memory so the flap-dampening statistics associated with it aren't lost.

Example 9-5. A history entry for a route experiencing flapping

```
BR1#show ip bgp 192.5.5.241
BGP routing table entry for 192.5.4.0/23, version 416923
Paths: (1 available, no best path)
  Not advertised to any peer
  40077 30099 3557 (history entry)
    192.0.2.50 from 192.0.2.50 (192.0.2.50)
      Origin IGP, localpref 100, valid, external
      Dampinfo: penalty 3295, flapped 4 times in 00:06:30
```

If a route shows up in the BGP table, this doesn't mean it's also present in the routing table. If you have synchronization enabled, BGP routes will fail to show up in the routing table until they are also present in an interior routing protocol, regardless of whether redistribution of BGP routes is enabled or if you even run an IGP. Since synchronization is the default, you should check whether your BGP configuration contains the *no synchronization* command. If it doesn't, synchronization is enabled. Another reason why a BGP-learned route may fail to show up in the routing table is because the next hop address is unreachable. This is usually the result of temporary problems in the internal routing protocol (when there are outages). It's also possible that the next hop address just isn't included in IGP routing. In that case, you need to modify your IGP (for instance, redistribute connected routes), use a static route towards the next hop address, or change the next hop address. For iBGP, this is simple: just configure *neighbor ... next-hop-self* on the router where the route enters the network. For eBGP, you need a route map to do this.

When routes are, in fact, present in the routing table, they may still not be used because another route takes precedence, either because it's more specific or because it has a lower distance. Remember that BGP has two default administrative distance values on a Cisco router: the value for eBGP (20) is lower (more preferred) than that for internal routing protocols, but the value for iBGP-learned routes (200) is higher than that for routes learned from internal protocols. If you suspect the routing table doesn't adequately represent the information present in BGP or other routing protocols, you can rebuild the routing table using the *clear ip route <address>* command, or even *clear ip route ** to clear all routes.

Black Holes

The situation in which you are receiving routes but are unable to use them to send traffic—a black hole—is pretty much the worst thing that can happen to a multihomed network. All other permutations of receiving routes and being able to send packets and receive return packets are better:

Receiving routes, able to send traffic
This is when everything works, so obviously it's the preferred situation.

Not receiving routes, able to send traffic
If for some reason the routes don't make it (for instance, because the BGP session is down), but you can still send traffic, a default route would still work. Even though the problem is reason for concern, the impact is limited.

Not receiving routes, not able to send traffic
A downed line or ISP failure are serious problems, but the impact should still be limited for a multihomed network: all traffic is rerouted over another connection, so everything still works, but the available bandwidth is lower than usual.

Receiving routes, not able to send traffic
In this situation, your router happily continues to send packets on their way towards nothingness, even if other routes that actually do work are available.

The really bad part is that multihoming doesn't protect you from black holes: you have to intervene manually or wait until the problem clears up. The first thing you should do is perform some traceroutes using your own addresses. If you do this on a border router, specify one of the addresses the router has from your own blocks. Save this information for later reference, along with what the associated route looks like in the BGP table. You should choose three or so networks you are familiar with as your traceroute destinations, so you can easily tell if the routes are different than usual. Then you have to decide whether the problem is bad enough to warrant shutting down the BGP session. Doing this may clear up the effects of the black hole, but it will slow down your troubleshooting efforts. If you are experiencing problems with only a few remote networks, you may want to leave the session up, but if many networks or even an entire ISP are effected, you'll probably want to shut down the BGP session:

```
!
router bgp 60055
 neighbor 192.0.254.17 shutdown
!
```

Depending on the speed of the router and the number of routes received from the peer, it will take a few moments to remove all these routes from memory. As the routes are removed, iBGP peers start sending replacement routes. Use the *show processes cpu* and *show ip bgp summary* commands to determine when the router is finished with this; the CPU load from noninterrupt tasks should be back to a few percent, and there shouldn't be any BGP messages waiting in queues. Now repeat the traceroutes.

If you are lucky, the second set of traceroutes will be successful. If this is the case, you should contact the ISP you've just shut down to ask what's going on. If you can't get through, it's because their single-homed customers are still unreachable, so their help desk and NOC will probably have their hands full. This would be the time you drink a cup of coffee and congratulate yourself on being multihomed. After a while, you should be able to ask them about the problem, and they should come up with one of two possible answers:

- We had a problem, but now it's solved.
- We have no idea what you're talking about; everything is fine here.

If they say something different, you haven't bugged them enough. When they finally decide on one of these answers, that's your cue to reenable the BGP session:

```
!
router bgp 60055
no neighbor 192.0.254.17 shutdown
!
```

You may want to do this during the part of the day when the network is least used, because if the problem wasn't resolved, your black hole will be back again.

If the black hole persists for five or ten minutes after shutting down the BGP session to one peer, either the problem is with the other ISP or with both. You may want to enable the shutdown peer again and shut down the other to see if this clears up the problem. On the other hand, this may break your remaining connectivity. You can also just go ahead with determining the traffic direction affected by the black hole— incoming, outgoing, or both.

Is the Black Hole Incoming or Outgoing?

If the black hole comes right back after reenabling the BGP session, you need to find out whether the problem is with incoming outgoing traffic. You can check this by logging on to two systems with a good *netstat* command and at least one TCP service open to the rest of the world. A good choice would be Unix or Linux boxes, but Windows will do, too, as long as you run a TCP service. This could be port 139, which is used for Windows file and printer sharing, if enabled.* One of the boxes should be inside your network, the other in a place that is unreachable because of the black hole. You'll probably have to dial in using a modem to have this second test machine. When both systems are in place, try to access the TCP service on one from the other. Suppose your internal test machine is a mail server at 192.0.2.103, and the external test machine is a Windows box running file sharing at 176.77.78.79. On the mail server, you would then type:

```
# telnet 176.77.78.79 139
```

---

* First perform a *telnet <address> <port>* command to make sure the service is running: there shouldn't be any "couldn't connect" or "connection refused" messages. Use the external address rather than the loopback address.

This creates a TCP session to the Windows box. If transmission of outgoing packets is successful, the Windows box will see a TCP session creation attempt, but it will be unable to complete the session because the return packet sent by the Windows machine doesn't make it back. You can see if this is the case with the *netstat* command in an MS-DOS window:

```
C:\WINDOWS>netstat -n
  Proto  Local address     External address  Status
  TCP    176.77.78.79:139  192.0.2.103:4810  SYN_RECEIVED
```

On the other hand, if outgoing packets don't make it, *netstat* won't show anything. If this happens, try the same procedure the other way around, by *telnet*'ing to the SMTP port on the mail server from the Windows box and checking for a TCP session from the Windows machine's IP address in SYN_RECEIVED state on the mail server. This will tell you whether incoming packets are allowed. Don't forget to run *traceroute* from the external system (using the *tracert* command on a Windows machine) to get an idea of where the problem area is. You should now have enough information to determine what type of black hole you're experiencing: transit from a nontransit AS, filtered traffic, or a broken upstream AS.

Transit from Nontransit AS

The classic way for black holes to be created is when two ASes set up a new BGP session, but neither correctly filters the routes exchanged over this session. The ISP then starts to use the customer for transit traffic, but because the customer usually doesn't have enough bandwidth to handle all this traffic, or there are antispoofing filters, the traffic will be lost. For reasons I have yet to fathom, it often takes many hours for this situation to be corrected.

In Figure 9-1, the routing information from AS Y is relayed to AS X, and AS X prefers to send the traffic for these destinations to the black hole AS rather than directly to AS Y. This happens if the black hole AS is a customer, because as a rule, customer routes are preferred over transit or peering routes.

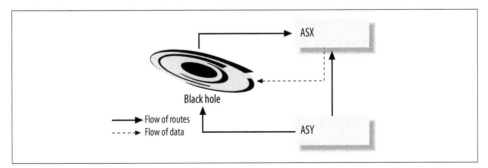

Figure 9-1. Black hole because of transit from nontransit AS

This type of black hole can work in just one direction or in both directions. If the problem affects outgoing traffic, you can diagnose this easily because there will be an unexpected AS number in the AS path for unreachable destinations. If the problem is with incoming traffic, you may see traffic disappear into a nontransit AS if you run *traceroute* from a network you can no longer reach back to your own network. On the other hand, the traceroute may provide inconclusive results, because it stops somewhere in the network of a valid transit AS without showing exactly what is going wrong. If the unreachable network has a looking glass, you can look up your own routes to see if the paths contain unexpected ASes.

It's possible that the problem affects only one of your ISPs. In that case, just shut down the BGP session with that ISP. However, if the problem is with incoming traffic, there is no way to be sure which ISP is the one with the problem. It's a bit more likely that it's the ISP you also use for outgoing traffic to the unreachable networks, but you can't be sure routing isn't asymmetric. However, if incoming traffic from one ISP is much lower than normal, this is probably the affected one.

An even nastier variation on this problem is when the badly configured network starts to announce the whole global routing table with its own AS as the source AS. This will happen if they redistribute BGP into an internal routing protocol and the IGP back into BGP. This is a lot worse than a simple missing BGP filter, because with the short path, these routes will attract all traffic from neighboring ASes. Also, filters on AS path aren't enough to protect you against a neighboring network that is experiencing this problem. But *maximum-prefix* will do the trick if it's a peer and not a transit AS (which are expected always to send you all routes).

Traffic Is Filtered

When the black hole persists over time, disappears when the BGP session is shut down, and reappears when the BGP session comes back up again, and it affects outgoing traffic while incoming traffic still works, it's likely that outgoing traffic is filtered. You may even be filtering yourself. The first thing you should do is remove all outgoing packet filters (not BGP filters). These are the *ip access-group ... out* lines in the interface part of the router configuration. Another thing to look for is the unicast RPF check. (Unicast RPF is explained in Chapters 11 and 12.) Remember, the RPF check fails if there is asymmetric routing, which happens all the time with multihoming, so remove all instances of *ip verify unicast reverse-path* from your router configurations. If you've done this, and you see the "packets output" counter steadily increasing, but the problem persists, either the black hole is of another type or the anti-spoofing filters are broken on the ISP's router at other end of the connection. Anyone with access to the router should be able to check this easily either by looking at the configuration or by using the *show ip interface ...* and *show access-list ...* commands, so don't let the fact that you're running BGP confuse them.

Filtering on TCP or UDP port numbers doesn't always work completely as expected. When a packet is fragmented, only the first fragment contains the TCP or UDP port number. So if the filter explicitly allows packets based on port number, only the first fragment will get through. If the filter explicitly denies packets based on port number, all fragments except the first will get through.

Broken Upstream AS

Temporary black holes when outages occur are unavoidable in BGP. When a link or a router goes down, it takes some time for BGP to notice this and tear down the session. In the meantime, traffic will be sent over a dead link. Such a temporary black hole shouldn't last for more than three minutes, Cisco's default BGP hold time. If you shut down the BGP session with the broken AS, outgoing traffic should start to flow again pretty much immediately. But because the router you're connected to is unable to inform the rest of the world that you're no longer reachable over it, you'll have to wait for the hold times in upstream routers to expire before you'll see incoming traffic return to normal.

Announcing Your Routes—With a Vengeance

If your incoming traffic keeps being black-holed over one ISP, you can try announcing your routes with more conviction than usual over the healthy ISP. If you have any path prepending in place, this is the time to turn it off and announce your routes with the shortest possible AS path. If both your ISPs share a transit ISP, and this transit ISP allows communities to set their Local Preference, set the right community so the Local Preference is as high as possible.

As a last resort, you can try to deaggregate. If you usually announce a /20, you may want to announce the two /21s that make up this /20 to your healthy ISP. This must be in addition to the regular /20 announcement: upstream networks may not accept the /21s, so if you don't announce the /20 as well, they'll have no choice other than to send all traffic to you over the broken ISP. This strategy will work only if your ISP accepts the longer prefixes. See Chapter 6 for more information on how to announce more specific routes.

DNS Problems

Because the Domain Name System is such a crucial part of the infrastructure of the Net, you will quickly notice when there are any problems with it. A name server is a pretty complex piece of software,* so there are many ways for it to fail. However,

---

* *DNS and BIND*, by Paul Albitz and Cricket Liu (O'Reilly) tells you everything you always wanted to know but were afraid to ask about the Domain Name System and the Berkeley Internet Name Domain software.

most problems boil down to someone not receiving an answer from the name server after sending it a query. Whether the BIND software is configured not to talk to you, the server is down, or the network is down, the results is pretty much the same. When the main local name server doesn't answer to queries, this creates a huge slow-down in all new sessions: the query to the first name server times out, and the host tries the second name server, if one is configured. This happens for all queries. Some protocols or applications, such as Telnet, FTP, and *ping*, do only a single DNS query when they start or connect, so there will be only a slight delay at the start of the session if the first DNS server is down. Others, like WWW clients, mail servers, and *traceroute*, go back to the name server all the time, so the delays accumulate. Things get really annoying when several name servers are configured, but none of them are reachable. Then the client has to wait for several time-outs for every query, only to fail after that.

A domain name should be served by at least two name servers. Many people still don't grasp the concept of redundant name servers and have both name servers share crucial infrastructure, such as location, power, IP address block, or network infrastructure. When none of the name servers for a domain responds to a query, the client assumes the requested record doesn't exist. For some applications, this doesn't matter much: whether the web browser says "host not found" or "host unreachable" when you're trying to access a web page on a server on an unreachable network doesn't make much of a difference. If you're doing a traceroute, on the other hand, it's nice if you can still find the IP address associated with a host, so you can see how far the trace gets. But for email, the difference is absolutely essential. When a name server returns an address that is unreachable, the sending server simply keeps the email and periodically tries to deliver it. But when no name server responds for the domain, the mail server thinks the domain doesn't exist, and the mail is returned with an error message.

It gets really bad when all the root name servers or all the servers for an important *top-level domain* (TLD, such as *.net*, *.com*, *.uk*, or *.fr*) fail. It's pretty much impossible for 13 root servers on 3 continents to fail at the same time, so the only way you're going to experience this effect is when your connection to all of them fails. To be connected to a reasonable subset of the Internet but at the same time unable to reach any of the root name servers is also pretty hard to do, but it can happen during widespread outages, especially if you're outside the United States. This is also what happens when you lose transit but still have some working peering connections. When your name server loses contact with all root servers, you will no longer be able to resolve any names, even if the name server containing the information you're looking for is still reachable. Because of all the caching that name servers do, you won't immediately notice this. Requests for information that is already in the cache will still be answered. Only when you request information that hasn't been requested recently will you notice the problem. Then the cached information starts to expire, and more and more domains become unavailable.

You may want to shut down the mail servers to keep mail from being returned because the domain supposedly doesn't exist. On the other hand, you may be receiving mail from networks that are still reachable. Another option is to forward DNS queries to another network that can still reach the root servers. If the name server on the other network is willing to perform recursive queries for you, you can simply list its address as a forwarder in the configuration for the BIND software.

CHAPTER 10
BGP in Larger Networks

This chapter deals with issues that are relevant for large networks. In larger networks, memory and especially CPU constraints become more important, because the difference in CPU speed between different routers in the network typically grows larger. In larger networks, internal BGP scalability quickly becomes an issue, and the interaction between interior routing protocols and BGP gets more complex.

Peer Groups

Some routers have a long list of BGP neighbors. It's then common to have several settings that are the same for each neighbor. In these cases, it's more efficient to create a peer group, assign the settings to the group, and have the neighbors share settings by making them members of the group. Example 10-1 shows two peer groups and several members.

Example 10-1. BGP peer groups

```
!
router bgp 60055
 network 192.0.2.0
 timers bgp 5 15
 neighbor ebgp peer-group
 neighbor ebgp prefix-list infilter in
 neighbor ebgp prefix-list outfilter out
 neighbor ebgp maximum-prefix 100
 neighbor ebgp filter-list 2 out
 neighbor ibgp peer-group
 neighbor ibgp remote-as 60055
 neighbor 192.0.2.68 peer-group ibgp
 neighbor 192.0.2.69 peer-group ibgp
 neighbor 192.0.2.254 peer-group ibgp
 neighbor 220.14.15.6 remote-as 1000
 neighbor 220.14.15.6 peer-group ebgp
 neighbor 220.14.15.6 description Net1000 noc@net1000.net
 neighbor 220.14.15.6 password abc def ghi
```

Example 10-1. BGP peer groups (continued)

```
neighbor 220.14.15.13 remote-as 2000
neighbor 220.14.15.13 peer-group ebgp
neighbor 220.14.15.13 description 2000net netmaster@2k.net
neighbor 220.14.15.13 maximum-prefix 1800 99
neighbor 220.14.15.160 remote-as 3000
neighbor 220.14.15.160 description Net3000 noc@net3000.com
neighbor 220.14.15.160 timers 10 30
neighbor 220.14.15.160 prefix-list infilter in
neighbor 220.14.15.160 prefix-list outfilter out
neighbor 220.14.15.160 maximum-prefix 100
neighbor 220.14.15.160 filter-list 2 out
!
ip as-path access-list 2 permit ^$
ip as-path access-list 2 permit ^60055$
ip as-path access-list 2 permit ^60055 60055$
!
ip prefix-list infilter description inbound filter
ip prefix-list infilter seq 5 deny 192.0.2.0/24 le 32
ip prefix-list infilter seq 10 permit 0.0.0.0/0 le 32
!
ip prefix-list outfilter description outbound filter
ip prefix-list outfilter seq 5 permit 192.0.2.0/24
!
```

In this example, all external peers are configured with three filters:

AS path access list 2
> To allow only outgoing announcements with just the local AS (possibly prepended once or twice) as the AS path

prefix list infilter
> To reject all incoming route announcements for the local address range or any subset

prefix list outfilter
> To reject all outgoing route announcements that aren't the local address range

In addition to the filters, the peer group ebgp also sets *maximum-prefix* to 100. Neighbors 220.14.15.6 and 220.14.15.13 belong to the group. They inherit the filters and *maximum-prefix* setting from the group, but they have the remote AS number and a description configured individually. Neighbor 220.14.15.6 has a password in addition to the settings inherited from the peer group, and 220.14.15.13 has a higher *maximum-prefix* setting.

Neighbor 220.14.15.160 doesn't belong to the peer group: it's a slow router, so the low BGP keepalive and hold times configured for the group are problematic. It isn't possible to configure an individual keepalive time for a peer group member, so this neighbor is kept outside the group, and the settings are all configured directly using *neighbor ...* statements.

The internal peers are part of the ibgp peer group, but they don't have any settings (such as filters) other than the remote AS number.

> Configuring a peer group when several neighbors share settings not only helps to keep your configuration tidy, but it also speeds up BGP processing. The router can send copies of a single update to all up-to-date members of the peer group rather than generate updates from scratch for each neighbor individually.

Using Loopback Addresses for iBGP

Since eBGP sessions are tied to a specific interface, it's actually a good thing that the BGP session goes down when the interface does: if the BGP session remained active, the information in BGP wouldn't reflect the current topology of the network, and there would be the potential for routing loops.

But in iBGP this is different: iBGP concerns itself just with where the traffic should leave the network. The decisions necessary to get the packets to the right border router over the internal network are left up to the interior gateway protocols. If a link goes down, the IGP will route around the failure, and the iBGP session should stay up. (When all links connecting a router to the rest of the network go down, the iBGP sessions with other routers will time out, of course.) However, when an interface goes down, its IP address is no longer reachable. So if this IP address is used in iBGP processing, the iBGP session goes down, even though the router itself is still perfectly reachable over other interfaces. This makes it necessary to configure iBGP sessions with addresses from interfaces that never go down. That's exactly the function of the loopback interface: to provide an interface that's always up. Example 10-2 configures the loopback interface for iBGP processing.

Example 10-2. iBGP using the loopback interface

```
!
interface Ethernet0
 ip address 192.0.2.67 255.255.255.192
 no ip directed-broadcast
!
interface Loopback0
 ip address 192.0.2.144 255.255.255.255
 no ip directed-broadcast
!
router bgp 60055
 no synchronization
 neighbor 192.0.2.145 remote-as 60055
 neighbor 192.0.2.145 update-source Loopback0
 neighbor 192.0.2.145 send-community
!
```

When configuring iBGP, don't forget the *no synchronization* command!

By giving the Loopback0 interface an IP address, it's automatically enabled. Because there are no other routers connected to the loopback "subnet," it's possible to use a single IP address (mask 255.255.255.255). The *neighbor 192.0.2.145 ...* statements in the BGP part of the configuration create an iBGP session to another router's loopback address, but the fact that this address belongs to a loopback interface on the remote router isn't visible here.

There is a last caveat: the router is obviously going to use an interface other than the loopback interface to send packets to its iBGP neighbor. Since, by default, the source address for outgoing packets is set to that of the interface the packet is transmitted over, the neighbor will see a BGP session coming in from an unexpected address. In this example, the router might set up a TCP session to its neighbor 192.0.2.145 using the source address 192.0.2.67 from the Ethernet0 interface. However, 192.0.2.145 doesn't have a BGP session configured with 192.0.2.67 but with 192.0.2.144, so it will refuse the connection. This is where the *neighbor ... update-source Loopback0* command comes in. When an *update-source* is configured, the router explicitly sets the source address for the BGP session to the address of the interface so the session can be initialized properly regardless of the particular interface used to reach the neighbor.

iBGP Scaling

BGP is an efficient, extensible, and scalable protocol. BGP-4 has served the Internet community well since 1994, and it will likely continue to do so for at least several more years. There is just one important limitation to the protocol: every BGP router within an AS must have an iBGP session with every other BGP router in the AS. In other words, BGP routers must learn all iBGP routes directly from the iBGP router where the information enters the AS. This is necessary: iBGP-learned routes are never propagated any further over iBGP, because iBGP can't use the AS path to avoid loops, as is done in eBGP. This limitation is already inconvenient in smaller networks, because whenever a new BGP router is attached, all other routers must be reconfigured. In larger networks, the huge number of iBGP sessions itself becomes a problem. This is illustrated in Figure 10-1: each of the eight routers has seven iBGP neighbors, making for a total of 28 iBGP sessions in the entire network.

There are two ways you can solve the iBGP scaling problem—route reflectors and confederations.

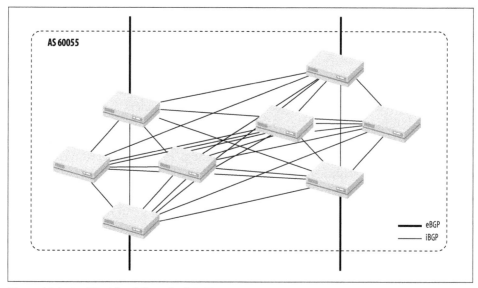

Figure 10-1. An AS with a full mesh of iBGP sessions

 Both confederations and route reflectors have serious drawbacks, such as complexity and less optimal routing. You should implement these methods only when your network is large enough to warrant it. Carefully read the release notes for your router's software and any vendor design recommendations to acquaint yourself with implementation-specific pitfalls.

Route Reflectors

The route reflection mechanism relaxes the rule that iBGP updates may not be sent to other iBGP speakers. Route reflectors send (reflect) all routes learned over iBGP to their clients. Thus, a route reflector client needs to have an iBGP connection only to a single route reflector, but it still receives the best route (as determined by the reflector) for each destination. A cluster of route reflector clients may be served by more than one route reflector, to avoid having a single point of failure. Route reflection has a big advantage over confederations: only the reflectors have to be aware of it. Clients and nonclient (regular) iBGP neighbors don't have to be configured in a special way or do anything other than regular BGP processing. Route reflectors are often used on a per–PoP basis, to hide the additional BGP routers in the PoP from the rest of the network. There must still be a full iBGP mesh between all route reflectors and nonclient peers. Also, route reflector clients must know all possible next hop addresses, so they have to participate fully in the IGP. Figure 10-2 shows the network from Figure 10-1 with route reflection.

Two routers are configured as route reflectors, with two clients each. The route reflectors and the two nonclient peers must still be fully meshed. The route reflector

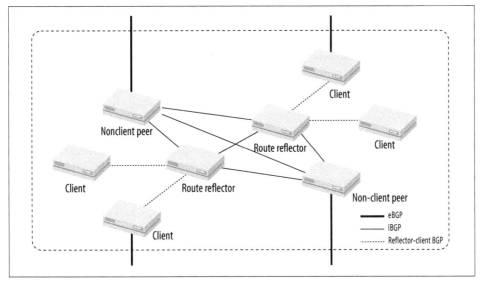

Figure 10-2. An AS with route reflectors

clients have only a single iBGP session (in the real world they would have at least two, for redundancy), the route reflectors have five sessions, and the nonclient peers have three. The total for the entire network is ten iBGP sessions: six regular iBGP sessions and four reflector-to-client sessions.

Because route reflectors perform the route selection algorithm on behalf of their clients, all route reflector clients share the reflector's view of which routes are best. This is usually not desirable in a large network: when such a network peers with another large network and receives copies of a route at opposite ends of the continent, the IGP metric makes fully meshed iBGP routers on the West Coast prefer the West Coast interconnect, while routers on the East Coast prefer the route learned there. If the entire network were to use a single route reflector, all routers throughout the network would use the route over the interconnect location closest to the route reflector. This problem can be mitigated by having several route reflectors in different parts of the network, but it's undesirable to have route reflector clients connect to large numbers of route reflectors; that defeats the purpose of the exercise.

Example 10-3 shows how a route reflector is configured to communicate with two clients. Note that the clients themselves don't need any configuration changes, other than removing iBGP sessions to all iBGP peers except the route reflector or route reflectors. And even that isn't really necessary.

Example 10-3. Route reflector configuration

```
!
router bgp 60055
 bgp cluster-id 257
```

Example 10-3. Route reflector configuration (continued)

```
neighbor rrclients peer-group
neighbor rrclients remote-as 60055
neighbor rrclients route-reflector-client
neighbor 192.0.2.66 peer-group rrclients
neighbor 192.0.2.66 description BR2
neighbor 192.0.2.67 peer-group rrclients
neighbor 192.0.2.67 description BR1
!
```

The *bgp cluster-id* command sets the Cluster ID for all the route reflectors sharing the same cluster of clients. This command takes a numerical value or an IP address-like value as its argument. By default, the Cluster ID is set to the BGP Router ID, which is usually the router's highest IP address. The purpose of the Cluster ID is to detect loops in the case of configuration errors, such as when two reflectors are configured to treat each other as clients. The *neighbor ... route-reflector-client* enables reflection towards an iBGP neighbor.

BR1 (192.0.2.67) has an eBGP session with AS 40077 and learns a route to 217.30. 16.0/20 over that session:

```
BR1#show ip bgp 217.30.16.0/20
BGP routing table entry for 217.30.16.0/20, version 28
Paths: (1 available, best #1, advertised over iBGP)
  40077
    192.0.254.17 from 192.0.254.17 (192.0.251.83)
      Origin IGP, localpref 100, valid, external, best
```

The fact that this router is now a route reflector client has absolutely no impact on eBGP processing. The route is propagated to the route reflector over iBGP, and there it looks a bit different:

```
RR#show ip bgp 217.30.16.0/20
BGP routing table entry for 217.30.16.0/20, version 4
Paths: (1 available, best #1)
  Advertised to peer-groups:
    rrclients
  40077, (Received from a RR-client)
    192.0.254.17 from 192.0.254.17 (192.0.2.67)
      Origin IGP, localpref 100, valid, internal, best
```

The route reflector distributes the route further to the other route reflector client:

```
BR2#show ip bgp 217.30.16.0/20
BGP routing table entry for 217.30.16.0/20, version 39
Paths: (1 available, best #1)
  40077
    192.0.254.17 from 192.0.254.17 (192.0.2.67)
      Origin IGP, localpref 100, valid, internal, best
      Originator : 192.0.2.67, Cluster list: 0.0.1.1
```

Now the route looks normal again, except for the last line: here the router shows that it knows it's dealing with a reflected route. The Cluster ID 0.0.1.1 is the same as the one configured on the reflector (257), but here it has been transformed into IP-address form.

Confederations

Another solution to the full iBGP mesh problem is splitting the network into several sub-ASes in a confederation. To the outside world, the confederation looks just like a single AS, and within each sub-AS, the regular iBGP rules apply. The BGP rules governing the interaction between sub-ASes are a mix of those for iBGP and eBGP: there is no need to maintain a full mesh of BGP speakers, but the next hop, MED, and Local Preference attributes are propagated unchanged, as in iBGP. Because the next hop attribute isn't changed, different sub-ASes would normally have to share interior routing information. However, by simply configuring inter-sub-AS links with *next-hop-self*, it's possible to remove this requirement and keep IGP information confined within each sub-AS. This makes confederations scale extremely well. Figure 10-3 shows the example AS from Figures 10-1 and 10-2 but now as a confederation of two sub-ASes. The two sub-ASes both have six iBGP sessions internally, and there are two sub-AS-to-sub-AS sessions; the total number of iBGP sessions is 14.

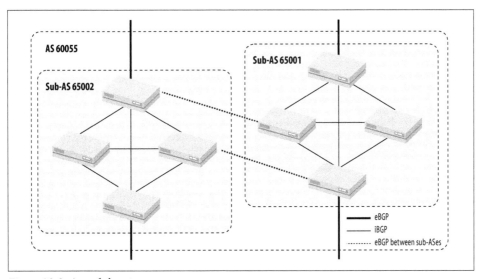

Figure 10-3. A confederation

I can't provide a full example of how confederations work, because this requires a much larger number of routers than I have at my disposal, but Example 10-4 shows how a router is configured to be part of a confederation.

Example 10-4. Configuring a confederation

```
!
router bgp 65003
 bgp confederation identifier 60055
 bgp confederation peers 65001 65002
 network 192.0.2.0
 neighbor 192.0.2.68 remote-as 65002
!
```

Because the AS numbers used for the sub-ASes are visible only within the confederation, it's not necessary to use "real" AS numbers here. The *router bgp ...* command now takes the local sub-AS number rather than the actual AS number for the confederation. This AS number is now called the "confederation identifier," and it's configured using the *bgp confederation identifier ...* command. The *bgp confederation peers ...* command lists the other AS numbers that are part of the confederation and completes the necessary confederation-specific configuration. This is how routes learned from other sub-ASes appear in the BGP table:

```
    Network     Next Hop     Metric LocPrf Weight Path
*> 192.0.2.0   192.0.2.68      0    100      0 (65002) i
*> 93.7.0.0    192.0.254.17         100      0 (65002 65001) 40077 i
```

The AS numbers that are part of the confederation are grouped between parentheses and are replaced by the confederation identifier (the real AS number) in nonconfederation eBGP sessions:

```
    Network     Next Hop     Metric LocPrf Weight Path
*> 192.0.2.0   192.0.254.18                    0 60055 i
```

> When implementing a confederation, include several extra internal AS numbers in the *bgp confederation peers ...* command. This way, you can easily add new sub-ASes without having to reconfigure all BGP routers throughout the network.

When engineering a confederation, it's generally best to have a "backbone" sub-AS that interconnects all other sub-ASes. This avoids unnecessary complexity.

Both route reflection and confederations adequately solve the iBGP full mesh problem. Route reflectors are easier to integrate into an existing network, but confederations make it easier to have several IGPs or several unrelated instances of the same IGP in an AS. It's possible to have multiple layers of route reflection or combine route reflection and a confederation.

Dampening Route Flaps

Routes that keep going down and coming back up make the BGP process use a lot of CPU time. This is especially problematic in a large network with many routers and many external connections; in that case, a remote route revocation can easily set a cascade in motion. The router with the best path is usually the first to receive the update, so the best path is revoked first. Then another router informs the rest of the network it now has the best route, only to receive a revocation for this route moments later. This is a variation of the count-to-infinity problem that Distance Vector routing protocols typically suffer from.

A router should obviously be able to handle a reasonable amount of routing table changes, but if a network becomes unstable, and routes continue to "flap," it puts an undue strain on the CPUs of routers throughout the rest of the network, and possibly those in other ASes as well. To avoid this, Cisco routers (and many other BGP implementations) support route flap-dampening. When flap dampening is configured, each time an eBGP route is revoked, it receives a penalty. When the penalty reaches a suppress-limit, the route is removed from the routing table and is no longer advertised to BGP neighbors. It will continue to be present in the BGP table, either as a "history entry" (when the last update was from up to down) or as "dampened" (when the last update was from down to up). The penalty is gradually lowered in accordance with the half-time value. The route is again advertised as usual when the penalty reaches the reuse-limit, and when it reaches half of the reuse-limit, the dampening information for the route is removed from memory. Example 10-5 enables flap dampening with the default values for the half-time (15 minutes), reuse-limit (750), suppress-limit (2000), and max-suppress-time (60 minutes) explicitly set.

Example 10-5. Enabling BGP flap dampening

```
!
router bgp 60055
 bgp dampening 15 750 2000 60
!
```

When a route flaps, it receives the default penalty of 1000. Suppose the penalty reaches 2800 after three flaps over the course of several minutes, and the route is suppressed. The penalty then has to halve nearly two times to reach 750, so it takes about 30 minutes for the route to be reinstated.

> There is no dampening of external routes received over iBGP: only the router receiving the routes over eBGP dampens them. When the BGP session to a neighbor is lost, all dampening information for routes received from this neighbor is purged from the router. However, this will count as a flap in ASes further up- or downstream.

RIPE document 229 describes a "Recommendation for Coordinated Route-flap Damping Parameters," because it was felt a more sophisticated approach with different penalties for different prefix sizes would be beneficial. Also, coordinated flap-dampening parameters makes dampening more consistent across networks, so problems are easier to find. Example 10-6 contains a route map taken from RIPE-229 that implements the recommendations (source: RIPE Network Coordination Center, *http://www.ripe.net*). The prefix lists that match the address ranges for the "golden networks" (the address prefixes the root and *gTLD* name servers are in) and the /24 and /22 – /24 prefix ranges have been omitted here. Consult RIPE-229 for more details: all current RIPE documents are available from the RIPE web site at *http:// www.ripe.net/ripe/docs/titletoc.html*.

Example 10-6. BGP flap dampening as recommended by RIPE-229

```
!
router bgp 65500
 bgp damp route-map graded-flap-damping
!
! don't damp golden networks,
! see http://www.golden-networks.net/
!
route-map graded-flap-damping deny 10
 match ip address prefix-list golden-networks
!
!   - /24 and longer prefixes: max=min outage 60 minutes
!
route-map graded-flap-damping permit 20
 match ip address prefix-list min24
 set damp 30 820 3000 60
!
!   - /22 and /23 prefixes: max outage 45 minutes but
!     potential for less because of shorter half life
!     value - minimum of 30 minutes outage
!
route-map graded-flap-damping permit 30
 match ip address prefix-list max22-23
 set damp 15 750 3000 45
!
!   - all else prefixes: max outage 30 minutes min
!     outage 10 minutes
!
route-map graded-flap-damping permit 40
 set damp 10 1500 3000 30
!
```

OSPF as the IGP

The task of selecting the right IGP (or even combination of IGPs!) for a large network is a difficult one, and discussing it in detail is well beyond the scope of this book. If you are implementing a large-scale IP network or have unusual requirements, you should definitely read up on all the protocols so you can make an informed decision. However, most small- to medium-sized networks running just IP should go ahead and select OSPF: it does the job, doesn't have any huge disadvantages, and is readily available.

It's important to keep in mind that the time it takes to execute the SPF algorithm OSPF uses for its route calculations increases faster than the number of links in the network. You can only have so many routers and/or links before the routers are spending all their time executing SPF. For this reason, OSPF allows you to divide your network into areas. When there is a link status change, the router needs to run the SPF algorithm only for the area this link belongs to. And you can aggregate routing information between areas to limit the number of routes in the routing table. Thus, dividing up your network in areas seems like a good idea. Unfortunately, there are also some disadvantages. Aggregation always leads to loss of information and thus to less efficient routing. But more importantly, there are certain rules on how areas are supposed to connect together. All areas must directly connect to area 0, the *backbone* area, and areas may never become partitioned: the two parts wouldn't be able to communicate with each other. The mechanism for assigning interfaces to areas is rather awkward: you need to define ranges of IP addresses and assign areas to them. Then the router matches the IP address for an interface to one of the ranges and assigns it to the associated area. This works well if every area has its own address range (which is a prerequisite for aggregation anyway), but if this isn't the case, you need to configure lots of address ranges to get the interfaces assigned to the right areas.

For reasonably small networks, it's much easier to just have a single area: there aren't any topology restrictions, and OSPF is easier to configure this way. But how large is "small"? Anything under 25 routers should be absolutely no problem; 25 to 100 routers should be doable if the routers are all fast enough, the network is stable, and the number of links isn't excessive. More than 100 routers in area 0 may work, but then again, it may not. Don't push your luck.

Redistributing Routing Information

On a network running both BGP and OSPF, there are three different types of routes:

- External routes, propagated through BGP
- Internal routes, propagated through OSPF
- Static and noninternal connected routes, which aren't propagated by default

When a router has an IP address in a subnet, it obviously has an interface connecting to it, so this subnet is connected. If the interface towards a connected subnet runs OSPF, the subnet is propagated through OSPF as an *internal* OSPF route. But if the interface doesn't fall within one of the ranges defined for one of the OSPF areas, the connected route for this interface doesn't show up in OSPF at all. This is one group of invisible routes. The second are static routes. Even with both BGP and OSPF running, you still need static routes: for instance, to direct traffic for an office network towards a firewall. ISP networks typically have large numbers of static routes. Rather than educate their users about routing or configure an instance of a routing protocol for each customer and risk problems, they configure routes to their customers statically.

The next question is: which routes should be redistributed into which protocol?

Redistributing static and connected into OSPF

It's customary to redistribute static and connected routes into the IGP. For OSPF, this is accomplished as in Example 10-7.

Example 10-7. Redistributing connected and static routes into OSPF

```
!
router ospf 1
 passive-interface Serial0
 redistribute connected subnets
 redistribute static subnets
 network 192.0.2.0 0.0.0.255 area 0
!
```

This example enables OSPF with process ID 1. Unlike the BGP AS number, the process ID has no function inside the protocol itself, but it can be used to differentiate between several instances of the protocol running on the same router. (But this is something you'll want to avoid if possible.) The *network* statement enables OSPF and puts the network 192.0.2.0/24 in area 0. Note the mask: it's in wildcard format, like an access list, rather than in netmask format, which is used in the BGP *network* command. OSPF processing is disabled for the Serial0 interface with the *passive-interface* command. The *subnets* keyword following the *redistribute* commands is necessary to include routes that don't match valid classful networks.

By default, the static routes show up in OSPF as external type 2 with a metric of 20. The difference between External type 2 (E2) and External type 1 (E1) routes is the way the metric is handled: in E1 routes, the external metric is added to all the link metrics in the path, and the path with the best total metric is chosen. For E2 routes, the external metric overrules all further metric calculations, and the path with the smallest external metric is always chosen, even if the internal part of that path is more expensive. Figure 10-4 illustrates this.

The network setup is the same in both pictures: two core routers (CR1 and CR2) route packets to an external network over border routers BR1 and BR2. The metric between both core routers is 15; the metric between core and border routers is 20. BR1 has a slightly "cheaper" connection to the external network: its metric is 40, while BR2's metric to the external network is 50. In the top picture, those external metrics are of type 1, so CR1 uses the path over BR1 with a total cost of 60 (20 + 40), and CR2 uses the path over BR2 with a cost of 70 (20 + 50). The cost of the alternative path for CR1 would be 15 + 20 + 50 = 85, and for CR2 15 + 20 + 40 = 75. In the bottom picture, however, the external metrics are type 2. This means the entire

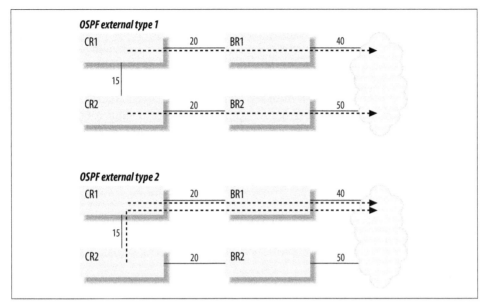

Figure 10-4. Differences between OSPF E1 and E2 metrics

network uses the link with the lowest metric, regardless of how far the traffic has to travel over the internal network. As a result, CR2 uses the path over CR1 now.

Redistributing BGP into OSPF

Redistributing the full BGP table into OSPF is almost never a good idea: it takes a lot of extra memory, CPU time, and bandwidth, and it certainly doesn't help keep OSPF running nice and smooth. The traditional reason for injecting BGP information into OSPF is that only border routers would talk BGP, but the internal routers should still be aware of the full routing information. However, this is much more easily accomplished by just running BGP on all routers that need a full view of the routing table. There are often routers that don't need a (semi-) full routing table; they can use the default injected into OSPF by one of the "big" routers. Example 10-8 injects a default route into OSPF (if one is available in the routing table) with metric 10. The type is External type 2 by default.

Example 10-8. Injecting a default route into OSPF

```
!
router ospf 1
 default-information originate metric 10
!
```

Even though full redistribution of all BGP routes in OSPF isn't advisable, it can sometimes be useful to redistribute a subset of the BGP information into OSPF or even RIP. For instance, a multihomed network might have two border routers, along with several smaller internal routers, or maybe a multilayer switch running IP. Because the non-BGP routers aren't aware of any routing information, they send all packets to one of the border routers. This border router then has to send a sizable chunk of all traffic to the other border router, because that one has the better BGP routes to these destinations. Obviously, it would be more efficient if the internal routers were to send this traffic directly to the second border router. This can be accomplished by having the first border router send out a default route over OSPF and then having the second border router inject more specific routes (along with a backup default route) into OSPF, as shown in Example 10-9.

Example 10-9. Limited redistribution of BGP into OSPF

```
!
router ospf 3
 redistribute bgp 60055 subnets route-map limitred
 default-information originate metric 20
 network 192.0.2.0 0.0.0.255 area 0
 !
ip as-path access-list 23 permit .+_.+_.+_.+
 !
access-list 33 permit 192.0.254.17
 !
route-map limitred deny 10
 match as-path 23
 !
route-map limitred permit 20
 match ip next-hop 33
 !
```

On this router, the OSPF process ID is 3, but this value is of only local importance. The area definitions match the interface used between the two routers, so they exchange OSPF information. The default route this router sends out has metric 20, so it's just a backup. Redistributed routes are external type 2 by default, which has the effect that the metric isn't increased as the route is passed from router to router, as is done with regular OSPF routes. The *redistribute* command takes routes from the BGP process with AS number 60055, including classless routes (supernets and subnets), and applies the route maps with tag limitred to them. The limitred deny 10 route map uses AS path access list 23 to match routes with an AS path of at least four ASes in it: four times the sequence "one or more characters" (.+) with a space (_) between. Because this is a *deny* route map, matching routes aren't redistributed. Nonmatching routes move on to the next route map, limitred permit 20. This route map matches BGP routes with the next hop 192.0.254.17 by means of access list 33, so those are allowed into OSPF. All other routes are implicitly denied when the *route-map* statements end. The net effect of these route maps is that only routes with an AS path of three hops or less and with the next hop set to 192.0.254.17 are redistributed from BGP into OSPF.

When redistributing BGP routes into another protocol, the router redistributes only eBGP-learned routes. Beginning in IOS Version 12.1 it's possible also to redistribute iBGP routes by configuring *bgp redistribute-internal*. However, this is dangerous: it can lead to routing loops because the IGP metrics will be inconsistent from router to router.

Redistributing OSPF into BGP

Redistributing IGP routes into BGP is generally a bad idea, so I don't even want to give an example of how to do it. When doing this, there will be many more specific routes in OSPF that shouldn't be announced over BGP, so there must be large filter lists, which are much harder to maintain than the list of *network* statements in the BGP configuration. (Filters lines have a specific order that must be preserved when changing them; *network* statements can be added and removed independently from others.) Redistribution also propagates any internal instabilities into the global routing table, which can lead to flap dampening further upstream and being unreachable for longer than necessary. But the main problem is that everything gets more complex as static routes are redistributed into OSPF and then from OSPF into BGP. This makes troubleshooting difficult: if a route is missing in BGP, the problem can be in many places. There may not be a static route, the static route may not be redistributed into OSPF, the OSPF route may not be redistributed into BGP, and the BGP route may not be announced to eBGP neighbors. Well, so far so good. But now we have to make sure that if the routers actually doing all this redistribution go down, others can take over, and the route remains visible.

If you want to redistribute an IGP into BGP, you may need to configure *no auto-summary* to make sure that networks smaller than the classful net they fall in are advertised. See Example 10-10 a little later in this chapter. Also take a look at the filtering of outbound BGP updates in this example, because this is also needed when redistributing IGP routes.

Redistributing BGP into OSPF into BGP

Redistributing BGP into the IGP and vice versa is extremely dangerous. Never *ever* do this!

If you redistribute BGP into OSPF and OSPF into BGP, there is a chance exterior BGP routes that are turned into OSPF routes are reannounced as interior BGP routes. Obviously there will be filters to prevent this, but experience shows that it's well within the realm of possibility that such a filter fails to do its job. And when this happens, you will start to announce thousands of routes with just your AS as the AS path. This path will, in almost all cases, be shorter than the AS paths the prefixes originally had, so neighbors that don't filter your prefixes or limit the number of prefixes they accept from you (filtering on AS path doesn't help here) will start to send you the traffic for nearly all the affected destinations. As a result, your AS becomes a huge black hole that sucks traffic in but doesn't let anything escape. This is about the worst thing that can happen to the global interdomain routing system.

These risks are far from academic: it has happened several times in the past. A study done at the University of Washington shows that nearly 75% of all new announcements that show up in the global routing table are the result of some kind of mistake or problem. One of the reasons for this is the practice of first removing an access list or set of route maps with *no access-list ...* or *no route-map ...* before entering a new version of the filter. The few moments before the new access list or route maps become active are enough for the router to start announcing random routes in the BGP table. But even changing filters the "proper way" is no guarantee against unwanted routers slipping through. Just recently, I replaced one filter with an identical one under another name. I didn't remove anything first, so there was a valid filter configured at all times. This still triggered the maximum prefix limit on the neighboring router, so routers that weren't allowed by either the old or the new filter must have slipped through during the change. You should never depend on a single filter.

The "Understanding BGP Misconfiguration" paper can be found at *http://www.cs. washington.edu/homes/ratul/bgp/index.html.*

Redistributing static and connected routes into BGP

Increasing numbers of internal routes mean OSPF has to do more and more work. For really big ISP networks, the number of static routes redistributed into OSPF may become a burden to the protocol. To avoid this, some ISPs don't redistribute these routes in OSPF (or their IGP of choice), but rather in BGP. Because BGP doesn't require exact synchronization between all routers within the AS unlike link state protocols such as OSPF, it can tolerate large numbers of internal routes much better. Also, when there is a topology change in the internal network, there are no changes in the BGP or routing tables as long as the router announcing the subnet remains reachable. Unlike an IGP, BGP doesn't concern itself with how, exactly, the route is reachable: it's sufficient that the router that is listed as the next hop is somehow reachable, even if this requires several levels of recursion. If 7,000 iBGP customer routes point to 500 iBGP connected routes that point to 80 OSPF routes for loopback addresses, OSPF has a lot less to do when a link goes down than if all those 7,000 customer routes had been present in OSPF. The router still has to recompute the routing table and route caches to adjust for the new IGP path towards the BGP next hop. However, this is done after OSPF has converged, so the time during which the network as a whole is in an inconsistent state (because OSPF is reconverging) is much shorter. Example 10-10 shows how to redistribute static and connected routes into BGP.

Example 10-10. Redistributing static and connected routes into BGP

```
!
router ospf 1
 network 192.0.2.64 0.0.0.63 area 0
 network 192.0.2.128 0.0.0.31 area 0
!
router bgp 60055
 no synchronization
 redistribute connected
 redistribute static
 neighbor 192.0.2.147 remote-as 60055
 neighbor 192.0.2.147 update-source Loopback0
 neighbor 192.0.2.148 remote-as 60055
 neighbor 192.0.2.148 update-source Loopback0
 neighbor 192.0.254.17 remote-as 40077
 neighbor 192.0.254.17 prefix-list no-internal out
 no auto-summary
!
ip route 192.0.2.0 255.255.255.0 Null0
!
ip prefix-list no-internal seq 5 permit 199.208.0.0/16
ip prefix-list no-internal seq 10 permit 192.0.2.0/24
!
```

Most of these configuration commands will be familiar by now. The address ranges
192.0.2.64/26 and 192.0.2.128/27 are put into OSPF area 0 because these are the
address ranges for internal router-to-router links. Redistribution of static and connected routes into BGP is enabled with the *redistribute connected* and *redistribute
static* commands. The *no auto-summary* command makes sure subnets are redistributed "as is" and aren't summarized into classful routes in BGP. For instance, the
route 192.0.2.64/26 would show up as 192.0.2.0/24 with *auto-summary* enabled, as
is the default.

When redistributing static and connected routes into BGP, it's more important than
ever to carefully filter announcements toward external ASes: if you don't, your transit ISPs, peers, and customers will receive all your internal routes. These routes are of
no interest to them, use up resources, and obscure what you really want to
announce, so troubleshooting gets harder than it needs to be. In this case, only 199.
208.0.0/16 and 192.0.2.0/24 are allowed. Note that there are no *network* statements
for these networks in the BGP configuration: the regular static routes to the Null0
interfaces for these prefixes (that normally serve to activate the *network* statements)
are now directly redistributed into BGP.

This is how the 199.208.0.0/16 network, redistributed into BGP by another router in
the local network, shows up in the routing table:

```
BR1#show ip route 199.208.0.0
Routing entry for 199.208.0.0/16
  Known via "bgp 60055", distance 200, metric 0, type internal
  Last update from 192.0.2.5 00:04:06 ago
  Routing Descriptor Blocks:
```

```
    * 192.0.2.5, from 192.0.2.147, 00:04:06 ago
        Route metric is 0, traffic share count is 1
        AS Hops 0
```

And in the BGP table:

```
BR1#show ip bgp 199.208.0.0/16
BGP routing table entry for 199.208.0.0/16, version 341
Paths: (1 available, best #1)
  Advertised to non peer-group peers:
  192.0.254.17
  Local
    192.0.2.5 (metric 128) from 192.0.2.5 (192.0.2.147)
      Origin incomplete, metric 0, localpref 100, valid, internal, best
```

The next hop address for 199.208.0.0/16 is 192.0.2.5, so to forward a packet, we have to go back to the routing table and look up this address:

```
BR1#show ip route 192.0.2.5
Routing entry for 192.0.2.4/30
  Known via "bgp 60055", distance 200, metric 0, type internal
  Last update from 192.0.2.147 00:06:40 ago
  Routing Descriptor Blocks:
  * 192.0.2.147, from 192.0.2.147, 00:06:40 ago
      Route metric is 0, traffic share count is 1
      AS Hops 0
```

But the next hop 192.0.2.147 still isn't a directly connected address, so we have continue looking up routes:

```
BR1#sh ip route 192.0.2.147
Routing entry for 192.0.2.147/32
  Known via "ospf 1", distance 110, metric 65, type intra area
  Redistributing via ospf 1
  Last update from 192.0.2.1 on Serial2, 00:06:57 ago
  Routing Descriptor Blocks:
  * 192.0.2.129, from 192.0.2.147, 00:06:57 ago, via Serial2
      Route metric is 65, traffic share count is 1
```

Fortunately, recursively looking up routes in the main routing table isn't something that has to be done for each individual packet. The Cisco Express Forwarding (CEF) table immediately leads to the right information:

```
BR1#show ip cef 199.208.0.0
199.208.0.0/16, version 764
0 packets, 0 bytes
  via 192.0.2.5, 0 dependencies, recursive
    next hop 192.0.2.129, Serial2 via 192.0.2.4/30
    valid adjacency
```

Now it's time to see if all this additional complexity pays off, by shutting down the Serial2 interface that is used for this route. The effect on the routing table is:

```
BR1#show ip route 199.208.0.0
Routing entry for 199.208.0.0/16
  Known via "bgp 60055", distance 200, metric 0, type internal
  Last update from 192.0.2.5 00:04:46 ago
```

```
Routing Descriptor Blocks:
* 192.0.2.5, from 192.0.2.147, 00:04:46 ago
    Route metric is 0, traffic share count is 1
    AS Hops 0
```

In other words, no change whatsoever. But traffic is rerouted all the same:

```
BR1#show ip cef 199.208.0.0
199.208.0.0/16, version 764
0 packets, 0 bytes
  via 192.0.2.5, 0 dependencies, recursive
    next hop 192.0.2.133, Serial3 via 192.0.2.4/30
    valid adjacency
```

This is exactly the intended effect of this configuration.

Redistributing static and connected routes into BGP has one major drawback: there must be stringent outbound filtering on all eBGP sessions, and these filters must be modified every time a new network is announced over BGP. The use of communities offers a way around this. Rather than having outbound filters that separate routes that should be visible externally from internal routes, external routes are tagged with a community at the point of origin:

```
!
router bgp 60055
 network 192.0.2.0 mask 255.255.255.0 route-map setexternal
!
route-map setexternal permit 10
 set community 60055:1
!
```

Outbound filtering on eBGP sessions is then limited to permitting routes with community 60055:1:

```
!
router bgp 60055
 neighbor 192.0.254.17 remote-as 40077
 neighbor 192.0.254.17 route-map external-only out
!
ip community-list 1 permit 60055:1
!
```

The filters for eBGP sessions never have to change in this scenario; whenever a new prefix is announced, only the router sourcing the route must be reconfigured. This minimizes the potential for mistakes.

Traffic Engineering in the Internal Network

Chapter 6 was all about traffic engineering for traffic to and from external networks. If you have a network spanning a significant geographic area (so that leased-line costs are considerable), you may need to do traffic engineering in the internal network. In one way, this is easier than interdomain traffic engineering: you have full control of all metrics for all links. But the down side is that IGPs aren't as sophisticated as BGP: they generally look only at a single metric, and this metric is applied to all prefixes that share a destination.

By default, Cisco routers set the metric for all interfaces to 100,000 divided by the interface speed in Kbps. So a T1 gets a metric of 65, and a 10-Mbps Ethernet interface gets a metric of 10. There are several problems with this. First, it doesn't allow for interfaces with a bandwidth of more than 100 Mbps. Also, all links are considered equal in this approach, while many topologies make the distinction between backbone and nonbackbone parts of the network. This means you have to override the default OSPF metrics. A good way to do this would be:

1. Assign the fastest backbone interfaces you imagine having in the foreseeable future a metric of 10.

2. Give all other backbone interfaces a metric relative to the fastest interfaces that have a metric of 10. For instance, if Gigabit Ethernet is 10, Fast Ethernet is 100, and 155-Mbps SONET is 65 (10 × 1000 Mbps ÷ 155 Mbps).

3. Give all nonbackbone leased lines a metric that is 10 times that of a similar backbone interface (so 650 for a 155-Mbps nonbackbone SONET connection).

4. Keep the defaults for local links within a building. Thus, those metrics are low so traffic stays within the building whenever possible.

Consider a network using the "ringed triangles" topology introduced in Chapter 3 with a backbone ring from New York to Chicago, San Francisco, Los Angeles, Dallas, Atlanta, Washington, DC, and back to New York. The picture on the left in Figure 10-5 shows this network with 10 as the IGP metric for all backbone links.

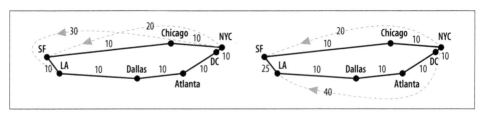

Figure 10-5. Adjusting a metric to influence traffic patterns

The problem in this example network is that there is a lot of traffic from New York to both San Francisco and Los Angeles, but it all takes the counterclockwise route over Chicago and San Francisco. It would be better for the traffic to Los Angeles to flow in the opposite direction, over Washington, Atlanta, and Dallas, because this part of the ring isn't as busy as the northern part. This is easily accomplished by increasing the IGP metric for the link between San Francisco and Los Angeles to a little more than double the usual value. If all backbone links have an IGP metric of 10, the San Francisco to Los Angeles link now gets 25. So now the northern path from New York to Los Angeles has a cost of 45 (three hops, one more expensive), while the southern path still has a cost of 40 (four hops). The picture on the right in Figure 10-5 illustrates the difference. The black lines are the backbone, metrics are the black numbers, and the traffic flows are the gray lines. Example 10-11 implements the necessary changes in interface metrics for the San Francisco router.

Example 10-11. Adjusting OSPF metrics for interfaces

```
!
interface POS0/0
 description OC12 backbone ring to Chicago
 ip ospf cost 10
!
interface POS1/0
 description OC12 backbone ring to LA
 ip ospf cost 25
!
interface POS2/0
 description OC3 link to Denver
 ip ospf cost 400
!
```

The *ip ospf cost* command accepts arguments in the range 1 to 65535.

Network Partitions

In simple cases, a network partition is similar to the situation in which a single-homed network finds itself when the connection to its ISP is down: part of the network is completely cut off from the rest of the world. If a multihomed network has two PoPs, one where both connections to the Internet terminate and another that depends on the first for its connectivity to the rest of the world, basically the first location serves as a single ISP for the second location. In these cases, it's easiest and often relatively cheap to get rid of the single point of failure by connecting to one ISP at the first location and to another ISP at the second location. This way, each location is still connected to the rest of the Net if the other location fails. The problems start when both locations are up but the connection between them is lost, so the internal network is partitioned. Consider the network depicted in Figure 10-6. No single failure will affect more than the failed component; e.g., if the entire Chicago location fails, New York and Washington will continue to be reachable over ISP 2 and MAE East. If the connection between Chicago and Washington fails, traffic for Washington entering the network in Chicago is rerouted over New York, and so on.

This network design doesn't address the possibility of two coinciding failures. Obviously, if both connections out of Washington are down at the same time, Washington will be pretty much unreachable from the rest of the world. But even if both connections out of Chicago fail, there will be problems. If the entire Chicago PoP disappears from the Net, New York and Washington continue to enjoy connectivity over ISP 2. But Chicago doesn't disappear: it continues to be reachable over ISP 1.

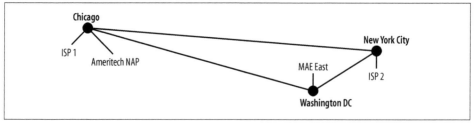

Figure 10-6. A geographically dispersed multihomed network

This works as long as Chicago announces only the addresses used there, and New York and Washington announce addresses only for systems reachable at or through those locations. If there is only a single address range, and it's announced at all locations, some packets destined for a host in one location will end up in another location with no means to transport them to their destination. For instance, if some of the packets for hosts in Chicago enter the network in New York, but the Chicago location is unreachable from there, the packets will either be dropped, or they'll be sent back to ISP 2, making them loop for a while until their TTL reaches zero.

Ideally, you would announce address ranges used in each location separately, from the location in question. In reality, this is an extremely hard thing to do, because either you need lots of fairly small address ranges—and those announcements will probably not be accepted by all networks throughout the entire Internet—or you must use artificially large ranges to pass route filters—but this conflicts with the address conservation policies enforced by the Regional Internet Registries. It's a good idea at least to try to assign addresses in such a way that they are easy to announce regionally, even if this means doing some extra renumbering now and then. When 70% of the first half of a /20 is assigned in one location and 80% of the second half in another location, you can announce the appropriate /21 at each location, and at least 70% of the systems in the first location and 80% of the systems in the other location will be reachable. Without any effort to assign addresses geographically, this wouldn't be much better than 50%.

IP Tunnels and Path MTU Discovery

Alternatively, or in addition to trying to get as much traffic as possible directly to the right destination by deaggregating your announcements, you can use IP tunnels to repair the partition. A *tunnel* is a virtual interface inside the router that can be used almost exactly like a regular interface. But there is no hardware attached to it: packets are transmitted by encapsulating them inside new IP packets, which are addressed to the router at the other end of the tunnel. When a router receives a tunneled packet, it first does some checks, and if the packet seems to be part of a valid tunnel, it's deencapsulated, and the original packet is routed just like a packet received over a physical interface. In the case of a network partition, it doesn't do any good to configure the tunnel between the regular addresses of the routers: these are exactly the unreachable addresses. It's always useful to have small address ranges from all your ISPs for these kinds of purposes, but if you don't, you can probably use the /30 subnet for the interface toward your ISP (if assigned by the ISP) for running BGP. Example 10-12 shows the configuration for an IP tunnel.

Example 10-12. Configuring an IP tunnel

```
!
interface Tunnel0
 ip address 220.37.15.253 255.255.255.252
 no ip directed-broadcast
 tunnel source 192.0.254.18
 tunnel destination 222.18.13.66
 tunnel mode ipip
!
ip route 222.18.13.66 255.255.255.255 Serial0
!
```

The *interface tunnel0* creates the tunnel. There is no real limit for the number of tunnels, other than the limits imposed by memory and general IOS limitations. The *tunnel source* specifies the source address used for the encapsulating packet. You can also list an interface rather than an IP address here, in which case the IP address configured on that interface is used. The *tunnel destination* is one of the destination router's addresses. Both addresses must match the respective destination and source addresses configured on the other side of the tunnel. You can have several tunnel interfaces, as long as you don't use the same combination of source, destination, and mode more than once. Use the *no interface tunnel0* command to remove the tunnel. There are several ways to encapsulate IP packets in tunnels. The most common are IP over IP (*tunnel mode ipip*) and Generic Route Encapsulation (*tunnel mode gre ip*). GRE has the advantage that it can encapsulate different protocols rather than just IP, and it has some other extras. When protocols other than IP aren't needed, IP over IP is a good choice, because it introduces the overhead only of a second IP header, while GRE needs at least another four bytes. The static route is there to make sure packets to the tunnel endpoint will always be sent directly to the ISP and not over the tunnel interface itself.

The overhead of an extra IP header is one of the main problems with tunnels, not so much because it eats away at usable bandwidth, but because packets grow too large to transmit for the router's interfaces. Most hosts are connected to the Net over Ethernet, so in pretty much all cases, at least one end of a TCP connection requests a Maximum Segment Size (MSS, the maximum number of user data bytes TCP can transmit in a single packet) of 1460 bytes. This makes for 1500-byte packets when the TCP and IP headers (both 20 bytes in the absence of options) are added. When such a packet enters a tunnel, the extra IP header increases the packet size to a total of 1520 bytes. In many cases, the path between the tunnel endpoints also includes Ethernet or other links with a 1500-byte MTU (it's also the default for PPP), so this packet can't be transmitted without fragmentation. And since sending smaller packets in the first place is a lot more efficient than having a router break up each packet into smaller ones and then reassemble them at the destination host, most systems implement Path MTU Discovery (RFC 1191). This works by setting the "don't fragment" (DF) bit in the IP header. If a router then encounters a packet that is too large to transmit, it drops the packet and sends back a "fragmentation needed and DF bit set" ICMP message, or "Datagram Too Big" in RFC 1191–speak. Upon receiving this ICMP message, the host lowers its idea of the path MTU to what the sending router reports, or it guesses, if the router doesn't include this information. This procedure works extremely well, as long as the sending host receives the "Datagram Too Big" messages. The RFC specifies, "Hosts using PMTU Discovery MUST detect decreases in Path MTU as fast as possible."

Most TCP implementations try to meet this requirement simply by always sending packets with the DF bit set. This makes communication impossible when, at some point, the packets are too large to traverse a link but the router doesn't send back a "Datagram Too Big" message or this message fails to reach the sending host. The host continues to retransmit packets of the same size with the DF bit set, each time with the same result: the packet is dropped. Eventually the TCP session times out. The reason why isn't immediately apparent to the casual observer. Because the initial packets of a TCP session aren't large, the session will be established without trouble. The problems start when the actual data transfer begins, and maximum size packets are sent, at which point the session stalls and times out.

Incorrect router configurations, firewalls, and Network Address Translation (NAT) can make it impossible for the "Datagram Too Big" messages to reach the source host, thereby triggering the problem. You should make sure that ICMP unreachable messages with the "fragmentation needed and DF bit set" code are always allowed through by filters, and that all routers connecting to networks with smaller than 1500-byte MTUs don't use private (RFC 1918) or otherwise unroutable addresses for any of their interfaces. You can diagnose the problem by sending both 1400- and 1500-byte pings with the DF bit set (*ping* with options on the router). If the 1400-byte pings make it but the 1500-byte ones don't, the path MTU is slightly smaller than 1500 bytes. If it's not possible to get the "Datagram Too Big" messages delivered correctly, you may want to either disable path MTU discovery or lower the MTU on the local Ethernets to that of the tunnel. The latter will make TCP sessions negotiate the use of smaller packets.

 All systems connected to a subnet (such as an Ethernet) must use the same MTU.

Depending on the IOS version, you may be able to use the *ip mtu 1500* command to set the MTU for the tunnel interface to an Ethernet-compatible size. But then the routers at both ends of the tunnel have to spend resources on fragmenting and reassembling fragments.

CHAPTER 11

Providing Transit Services

Being a multihomed ISP with BGP-speaking customers isn't very different from just being a multihomed network in most regards, but some things need extra attention. A regular multihomed network sends out just its own routes, which makes for easy outbound filtering: allow out the BGP announcements you're trying to send, and nothing else. When you're providing transit services, it gets a bit more complex. You can, of course, filter out any announcements that don't fit your idea of how your customers should announce their routes. That way, however, you don't leave any room for traffic engineering or BGP-based anti-DoS measures. A better solution is to accept all reasonable announcements. You should also have a solution for customers with two connections to your network. And expect customers to come to you with questions about IP multicast and IPv6.

The examples in this chapter all use AS 40077 as the local AS number with different customer and upstream ISP connections in each example.

Route Filters

Outbound route filters to upstream networks (peers and transit ISPs) are important to make sure you send only the routes you want to source and those of your customers to your peers and upstream ISPs. You need two types of outbound route filters: AS path and prefix filters. Having both prefix and AS path filters is redundant in theory, but in practice there are many ways in which faulty routes can escape one check, so they must be filtered out by the other. Example 11-1 shows both plus an inbound prefix list filter and how the filters are applied to an individual BGP session and a peer group.

Example 11-1. Filtering outbound routes to transit ISPs and peers

```
!
router bgp 40077
 network 192.0.224.0 mask 255.255.224.0
 network 223.15.0.0 mask 255.255.0.0
 neighbor nap peer-group
 neighbor nap prefix-list in in
```

Example 11-1. Filtering outbound routes to transit ISPs and peers (continued)

```
neighbor nap prefix-list out out
neighbor nap filter-list 10 out
neighbor 169.254.30.8 remote-as 30088
neighbor 169.254.30.8 prefix-list in in
neighbor 169.254.30.8 prefix-list out out
neighbor 169.254.30.8 filter-list 10 out
!
ip route 192.0.224.0 255.255.224.0 Null0
ip route 223.15.0.0 255.255.0.0 Null0
!
ip as-path access-list 10 permit ^(40077_)*$
ip as-path access-list 10 permit ^(40077_)*(60055_)+$
!
ip prefix-list out description outbound route filter
ip prefix-list out seq 5 permit 192.0.224.0/19 le 22
ip prefix-list out seq 10 permit 223.15.0.0/16 le 19
ip prefix-list out seq 15 permit 192.0.2.0/24 le 27
ip prefix-list out seq 20 permit 220.37.0.0/20 le 23
!
ip prefix-list in description inbound route filter
ip prefix-list in seq 5 deny 192.0.224.0/19 le 32
ip prefix-list in seq 10 deny 223.15.0.0/16 le 32
ip prefix-list in seq 15 permit 0.0.0.0/0 le 24
!
```

In this example, there are four address ranges: a /19 and a /16 announced by the local AS (AS 40077), and a /24 and a /20 announced by a customer (AS 60055). There are *network* statements for the locally sourced /19 and /16 announcements, but not for the customer routes: they must announce these address blocks themselves. The out prefix list allows all four address ranges and routes for prefixes that are up to three bits longer. This way, some deaggregation is possible to counteract DoS attacks or black holes, but the blocks can't get too small (and thus their number too large) to avoid running into trouble with upstream maximum prefix settings. The inbound in prefix list filter makes sure the router doesn't listen to others announcing the network's own address space by filtering out all prefixes matching the locally sourced address blocks or subsets thereof. (External announcements of customer address ranges are allowed so that they can reach the customer when their connection to this network is down.) The last line of the in filter permits all prefixes that aren't longer than 24 bits. The first line of AS path access list 10 allows all AS paths consisting of zero or more times the sequence 40077_ (the local AS number and a space character). The second line allows all AS paths with the local AS number zero or more times followed by one or more (+) times the customer AS number. The * and + wildcard characters are made to work on multicharacter strings (atoms in *regexp* speak) by enclosing them in parentheses. The ^ (beginning of the line) and $ (end of line) special characters make sure the regular expressions match only lines consisting entirely of the desired expression and not all lines that include the desired expression.

If you have multihomed customers (or even ex-customers) announcing routes that fall within your address ranges, you must explicitly allow these ranges in your inbound prefix list before denying your own ranges. Otherwise, these customers will be unreachable when your direct connection to them is down, because the route over their alternate ISP will be filtered out.

Filtering outgoing route updates to peers and transit ISPs makes sure they can't receive any faulty announcements from you, but it doesn't protect your own network from mistakes made by your customers. It's important to also perform incoming filtering on the BGP sessions with customers. Example 11-2 does this.

Example 11-2. Filtering inbound routes from customers

```
!
router bgp 40077
 neighbor 192.0.254.18 remote-as 60055
 neighbor 192.0.254.18 prefix-list as60055-in in
 neighbor 192.0.254.18 filter-list 32 in
!
ip as-path access-list 32 permit ^(60055_)+$
!
ip prefix-list as60055-in description filter for 60055
ip prefix-list as60055-in seq 5 permit 192.0.2.0/24 le 32
ip prefix-list as60055-in seq 10 permit 220.37.0.0/20 le 32
!
```

Unlike the outgoing filters, these inbound filters allow long prefixes, all the way up to a /32. This is necessary for customers to announce individual IP addresses with the "black hole" community, so they can easily get rid of DoS attacks. This is discussed in more detail later this chapter.

Communities

As discussed in earlier chapters, the community attribute that can be attached to BGP routes is extremely helpful in two ways. First, it can instruct upstream networks to perform certain actions for each announced prefix. The second use is to aid a multihomed customer in selecting the better route to a destination from the two received from both transit ISPs.

Setting the Local Preference

The oldest use of the community attribute is to adjust the Local Preference of a route in an ISP network, to avoid having to rely on the "weak" MED metric. This is outlined in RFC 1998, "An Application of the BGP Community Attribute in Multi-home Routing." This RFC uses an example with the Local Preference values listed in Table 11-1.

Table 11-1. RFC 1998 Local Preference values

Category	Local Preference
Customer routes	100
Customer backup routes	90
Other ISP routes	80
Customer-provided backup	70

This has the advantage of using 100 (the default Local Preference) for customers, so it's impossible to make a mistake and give customer routes the wrong Local Preference. Because this example comes from MCI, a tier-1 ISP, there is no difference between transit and peer routes for "other ISP routes," so to apply this to smaller networks it's necessary to add a "peer routes" category with a Local Preference of 85. This way, routes from peers are always preferred over those received from transit ISPs, which have a slightly lower Local Preference of 80. Customers can set the Local Preference for their announcement to two values, 90 and 70, in addition to leaving it at the default of 100. A Local Preference of 90 is useful for backup routes to the same ISP, because it still preempts routes received over transit or from peers. The Local Preference value of 70 is even "weaker" and kicks in only when there aren't any other routes, so it's useful for backup links that connect to a different ISP than the main one. If your network provides transit services to ISPs with BGP customers of their own, you may also want to have communities that set the Local Preference to the values for transit (80) and peer (85) routes. This way, such an end customer can avoid having you send all traffic to them over one of their ISPs, so they can make better use of AS path prepending.

Example 11-3 shows a configuration that looks for the communities 40077:90 and 40077:70 and adjusts the Local Preference accordingly.

Example 11-3. Allowing customers to set the Local Preference

```
!
router bgp 40077
 neighbor 192.0.254.18 remote-as 60055
 neighbor 192.0.254.18 prefix-list cust60055-in in
 neighbor 192.0.254.18 route-map customer-in in
 neighbor 192.0.254.18 filter-list 32 in
!
ip bgp-community new-format
ip community-list 70 permit 40077:70
ip community-list 90 permit 40077:90
!
ip prefix-list any description prfx-lst to match all routes
ip prefix-list any seq 5 permit 0.0.0.0/0 le 32
!
route-map customer-in permit 70
 match community 70
```

Example 11-3. Allowing customers to set the Local Preference (continued)

```
 set local-preference 70
 set comm-list 70 delete
!
route-map customer-in permit 90
 match community 90
 set local-preference 90
 set comm-list 90 delete
!
route-map customer-in permit 100
 match ip address prefix-list any
!
```

Because there are already customer-specific filters for each BGP session, the inbound route map customer-in can be the same for all customers. The first *route-map* statement (*permit 70*) applies community list 70 to the communities present for the route, and if the list matches (which it will do if the community 40077:70 is present), it sets the Local Preference to 70, removes the community from the route, and installs the route in the BGP table. The syntax for removing communities is slightly counterintuitive: the *set comm-list ... delete* command applies a community list to the communities attached to the route, then it removes the communities matched by the list. Removing the community after it has done its job isn't strictly necessary, but it helps keep the number of communities for this route down to something reasonable.

The second statement (*permit 90*) works exactly the same way, by using community list 90 to match community 40077:90 to set the Local Preference to 90, remove the community, and install the route. The last statement (*permit 100*) matches all remaining routes and doesn't perform any actions. Because route maps have an "implicit deny" like all other Cisco filters, this statement is necessary to install all routes that didn't match any of the previous statements in the BGP table.

Fine-Grained Path Prepending

Prepending the AS number in route announcements is an effective but somewhat crude mechanism for customers to influence their incoming traffic. You can help them better balance their traffic by providing communities to do path prepending for each transit ISP or peer individually. Since the number of peers can grow large, you probably shouldn't provide communities for each individual peer, but rather per exchange point, with the possible exception of a few important peers. Table 11-2 shows example communities for path prepending, along with extra communities to completely avoid announcing a route to an ISP or exchange.

Table 11-2. Per-peer or per-exchange action communities

Community	Peer/location	Action
40077:2001	Transit AS 30088	Prepend once
40077:2002	Transit AS 30088	Prepend twice

Table 11-2. Per-peer or per-exchange action communities (continued)

Community	Peer/location	Action
40077:2003	Transit AS 30088	Prepend three times
40077:2009	Transit AS 30088	Don't announce
40077:4001	Chicago NAP	Prepend once
40077:4002	Chicago NAP	Prepend twice
40077:4003	Chicago NAP	Prepend three times
40077:4009	Chicago NAP	Don't announce

Unlike the route maps for communities discussed earlier in this chapter, these route maps must not be applied to customer BGP sessions, but to sessions with transit ISPs and peers. Example 11-4 shows this for a single transit ISP.

Example 11-4. Communities for path prepending towards a transit ISP

```
!
router bgp 40077
 neighbor 169.254.30.8 remote-as 30088
 neighbor 169.254.30.8 send-community
 neighbor 169.254.30.8 route-map as30088-out out
!
ip community-list 21 permit 40077:2001
ip community-list 22 permit 40077:2002
ip community-list 23 permit 40077:2003
ip community-list 29 deny 40077:2009
ip community-list 29 permit
!
route-map as30088-out permit 10
 match community 21
 set as-path prepend 40077
 set comm-list 21 delete
!
route-map as30088-out permit 20
 match community 22
 set as-path prepend 40077 40077
 set comm-list 22 delete
!
route-map as30088-out permit 30
 match community 23
 set as-path prepend 40077 40077 40077
 set comm-list 23 delete
!
route-map as30088-out permit 90
 match community 29
!
```

The community lists 21, 22, and 23 match the communities for prepending the path once, twice, and three times, respectively, and the appropriate actions are taken in the route maps with tag as30088-out. Community list 29 is a different beast: this one matches everything except routes with the community attribute 40077:2009. The final as-30088-out route map matches this community list without taking any actions. This results in all routes without the community 40077:2009 being announced to AS 30088. Because the *send-community* keyword is specified for this neighbor, all communities still attached to the route are communicated to this AS. This allows customers (and you) to set communities that trigger special actions in AS 30088.

Setting Communities on Incoming Routes

Your multihomed customers will be happy to receive all additional information you can provide for a route; this enables them to pick the best route for a destination from the ones received from their transit ISPs. So if it's not too hard to supply a certain piece of information by setting a community, take a few minutes to configure it, even if you don't think this information is of great value. The most basic information you can provide using communities is where a route entered your network. Table 11-3 shows some example communities for doing this.

Table 11-3. Communities to convey route origin information

Community	Location	Source
40077:2000	Chicago	Transit AS 30088
40077:3000	New York	Transit AS 30088
40077:4000	Chicago	Ameritech NAP
40077:5000	DC area	MAE East

Having communities to indicate the source AS may seem redundant: customers could also use the Cisco regular expression ^40077_30088_ to determine which routes were learned from transit AS 30088 by AS 40077. But this doesn't tell them where this happened if you have multiple connections to this ISP. Also, it's often more convenient to use community filters rather than AS path filters. Example 11-5 shows a configuration example for setting these communities on the router connecting to AS 30088 and the NAP in Chicago.

Example 11-5. Setting the Local Preference and communities for inbound routes

```
!
router bgp 40077
 neighbor nap peer-group
 neighbor nap route-map nap-in in
 neighbor 169.254.30.8 remote-as 30088
 neighbor 169.254.30.8 route-map as30088-in in
!
route-map as30088-in permit 10
 set local-preference 80
 set community 40077:2000 additive
!
```

Example 11-5. Setting the Local Preference and communities for inbound routes (continued)

```
route-map nap-in permit 10
 set local-preference 85
 set community 40077:4000 additive
!
```

Because these route maps set the community and Local Preference for all routes received over a session, there is no need for a *match* clause. The *additive* keyword prevents existing communities received from the peer from being deleted.

Nobody likes to admit it, but most networks experience instability or congestion at some time. In these cases, you may want to add a community to the affected routes to inform your BGP customers of the situation. It may not be pleasant to have to tell your customers your network isn't running the way it should be, but this is nothing compared to the discomfort you'll experience when a customer demands an explanation of why you let her use "bad" routes rather than inform her about the problem (by setting a community), so she could reroute over her other ISP. In the case of congestion, it's also in your best interest to have multihomed customers reroute their traffic, because this frees up the circuit for other traffic. Example 11-6 lists the route maps used in Example 11-5, now modified to also attach the community 40077:2 to the incoming routes to indicate degradation of service.

Example 11-6. Setting a community to indicate degraded routes

```
!
route-map as30088-in permit 10
 set local-preference 80
 set community 40077:2 40077:2000 additive
!
route-map nap-in permit 10
 set local-preference 85
 set community 40077:2 40077:4000 additive
!
```

Don't forget to clear the BGP sessions to have the changes take effect. The easiest way to do this is by issuing the *clear ip bgp * out* command if your router and those of your peers support the route refresh capability. This way, the routes aren't first revoked before the new information is sent, so this doesn't count as a flap if routers in neighboring ASes or further upstream have flap-dampening enabled.

Community Overview In Routing Registry

It's customary to outline the use of communities in your network in the "remarks" part of your AUT-NUM object in the Routing Registry, so others can easily find this information when they need it. Example 11-7 shows such a remarks section.

Example 11-7. Remarks section of an AUT-NUM object

```
remarks: ----------------------------------------------------
remarks: abuse contact:        abuse@example
remarks: peering contact:      peering@example
remarks: operational issues:  noc@example
remarks: ----------------------------------------------------
remarks: communities sent to customers:
remarks:
remarks: 40077:2    route over degraded circuit
remarks: 40077:2000 transit routes from AS30088 in CHI
remarks: 40077:3000 transit routes from AS30088 in NYC
remarks: 40077:4000 peer routes from Chicago NAP
remarks: 40077:5000 peer routes from MAE East
remarks: ----------------------------------------------------
remarks: communities accepted from customers:
remarks:
remarks: 40077:13 set next hop to null interface
remarks:          (use to blackhole DoSed ip addresses)
remarks: 40077:70 set local preference to 70
remarks: 40077:80 set local preference to 80
remarks: 40077:85 set local preference to 85
remarks: 40077:90 set local preference to 90
remarks:
remarks: default local preference values:
remarks: customers: 100, peers: 85, transit: 80
remarks:
remarks: 40077:2001 prepend once to AS30088
remarks: 40077:2002 prepend twice to AS30088
remarks: 40077:2003 prepend three times to AS30088
remarks: 40077:2009 don't announce to AS30088
remarks: 40077:4001 prepend once to Chicago NAP peers
remarks: 40077:4002 prepend twice to Chicago NAP peers
remarks: 40077:4003 prepend three times to Chicago NAP peers
remarks: 40077:4009 don't announce to Chicago NAP peers
remarks: ----------------------------------------------------
```

Anti-DoS Measures

As an ISP, it's an important part of your job to assist customers as well as you can when they fall victim to denial-of-service attacks. There are two things you can do to anticipate attacks: provide your users with a community they can set to have traffic to certain addresses filtered out before it reaches them, and rate limiting of traffic types that are used often in attacks. In the end, though, it comes down to picking up the phone in the middle of the night when your customers need your assistance.

A Community for Black-Holing

If there is a DoS attack targeting a single address or a small number of addresses, a customer may choose to have all traffic for these addresses filtered out, rather than having their entire bandwidth saturated. As an ISP, you can enable them to have your network automatically discard all traffic for certain addresses by manipulating the next hop attribute. Example 11-8 expands the `customer-in` route map from Example 11-3 for this purpose.

Example 11-8. Filtering inbound routes from customers

```
!
ip route 192.0.255.13 255.255.255.255 Null0
ip community-list 13 permit 40077:13
!
route-map customer-in permit 10
 match community 13
 set ip next-hop 192.0.255.13
!
```

If the `customer-in permit 10` route map finds the community `40077:13` attached to a route, it sets the next hop address for this route to `192.0.255.13`. In itself, this address has no special meaning: it's just an address from one of the local PA blocks. But because it's routed to the null interface, all routes with this address as their next hop are effectively black-holed. By routing this address to the null interface on all routers in the network, you can make sure the attacking traffic is immediately dropped as soon as it enters the network, so it doesn't take up bandwidth in the internal network.

Preemptive Anti-DoS Measures

To lessen the impact of DoS attacks when they happen, and to avoid having to make configuration changes immediately, you can install permanent rate-limiting for typical DoS traffic. There can never be a "one size fits all" solution for this, however, because some customers may have more legitimate traffic falling within a DoS-like traffic category than others. For instance, a site doing mainly web hosting will have a significant number of SYN packets, and a customer involved in streaming audio or video (either sending or receiving) will have more UDP traffic than average. So you should ask your customers (in terms they can understand) if they have any specific traffic patterns and if they want anti-DoS rate-limiting. Also, don't try to be overly restrictive: limiting the DoS traffic to 25% of the available bandwidth or to 50% doesn't make a big difference in user experience, but in some cases, 25% may be dangerously close to the needs of legitimate traffic. When an attack happens, you can always adjust the rate limiting to better suit the circumstances.

Rate limiting doesn't use all that much CPU time, so for low-to-medium bandwidth customers, there shouldn't be much of a problem implementing it. Try to make the filters as general as possible, to keep the router configuration easy to understand and maintain. Example 11-9 defines three access lists that should cover most situations and applies them to several customers.

Example 11-9. Preemptive anti-DoS rate limiting

```
!
interface Serial0
 bandwidth 1544
 rate-limit output access-group 171 384000 8000 8000 conform-action transmit exceed-action
drop
!
interface Serial1
 !
 bandwidth 1544
 rate-limit output access-group 172 768000 8000 8000 conform-action transmit exceed-action
drop
!
interface Serial2
 bandwidth 128
 rate-limit output access-group 173 32000 8000 8000 conform-action transmit exceed-action
drop
!
access-list 171 remark match icmp for rate limit
access-list 171 permit icmp any any
!
access-list 172 remark match udp+icmp for rate limit
access-list 172 permit udp any any
access-list 172 permit icmp any any
!
access-list 173 remark match tcp/syn+udp+icmp for rate limit
access-list 173 deny    tcp any any established
access-list 173 permit tcp any any
access-list 173 permit udp any any
access-list 173 permit icmp any any
!
```

The first customer (Serial0) works a lot with streaming audio, so they want protection only against excessive ICMP messages. This is accomplished by rate-limiting traffic matched by access list 171 to 384 Kbps, a quarter of their bandwidth. The second customer does mostly web hosting, so they don't want to limit TCP SYNs, but incoming ICMP and UDP (access list 172) traffic is limited to 50% of the available bandwidth. The third customer has a 128-Kbps fractional T1 line, and they don't run any services, so they can safely have a limit on TCP SYNs, UDP, and ICMP of 25% of their bandwidth.

Customers who are a frequent target of DoS attacks may want to run BGP with a private AS number, even if they have only a single connection. This way, they can take advantage of black- hole communities to lessen the impact of the attacks.

Customers with Backup Connections

At some point, you may encounter customers who like your service so much that they want two connections to your network. In other words, they want to multi-home, but not to two different ISPs. This isn't as robust as "real" multihoming, but it saves the customer a lot of BGP-related complexity.

Simple Backups

If simplicity is key, the customer shouldn't run any routing protocols but should depend on the interface status to determine whether a connection is viable or not, simply by pointing two default routes to two interfaces. This works well for point-to-point circuits, because they use a keepalive mechanism. For Ethernet and ATM, it works only when there is a direct connection between the customer and ISP equipment routers, without any switches (or hubs) in between.

If you configure both connections to a customer the ordinary way, it depends on the IGP whether there is any load balancing and which connection receives most or all of the traffic. Sometimes this is good enough, but often customers have a high-bandwidth primary connection and a slower backup. In these cases, they'll want all traffic to flow over the primary connection and have the backup kick in only when the primary is offline. You can probably get this working by using a route map to adjust the IGP metrics, but this is a lot of work. A much simpler way is just to split the address blocks for the customer in half and route both halves to the primary connection, in addition to routing the "full" routes to both the primary and the backup. So the primary connection is configured like this:

```
!
ip route 192.0.2.0 255.255.255.0 Serial0
ip route 192.0.2.0 255.255.255.128 Serial0
ip route 192.0.2.128 255.255.255.128 Serial0
!
```

And on the router connecting the backup circuit, the static route is the same as for regular customers:

```
!
ip route 192.0.2.0 255.255.255.0 Serial3
!
```

Due to the longest-match-first rule, the more specific routes will always be preferred, regardless of the IGP metrics, and traffic will flow over the primary connection as long as it's available. Only with the primary connection down will the traffic start flowing over the backup.

More Complex Backups: BGP

If statically routed backups relying on the interface status for failover aren't enough, you need to run a routing protocol between your routers and those of the customer. You can use any routing protocol for this, but because of the slow convergence of RIP and the complexity of OSPF, it's usually best to do this with BGP.

The customer should use a private AS number from the 64512–65535 range for this. On the router connecting to the customer, you configure this exactly like any other customer BGP session; you just don't configure anything on the border routers. This way, the routes the customer announces are present in your own network, but they aren't sent to peer and transit networks because the outgoing AS path filter stops them. You may also want to configure a static route, so the customer is still reachable when there is a problem with BGP:

```
!
ip route 192.0.2.0 255.255.255.0 Serial3 250
!
```

Note the explicit administrative distance value of 250. Without it, the route has an administrative distance of 1, and the router ignores all BGP routes (with a distance of 20 or 200) for this prefix. With the distance value 250, the static route is a floating static and becomes active only when there are no BGP or OSPF routes to this destination.

Some ISPs have a dedicated "real" AS number for shared use between customers who want to run BGP but don't qualify for an AS number of their own. By default, a BGP router filters out any incoming routes with its own AS number in it, so these customers won't see each other's routes, but apart from this, there are no real problems in sharing an AS number.

Providing IPv6 and Multicast

It's hard to predict when IPv6 will become an important factor in production networks, but when this happens, your customers will be asking for it, so preparation is key. The traditional way to handle IPv6 is to create tunnels between "IPv6 islands" in the sea of the IPv4 Internet, but native IPv6 interconnects between networks are no longer a rarity. It's expected that the introduction of large numbers of IPv6-enabled mobile devices will generate a lot of momentum for IPv6 elsewhere on the Net: rather than having to sit behind a service provider's IPv6-to-IPv4 translator, content providers will likely want to interact directly with the mobile devices over IPv6. The decisions you need to think about are these:

IPv6 or no IPv6 in your network
> If you feel you won't be able to do a good job providing IPv6 services, you may want to decide against it altogether. Customers can always use tunnels to connect to the IPv6 backbone.

Native IPv6 or tunnels

If you have IPv6 in your network, you'll have to decide whether you want to run it on all (or most) of your routers. If customers connect to IPv4-only routers, they must use tunnels to one of your IPv6 routers for their IPv6 connectivity.

Running IPv6-to-IPv4 translators

Customers may ask you to do IPv6-to-IPv4 translation for them. If they need protocol-independent translation (which is pretty much the same as NAT), they (and you) are probably best off if they do this themselves. However, if you already run proxies for WWW and possibly other protocols, you may want to make those available over IPv6 too, so IPv6 users can use them to access IPv4 resources.

At the time of this writing, most IPv6 protocols have been finalized, and many vendors implement them, but the policies for address assignment and operational procedures are still in a state of flux. The web site of the 6bone, the global IPv6 testbed, has more information about this at *http://www.6bone.net*.

 All hosts automatically create "link local" addresses for themselves if IPv6 is enabled (these are the addresses starting with "FE80"). This means the host is reachable over IPv6 from all systems connected to the local subnet (such as an Ethernet), possibly allowing access to services that are firewalled or filtered in IPv4.

IPv6 Multihoming

Traditional IPv4-style multihoming is also possible in IPv6: just get an IPv6 address block and announce it over multiple ISPs using Multiprotocol BGP. But this may be hard or even impossible to do, because this breaks the very hierarchical IPv6 address allocation scheme. In other words, nobody wants people shooting holes in their IPv6 address blocks. The reasoning is that IPv4-style multihoming doesn't scale well because each multihomed network injects a route into the global routing table. To avoid this, there is work going on to find better ways to multihome in IPv6. One way to do it would be to take addresses from an ISP and have this ISP reroute traffic for those addresses over a second ISP when the direct link with the multihomed customer goes down. This is what RFC 3178, "IPv6 Multihoming Support at Site Exit Routers," proposes.

Having several addresses, some of which may be deprecated, is a basic IPv6 capability, so it's also possible to do multihoming at the host level. Ideally, higher-layer protocols (such as TCP) would jump from one address to another when outages occur, but so far this isn't possible.

Multicast

Most networks that participated in the MBone experimental multicast network now run "native" multicast, and the MBone as an experimental network using tunnels has as much as disappeared. If you want to engage in global multicast routing with your network, you must either connect to an ISP or Internet Exchange offering multicast service, or find a network willing to connect you over a tunnel.

CHAPTER 12

Interconnecting with Other Networks

When your network has a low traffic volume, it makes sense to pay one or more ISPs to handle traffic you exchange with all destinations on the Net. Because the amount of traffic you exchange with each individual destination network is very small, there is no point in arranging direct connections to these networks. But as your traffic volume grows, at some point the economy of interconnecting with other networks swings the other way. For networks with a high traffic volume, it doesn't make much sense to pay ISPs to handle all this traffic. Few ISPs differentiate between "cheap" traffic that can be delivered to another network locally or regionally, and "expensive" traffic that has to be carried over great distances. Handling the cheap traffic yourself will cost less than paying your ISP the average traffic costs over it. In addition, the economies of scale are a little peculiar for networking. At first, the cost per unit of traffic goes down as the amount of traffic goes up, but at some point, the cost per unit starts to go up again because the fastest routers and the fastest interfaces are more expensive than a combination of several midrange routers and slower interfaces with the same aggregate bandwidth. At some point, a larger number of direct connections will become more attractive than one or two big pipes to ISPs.

Peering

Although the word "peering" is used for different things, it's usually assumed in the Internet business to mean "exchanging traffic without money changing hands." In telco terms: settlement-free interconnection. In the telephony world, things are usually done differently. A common scenario is that the originating network of a long-distance call pays a per-minute fee to the next network in the path of the phone call. In many cases, the next network will be the network that terminates the call, but it's also possible for a call to traverse several networks. In this case, each network keeps some money for itself and pays the rest to the next network.

People with a telco background often use the term "sender keep all" for the settlement-free peering used in the Internet business: the sender of the traffic doesn't compensate the next network in line but keeps the entire sum. However, this doesn't adequately describe what happens when two IP networks peer. When someone calls someone else on the phone, the calling party pays, and the party being called doesn't. But in the IP world, both the source and destination parties pay: the usual pricing for ISP services is based on access speed, regardless of whether a connection is used for inbound traffic or outbound traffic. So the correct term would have to be "both sender and receiver keep their part."

Internet Exchanges, NAPs, and MAEs

There are basically two ways to interconnect (peer) with other networks: using a direct connection or through an Internet Exchange, Network Access Point, or Metropolitan Area Exchange (MAE). IXes, NAPs, and MAEs all boil down to the same thing: a single location or a small number of locations where ISPs can connect a router to a switched network in order to exchange traffic with all other connected parties.

Peering over a direct connection is straightforward: it's exactly the same as connecting to an ISP for transit. Because both parties announce only local and customer routes, however, the only traffic flowing over the peering link is between the two networks and/or their customers. Traffic volume to a single peer is usually not enough to justify the cost of a telco circuit for small to medium-sized networks, but networks of this size may want to peer over a direct connection if they both happen to be present in the same building. In that case, the costs of the connection are limited to a spare router or switch port and some length of cable. The rest of this chapter will deal with peering over an IX.

Connecting to an Internet Exchange

Connecting to an IX is often a daunting task. Apart from the technical intricacies, which can be complex enough, especially when the exchange uses ATM or another virtual circuit-oriented technology, you must also manage the business and political aspects of peering with other networks.

 IXes often limit membership to ISPs or closely related businesses.

The Business of Peering

It's a good idea to have a reasonable number of peering agreements in order before you connect to an IX. If you don't, you may later find yourself in the situation where you have spent a great deal of money to connect to an IX, but you are unable to exchange much traffic there.

Even if connecting to an IX doesn't immediately save you money every month, there are two possible reasons to do it anyway. If you are about to hit a major threshold in router or interface speed, getting an additional connection at the speeds you're currently using can be cheaper than upgrading to faster equipment. For instance, if you have two 45 Mbps T3 connections to two ISPs, you may want to get a T3 connection to an IX rather than upgrading to SONET OC-3 speeds. The other possible reason is that your ISP connection may be limited to a speed relatively close to your average bandwidth requirements, while an IX connection can be much faster without costs increasing accordingly. For instance, if your average traffic is 10 Mbps, you probably have 12 Mbps or so worth of bandwidth to your ISP(s). Getting more would mean paying all the time for bandwidth you need only a few times a month. However, when you connect to an IX, extra speed is relatively cheap, because there are no bandwidth charges.

To make sure connecting to an IX makes sense from a business point of view, you have to look at the traffic volume towards your intended peering partners. Saving a few hundred kilobits worth of traffic on your existing ISP connections won't let you downgrade those connections and save enough money to pay the costs of connecting to the IX. To see if it makes sense to connect to an IX business-wise, you should:

1. Get a good idea of where most of your traffic goes to or comes from. Make a list of all networks that are the source or destination of 3% or more of your traffic. Look only at outgoing traffic destinations if most of your traffic is outgoing; look at the sources of inbound traffic if most of your traffic is incoming.

2. Get quotes for the equipment, leased line, IX connection, and housing/co-location costs, and determine the total monthly costs of connecting to the IX.

3. Determine how much traffic you need to reroute over the IX to be able to downgrade (or not upgrade) the connections to your ISPs to save the amount of money that connecting to the IX will cost.

4. See whether the high-traffic networks on your list connect to the exchange and whether the traffic volume to or from these networks matches the needs of Step 3. If the traffic you can exchange with these networks over the IX (assuming they'll peer with you) is less than what you need to save on your regular connections, connecting to the IX will be more expensive than having your ISPs handle the traffic.

5. Contact the networks on the list and ask if they'll peer with you at the IX of your choice. Remove all the networks that don't want to peer from the list and repeat Step 4.

When you have repeated Step 4 for all potential peering partners, you'll know how much money connecting to the IX will cost or save you each month. Figure 12-1 shows a graph of the average per-megabit bandwidth cost for a transit-only and a transit + IX setup with an increasing number of peers.

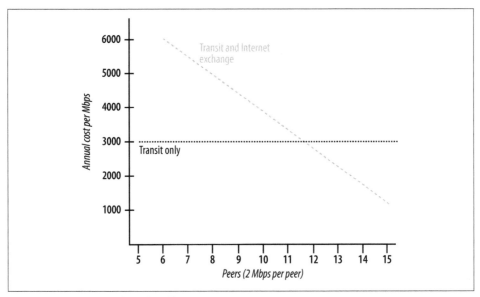

Figure 12-1. Cost per Mbps of traffic over an IX

The monthly cost of transit is assumed to be $250 per Mbps, the monthly costs for connecting to the exchange, $3,000. The picture clearly shows that connecting to an Internet Exchange is attractive only when you can exchange a lot of traffic there.

Where Does the Traffic Go?

Getting good traffic statistics can be hard, but it's essential if you want to know in advance how much traffic you can route over an IX. There are products that create traffic statistics, such as Cisco's Netflow. With such a tool, you'll probably still need to do some additional processing to be able to see the traffic for an entire AS or group of ASes.

The most accurate way to measure the traffic volume is to set up a tunnel to the network in question, create a BGP session, and gather statistics from the tunnel interface. Obviously, you'll need the cooperation of the network in question for this. You can also gather some example traffic using a tool such as *tcpdump* (be sure to do this over a long enough period of time so a single download doesn't skew the results), and write a script to total the traffic per source or destination AS.

Another approach is to incorporate explicit permit lines for the traffic to and from a certain network in the antispoofing access lists on the interfaces that connect to your ISPs. You can then use the *show access-list* command to see how many packets were matched by the lines for the target network and how much for the rest of the Internet (the last *permit* line). These must be extended access lists; standard access lists don't gather statistics. Example 12-1 shows the IP address ranges advertised by a network.

Example 12-1. IP address ranges for an AS

```
BR2#show ip bgp regexp _34_
BGP table version is 706608, local router ID is 192.0.2.66
Status codes: s suppressed, d damped, h history, * valid, > best, i - internal
Origin codes: i - IGP, e - EGP, ? - incomplete
  Network        Next Hop    Metric LocPrf Weight Path
* 48.5.96.0/20  219.2.19.1      25            0 50066 34 8 i
* 48.73.12.0/20 219.2.19.1      25            0 50066 34 i
* 218.8.0.0/16  219.2.19.1      25            0 50066 34 i
```

Example 12-2 shows the corresponding access lists after some traffic has passed through them.

Example 12-2. Antispoofing access lists with explicit permits

```
BR2#show access-lists
Extended IP access list 101
    deny ip 192.0.2.0 0.0.0.255 any
    deny icmp any any redirect
    permit ip 48.5.96.0 0.0.15.255 192.0.2.0 0.0.0.255 (7388 matches)
    permit ip 48.73.0.0 0.0.15.255 192.0.2.0 0.0.0.255 (830 matches)
    permit ip 218.8.0.0 0.0.255.255 192.0.2.0 0.0.0.255 (11334 matches)
    permit ip any 192.0.2.0 0.0.0.255 (298184 matches)
    deny ip any any
Extended IP access list 102
    permit ip 192.0.2.0 0.0.0.255 48.5.96.0 0.0.15.255 (8930 matches)
    permit ip 192.0.2.0 0.0.0.255 48.73.0.0 0.0.15.255 (783 matches)
    permit ip 192.0.2.0 0.0.0.255 218.8.0.0 0.0.255.255 (13368 matches)
    permit ip 192.0.2.0 0.0.0.255 any (353671 matches)
    deny ip any any (6 matches)
```

The total number of packets matched by access list 101 (inbound traffic) is 317,736 packets, of which 19,552 (6%) were from AS 34 or its customer AS 8. Access list 102 (outbound traffic) matched 376,752 packets, of which 23,081 (also 6%) were for AS 34. It's reasonable to assume that AS 34 doesn't use a different average packet size from other traffic, so if 6% of the packets are to and from AS 34, this network is responsible for about 6% of the traffic volume. However, it's impossible to see if most of the traffic volume is to or from AS 34; the number of packets in both directions is usually similar for TCP traffic. But packets in one direction carry the actual data; packets in the other direction are acknowledgments, so the volume in Mbps will usually be very different.

The Politics of Peering

When you approach other networks with a peering request, you will soon notice that not everyone wants to peer with you. Don't take it personally: this is politics. The two most common reasons why other networks refuse to peer are:

- Your network is so small that it just isn't worth the trouble to set up a peering session with you. This is especially likely to happen if your intended peering partner already peers with one of your ISPs and/or is very large.

- The other network sells transit service, and they feel they would be giving away free service by peering with you. This is likely when the other network spans a large geographic area and is connected to several IXes, while you connect to just one. In this scenario, they would bear the costs of transporting the traffic over large distances.

Some networks have their peering policies set in stone. Trying to get them to peer when you don't meet the criteria listed in the policy is like trying to teach a pig to sing: it wastes your time and annoys the pig. (Referring to intended peering partners as "pigs" doesn't help, either.) There are some things you can do that may help:

- Know your stuff and be professional. If your prospective peering partner gets the idea you know exactly what you're doing and won't waste their time, you've won half the battle.

- If peering with a certain network isn't essential for your decision to connect to the IX, revisit the issue once you're connected. Configuring the router and being done with it is a more attractive proposition than promising to peer with a newbie network that may or may not connect at some point in the future.

- Be visible. Hosting something on your network that people know and recognize will put you on the map. This can be an interesting (for your target audience) FTP archive or web site, or the webcast or connectivity for an event.

- Make sure you have a 24×7 NOC, or at least the outward appearance of a 24×7 NOC. If the other party feels they can easily reach you when there is a problem, they will be more inclined to peer.

- Try to get a customer of the network you want to peer with on your side. Having a customer ask why their traffic to you has to take a detour is more likely to show up on their radar screen than one of the many peering requests from networks trying to save a few bucks—especially when the customer conveniently happens to know that a direct peering session is possible at the IX where both of your networks are present and that this will mean a large speed increase. (Hinting at a bandwidth upgrade may be required, bringing in more money for their ISP.)

- Remember: this is politics. Schmoozing helps, so attend meetings and trade shows, participate on mailing lists, and so forth.

Multilateral Peering

On large exchange points where many networks interconnect, setting up peering sessions with other networks can get time-consuming. To get around this, some IXes have a Multi-Lateral Peering Agreement (MPLA) in place. With an MPLA, everyone who is part of the MPLA sets up a BGP session to a route server operated by the MPLA organization. Then the route server distributes all the routes it learns to all MPLA members. Because all the routers share a common IP subnet (the IX subnet), the BGP next hop attribute points to the router the MPLA route server learned the route from and not to the route server itself. So even though the routing information passes through the route server, the traffic is delivered directly to the right peer's router. Multilateral peering has the advantage of simplifying the peering process, but there is also a major drawback: it's impossible to prevent having to peer with a certain network unless you can get the appropriate filters set on the route server. In most cases, MPLA peering is all or nothing. This means that larger players aren't interested in joining MPLAs. The Routing Arbiter project was intended to provide the NAPs with route servers and apply the policies in a Routing Registry to overcome this limitation.

There is nothing to prevent you from joining an MPLA and then setting up bilateral peering agreements (and thus direct BGP connections) to the networks present at the IX that aren't part of the MPLA. Not every IX has an MPLA, either because of lack of interest among the IX member networks, or because the IX policy enforces use of the *next-hop-self* command, which makes multilateral peering much more difficult.

Connecting to the Exchange

The individual steps in the process of connecting to an IX aren't difficult. But because you have to deal with many different organizations (the IX, the housing location, the telco, peering partners) and many things influence each other, it's easy to lose track of the big picture. The solution is simple: make sure you know what you want to do before you start doing it. It also helps to do everything in the right order:

1. Make sure essential peerings are arranged. Many networks don't require a signed peering contract, and when peering with many small networks, this isn't a problem. On the other hand, for peerings that make or break your business case for connecting to the exchange, it's a good idea to have a signed contract.

2. Determine the bandwidth you need for the IX connection and the telco connection from your router at the IX back to your network.

3. If you don't have an AS number and IP addresses of your own, get them now.

4. Get quotes for housing your router at each IX location (if there is more than one) and for telco circuits to each location.

5. Select a housing location and telco.

6. Sign the necessary agreements and contracts with the IX organization, the housing facility (if different from the IX organization), and the telco.

7. Get an IP address in the IX subnet (and PVC numbers, if necessary).

8. Get a router, configure it, and install it.

9. Configure a few BGP sessions to networks that don't mind helping you out a bit with things like sending back their view of your network. Test that everything works as it should.

10. Approach additional potential peering partners. Once you're connected, you'll also want to peer with networks you didn't approach before, because they were too small to factor into the decision to connect to the exchange.

11. Configure BGP sessions to the rest of your peers.

It's considered good form to inform your peering partners before performing any actions that may disrupt the flow of routing information or traffic over the peering connection. It's a good idea to keep an up-to-date list of operational (NOC) contact email addresses for this purpose, unless the IX has a mailing list for this. However, peers aren't customers: if the peering connection is down, traffic flows over an alternate path, so the impact is small and there is no need to announce maintenance weeks in advance. A message one or two days in advance won't be forgotten by the time you perform your maintenance. And when an unexpected situation arises, you can suffice with sending a message saying, "We have problems" and a later one, "We're up and running again," or even just the last one. Continuous, detailed status updates aren't necessary, unless the amount of traffic your partners exchange with you is a significant portion of their total traffic.

Connecting to More Exchange Points

Peering with the same network in more than one location introduces additional complexity: where do you deliver the traffic to your peer? The most often used solution is to deliver the traffic to the peer as soon as you can. This is called "early exit" or "hot potato" routing. This method has several advantages:

- No configuration necessary: BGP will do this automatically.
- Cost-effective: the peer has to transport the traffic most of the way.
- Traffic will most likely follow the shortest geographical path.

Figure 12-2 shows how early exit routing is successful in keeping regional traffic within the region.

The disadvantages of early exit routing are:

- Asymmetric routing: packets from you to the other network travel most of the way over your peer's network, and packets in the other direction travel most of the way over your network, so leased lines are mostly used in one direction.

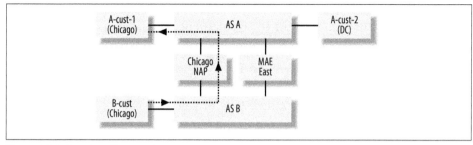

Figure 12-2. Local traffic in early exit routing

- The burden of transporting packets over great distances falls on the network that receives the traffic.
- Detours are possible when the closest exchange is in the wrong direction. For instance, a packet originating in Denver might be transported to the West Coast because the PacBell NAP is closer (in network terms) than the Chicago NAP, even though the destination of the packet is the East Coast.

Figure 12-3 shows how early exit routing causes traffic flows to take asymmetric routes when the source and destination are close to different IXes.

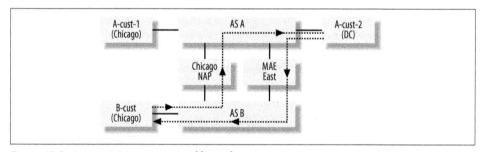

Figure 12-3. Asymmetric routing caused by early exit

Early exit is used more often, because despite the disadvantages, it's the only way to use several interconnects between networks in a way that is straightforward to configure. But if one exchange point is highly preferable over another, you might want to set the Local Preference for routes learned over the "better" exchange point higher so outgoing traffic will flow over this one by default. The traffic will then flow over the other exchange point only if routes over the better one aren't available, either because of a temporary problem or because another network isn't present there. Incoming traffic is unaffected. Figure 12-4 shows how preferring a distant exchange point causes longer physical paths.

Some networks try to influence inbound traffic flows by announcing more specific routes with different properties at different exchange points, usually routes to customers close to the region of the exchange point. Traffic within the exchange point region itself should already take the shortest path if early exit routing is used, so this

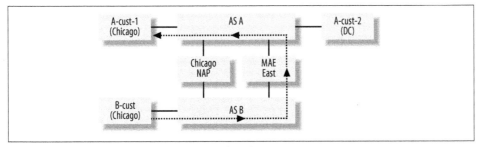

Figure 12-4. Traffic flowing over a remote preferred IX

technique is relevant mostly for traffic to locations not served by an IX and for networks that want to use "best exit" or "longest exit" routing (source network carries the packet most of the way). The main reason for not wanting to use early exit is that it favors networks with a lot of outgoing traffic. For instance, a large web hosting business with massive amounts of outgoing traffic but no incoming traffic to speak of could get a big pipe to the closest IX and connect to the other main IXes using cheap, low-bandwidth connections. Using the early exit strategy, they are able to offload their outgoing traffic at the exchange point of their choice and have to transport only the initial HTTP requests, TCP acknowledgments, and the occasional incoming email message from IXes far away. This is the reason many large backbone networks want to peer with others only if the amounts of incoming and outgoing traffic are more or less equal.

Rejecting Unwanted Traffic

When attackers try to flood a network with huge amounts of traffic to disrupt it (a DoS attack), they tend to use falsified addresses. This makes it harder to find where the abusive traffic is coming from, as well as making it impossible to create effective filters. To make sure you won't receive packets with falsified source addresses, you can create a filter for each peer and allow only packets with legitimate source addresses. This filter will look a lot like a combination of all prefix filters used to filter the IP address announcements from all the peers you connect to over your IX connection. Alternatively, you can make the router check the source IP addresses of incoming packets against the routing table using the *unicast reverse path forwarding* (RPF) feature. When configured, an RPF check is done for each incoming packet. If the interface the packet was received on is the same as the interface the router uses to transmit packets directed to the address listed as the packet's source, the packet is allowed through. If the check fails, the packet is dropped. Example 12-3 enables the unicast RPF check for the Ethernet0 interface.

Example 12-3. Enabling the unicast RPF check for an interface

```
!
ip cef
!
```

Example 12-3. Enabling the unicast RPF check for an interface (continued)

```
interface Ethernet0
 ip verify unicast reverse-path
 no ip route-cache cef
!
```

The *ip cef* command enables Cisco Express Forwarding (CEF). Unicast RPF employs the Forwarding Information Base (FIB) created by CEF. It's not actually necessary to use CEF on the interface performing unicast RPF. In this example, CEF is disabled for the interface, so the router reverts to regular fast switching. Unicast RPF is an interface-wide feature and can't be configured for individual BGP peers.

 Unicast RPF should be enabled only on interfaces that connect to peer and customer networks. Traffic patterns over the internal network and to and from transit ISPs are often asymmetric, so the RPF check will fail even though the traffic is perfectly legitimate.

If you configure unicast RPF on a router interface connecting to an exchange point, you should make sure the router will always prefer to send packets over the exchange if there is a route over the exchange. In the situation outlined back in Figure 12-4, the Chicago NAP router in network B probably prefers the path over MAE East, just like other routers in the network. But when network A sends a packet over the Chicago NAP to network B, the RPF check fails, and the packet is dropped: the route to network A points to a MAE East router. The BGP table also contains a route to network A over the NAP, but the routing table, which is what unicast RPF looks at, doesn't. So if unicast RPF is to be used in such a setup, the border router at the Chicago NAP should be configured to prefer the path to A over the NAP, rather than over MAE East. Other routers in the B network may still prefer the path over MAE East. The easiest way to do this is with Cisco's proprietary weight attribute, as is done in Example 12-4.

Example 12-4. Configuring unicast RPF and the weight attribute

```
!
interface FastEthernet0
 ip address 193.148.15.32 255.255.255.0
 ip verify unicast reverse-path
 no ip directed-broadcast
 full-duplex
 no cdp enable
!
router bgp 40077
 no synchronization
 bgp always-compare-med
 bgp log-neighbor-changes
 timers bgp 5 15
 neighbor amsix peer-group
 neighbor amsix weight 10
```

Example 12-4. Configuring unicast RPF and the weight attribute (continued)

```
 neighbor amsix route-map setlp83 in
 !
route-map setlp83 permit 10
 set local-preference 83
 !
```

All routes learned over the exchange will now have a weight of 10 and a Local Preference of 83. Thus, these routes are preferred over all others with the default weight of 0, even if these other routes have the regular Local Preference for peers of 85 or an even higher Local Preference. Figure 12-5 shows the Local Preference (LP), weight (W) and next hop (NH) information for a route learned over two IXes (X and Y).

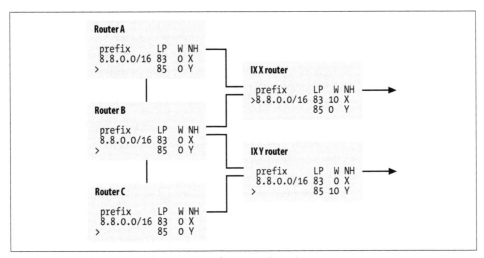

Figure 12-5. Preferences based on Local Preference and weight

Because the route gets a higher Local Preference when it enters the network at exchange point Y, all routers except the router at exchange point X prefer this route. Router X bases its decision on the higher weight value that is local to the router. So it's now safe to enable the unicast RPF check.

Using unicast RPF on an interface connecting to an IX also makes it impossible for others to (successfully) direct traffic to your router if they don't peer. In the past, rogue networks have been known to point a default route towards another network's IX router to get free transit service for outgoing traffic. If you don't peer with the network in question, the RPF check will fail, so the other network will be unable to abuse your network in this way. Traffic from peers pointing a default to your router will pass the RPF check, but this traffic can easily be stopped by an input filter on the interface connecting to the IX switch that just allows packets with your network as their destination.

If you subject peering traffic to the unicast RPF check, make sure your peers know this. A peer may have reasons (good or otherwise) to send you traffic for which they don't announce a route with the return path, making the RPF check fail.

IX Subnet Problems

If you connect to an IX, there will be many routes with a next hop address inside the exchange subnet in your network. In order for these routes to work, the subnet used on the exchange must be present in your IGP or in iBGP. However, often these ranges are individual Class C networks that don't fall within a larger block. Thus it's relatively common to see these subnets show up in the global routing table. That's not good: this way, routers receiving this subnet over eBGP will install the eBGP route in their routing table, because the administrative distance for eBGP is lower than the distance for IGPs or iBGP. So now all peering traffic is routed over a transit link by this router. Fortunately, this problem is limited to routers receiving the exchange subnet over eBGP, because elsewhere in the network, the route receives the much higher administrative distance for iBGP routes.

There is much debate over whether the IX subnet should be visible in the global routing table at all, but the reality is that it happens, so you must be prepared. There is no elegant solution to this problem, so you'll have to use a less elegant one, such as configuring all iBGP sessions from exchange routers to the rest of the network with *next-hop-self* or filter out announcements for the subnets of IXes you connect to on all eBGP sessions.

Talking to Other Network Operators

It can be extremely useful to talk to people doing the same work in other organizations. A good way to do this is to subscribe to the North American Network Operators (NANOG) mailing list. This mailing list is intended for operational discussions, and there are many of those. For instance, when there is a telco outage, the NANOG list is usually the first place this information shows up. The list is also extremely useful in finding the right contact for other organizations if traditional methods fail. There are also a lot of off-topic discussions that can get pretty heated, so have a look at the archives to see if this is a place you want to hang out. Several times a year, there are NANOG meetings at which everyone can meet face to face, and there are always interesting presentations. In Europe, RIPE meetings perform the same function. See *http://www.nanog.org* and *http://www.ripe.net/ripe/meetings/index.html* for more information.

Exchange Point Future

In the early 1990s, many people believed IXes would be a short-lived phenomenon because, in the future, networks would interconnect over broadband-ISDN (which isn't the same thing as ATM, but they are related). Obviously, this hasn't happened. Right now, the fastest ways to transport IP packets are Packet over SONET (POSIP) and 10 Gigabit Ethernet. It seems unlikely that broadband-ISDN/ATM will surpass POSIP and Ethernet developments, but it's certainly possible that other technologies will fill the gap.

For instance, the fact that 10 Gigabit Ethernet has a WAN PHY that uses SONET framing makes it easy for telcos to offer Ethernet long-distance service. This may not be immediately obvious to them, because Ethernet lacks the sophisticated QoS features of ATM, and traditional billing methods are unusable. But as soon as they realize that providing the extra bandwidth that makes congestion impossible is cheaper than engineering elusive QoS guarantees, and that the billing problem is solved by using a flat fee or (possibly per-destination) traffic volume charge, it's likely that telco Ethernet services will start to emerge. Then there is Dense Wavelength Division Multiplexing (DWDM). By using a different laser light wavelength (frequency or color) for each communication stream, it's possible to multiplex many streams over a single fiber pair. It's entirely possible that a "switched wavelength" service will be developed, allowing the subscriber to create multigigabit communication sessions to remote destinations the same way that ISDN service allows us to create 56- or 64-Kbps sessions today.

These possible developments, coupled with the private interconnect trend among the larger network, suggests IXes will not be around forever. Still, the developments over the past decade or so have taught us that older technologies keep being used long after new ones have been deployed. Also, when several networks are present within a building or a group of buildings close together, it makes sense to interconnect these using cheap LAN technology. Thus, even if IXes dwindle in the future, it's likely this will mostly be a problem for exchanges in which ISPs can only interconnect and not house any additional equipment. It seems unlikely that there will no longer be any need for full-fledged "carrier hotels" where networks can colocate servers and dial-up, DSL, and leased-line equipment. On the contrary, as the power and cooling requirements of both hosts and network equipment continue to increase, specialized facilities to house them are becoming more of a necessity. This means that facilities that combine an IX with colocation services are in the best position to survive a possible IX shakeout.

Cisco Configuration Basics

To configure a Cisco router, you must first be able to talk to it. Out of the box, the router doesn't have any IP addresses yet, so the only way to access it is over the console port. On some models, the console port is an RJ-48 connector (identical to that of an UTP Ethernet port), on others, a 25-pin RS-232c connector. Use the supplied cable and connectors to connect the console port of the router to a terminal or a computer running a terminal emulation program. The terminal emulation program doesn't have to be anything fancy; something like the Hyperterminal program that comes with many versions of Windows is good enough. The communication settings should be 9600 bps, 8 bits, no parity, no flow control, and full duplex/no local echo.

When you turn on the router, there should pretty much immediately be a message on the screen. If the message doesn't appear, your cable probably needs to be "null-modemed," or your communication settings are wrong. The router needs a minute or so to boot, and then it will ask you if you want to execute the initial setup dialog. Say "no." Doing the initial configuration manually is easier and faster. The router should now display a prompt:

```
Router>
```

This is your cue to type "enable" to enable privileged mode, so you are allowed to perform configuration changes. This is something you'll be doing a lot from now on.

```
Router>enable
Router#
```

Normally, the router will ask for the enable password, but since the configuration is empty, you can enter enable mode without a password. The # prompt indicates you are in privileged (enable) mode. If the prompt ends with >, you aren't allowed to view the configuration or execute any commands that influence the behavior of the router, but you can still examine what the router is doing in much detail.

In this book, example configurations are presented with an exclamation mark as the first and last lines. This is also how configuration commands show up in the configuration file. For instance, this configuration example sets a new system name for the router:

```
!
hostname BR1
!
```

You must enter these configuration samples by first entering configuration mode using the *configure terminal* command. After this, the prompt changes to indicate you are now in configuration mode. Then, you can enter the configuration commands as shown in the example, leaving the exclamation marks out if you want, and finally type Ctrl-Z (^Z) to leave configuration mode. Entering the previous example looks like this:

```
Router#configure terminal
Enter configuration commands, one per line.  End with CNTL/Z.
Router(config)#hostname BR1
BR1(config)#^Z
BR1#
%SYS-5-CONFIG_I: Configured from console
```

As you can see, when you entered the *hostname BR1* command, the router immediately executed it: you aren't editing a configuration file but working directly on the active configuration itself. This is very important to remember.

The line that gets printed to the screen a moment after you leave configuration mode is a log message. By default, the router logs all kinds of information (such as the fact that someone changed the configuration) to the console.

The first thing the router needs, apart from a hostname, is an IP address. To set one, you must first enter the interface subconfiguration mode:

```
BR1#conf t
Enter configuration commands, one per line.  End with CNTL/Z.
BR1(config)#interface Ethernet0
BR1(config-if)# ip address 192.0.2.65 255.255.255.192
BR1(config-if)#
```

Rather than type the entire command, you can enter just enough letters so the router knows which command you want to execute; *conf t* is short for *configure terminal*. Notice that the prompt changes again after entering the *interface ...* command: first it was just BR1#, then BR1(config)# to indicate the router is ready for configuration commands, and then BR1(config-if)# to indicate the router expects commands to configure a specific interface. There are several other subconfiguration modes. They are indicated in the configuration file by a space before the commands, like the one in front of the *ip address ...* command in this example:

```
!
interface Ethernet0
 ip address 192.0.2.65 255.255.255.192
!
```

This sets the IP address for the Ethernet0 interface to 192.0.2.65 with a netmask of 255.255.255.192. Obviously, you should substitute something appropriate within your network. After entering these configuration commands, the router has an IP address. You can now test connectivity with the *ping* command. *ping* isn't a configuration command, so you can execute it without entering configuration mode:

```
BR1#ping 192.0.2.93
Type escape sequence to abort.
Sending 5, 100-byte ICMP Echos to 192.0.2.93, timeout is 2 seconds:
.!!!!
Success rate is 80 percent (4/5), round-trip min/avg/max = 1/3/4 ms
BR1#
```

The router doesn't yet have an ARP entry for IP address 192.0.2.93, so the first ping packet is lost, as indicated by the . character. But the remaining ping requests are answered and result in a ! character.

If you configure the router with passwords, you can disconnect the console cable and use the Telnet protocol to connect to the router. You need to configure three types of passwords, and optionally a fourth:

- The enable secret is the password the router asks for when you want to enter privileged mode. The enable password is encrypted using a strong, irreversible encryption algorithm in the configuration file, so don't forget it. If you do, you'll have to go through a complex password-recovery procedure before you can set a new one.

- The enable password has the same function as the enable secret, but it's used when the router runs very old software (such as the software in the boot ROMs of older routers) that can't perform the enable secret encryption. If you don't set either an enable secret or an enable password, anyone with command-line access to the router can enter enable mode.

- The vty password authenticates Telnet access. If you don't set a password or another authentication mechanism, incoming Telnet sessions will be denied. The vty passwords are encrypted in the configuration, but the encryption algorithm used for this is weak and easily broken.

- The console password. By default, the console doesn't need a password, but you can set one if you want.

The following configuration sets the first three types of password and limits access to the router over the network to just telnet from IP addresses within the 192.0.2.0 Class C net:

```
!
enable secret leavemyrouteralone
enable password cisco
!
access-list 99 permit 192.0.2.0 0.0.0.255
!
```

```
line vty 0 4
 access-class 99 in
 password leavemytelnetalone
 transport input telnet
 !
```

You can now use Telnet to access the router:

```
$ telnet 192.0.2.65
Trying 192.0.2.65...
Connected to 192.0.2.65.
Escape character is '^]'.

User Access Verification

Password:
BR1>enable
Password:
BR1#
```

Use *copy running-config startup-config* to save the current configuration in the router's nonvolatile RAM. This saves you from doing the whole thing again when the router loses power or reboots. You can display both configurations onscreen by using the *show running-conf[i]gation* and *show startup-conf[i]gation* commands. Note that every command has its own place in the configuration file; the order in which you type them is irrelevant for most commands. (There are exceptions to this.)

 If you can't remember the exact command or option you want to enter, type ? at any time, and the router will show you what's available in the current context.

IP Configuration Essentials

Example A-1 shows the relevant parts of a simple non-BGP Cisco router configuration. Settings necessary for managing the router, such as passwords, have been omitted.

Example A-1. Most important parts of a non-BGP Cisco configuration

```
!
version 12.0
!
hostname BR1
!
ip subnet-zero
no ip source-route
!
interface Ethernet0
 ip address 192.0.2.65 255.255.255.192
 no ip directed-broadcast
!
```

Example A-1. Most important parts of a non-BGP Cisco configuration (continued)

```
interface Serial0
 description ISP A
 encapsulation ppp
 ip unnumbered Ethernet0
 ip access-group 101 in
 ip access-group 102 out
 no ip directed-broadcast
!
ip classless
ip route 0.0.0.0 0.0.0.0 Serial0
!
access-list 101 deny    ip 192.0.2.0 0.0.0.255 any
access-list 101 deny    icmp any any redirect
access-list 101 permit ip any 192.0.2.0 0.0.0.255
access-list 101 deny    ip any any
access-list 102 permit ip 192.0.2.0 0.0.0.255 any
access-list 102 deny    ip any any
no cdp run
!
```

Even though this book isn't about router configuration in general, there are some network security settings that are too important to ignore here. All border routers (routers that connect to outside networks) must protect the network itself against attacks and abuse, even if the hosts on it are well-firewalled.

Source Routing and Directed Broadcasts

The *no ip source-route* command disables source routing. The IP source route option is a potential security risk, because the sender of a source routed packet gets to select the route the packet takes, possibly bypassing firewalls. Because source routing isn't generally used on the Internet, there is no harm in disabling it on the router. When it's disabled, all packets with the source route option set are dropped (thrown away). The *no ip directed-broadcast* command prevents packets that a remote host sends to the network or subnet broadcast address from being turned into broadcasts by the router. For the 192.0.2.64/26 network, the broadcast address is 192.0.2.127; this is the address with all the bits in the host part set to one. When the router receives a packet directed to such an address, it turns a regular packet into a broadcast. This behavior can be exploited to launch so called "Smurf" attacks, so unless there are legitimate applications on the network that use directed broadcasts (which is rare), this feature has to be disabled. This must be done on every interface of every router, because border routers can't always determine which packets are potential broadcasts and which aren't.

Another unnecessary service is the Cisco Discovery Protocol. It detects the presence of different types of equipment built by Cisco on the network. This is usually not desirable on connections to other networks, so it's best to disable the protocol using *no cdp run.*

Antispoofing Filters

The *ip access-group* commands enable incoming and outgoing filters on interface Serial0. Access list 101 is an incoming filter against address-spoofing that keeps packets with obviously falsified header information out. First, it filters out any incoming packets that claim to have a local source address, something that can't possibly be correct, with the following line:

```
access-list 101 deny    ip 192.0.2.0 0.0.0.255 any
```

The action of this line is to deny (filter out) packets. The *ip* keyword matches IP packets of all kinds (TCP, UDP, ICMP and some more esoteric protocols that run over IP). 192.0.2.0 is the first address of the range of source addresses that will match, and 0.0.0.255, the wildcard bitmask that determines the size of the range. The end of the range is 192.0.2.0 OR 0.0.0.255, which equals 192.0.2.255. (See Appendix B for an explanation of the binary math involved.) The final *any* keyword makes sure the line matches all destination addresses.

All ICMP redirect messages are dropped, because these messages (that tell a host that another router has a better path to a certain destination) should only be generated by routers on the local subnet:

```
access-list 101 deny    icmp any any redirect
```

This line matches ICMP packets without looking at either the source or destination addresses, but the ICMP type must be "redirect." After that, all packets to local destinations are allowed through:

```
access-list 101 permit ip any 192.0.2.0 0.0.0.255
```

This line permits any type of IP packets to be forwarded by the router regardless of the source address (packets with falsified source addresses have already been caught by the first line of this access list) if they have an address in the 192.0.2.0–192.0.2.255 range as their destination.

The final line in access list 101 throws away all IP packets with all source and destination addresses that haven't matched any of the earlier lines:

```
access-list 101 deny    ip any any
```

Access list 102 allows only packets with local source addresses to leave the network. This makes it impossible to launch untraceable DoS attacks from local hosts, making the network less appealing to intruders.

CIDR and VLSM

The *ip subnet-zero* and *ip classless* commands are a necessary part of every Cisco IP configuration. Without them, the router reverts to early 1990s pre-VLSM and pre-CIDR behavior. More specifically, without *ip subnet-zero*, the router will complain if you try to use the first subnet, the one that has all zeros in the subnet bits of the address. Without *ip classless* it's not possible to have a route for just part of a classful network: there must always be routes that cover the full classful network. The *version* command at the beginning of the configuration is added by the router for informational purposes; it doesn't have any effect.

A few final tips:

- List a DNS server in the router configuration using the *ip name-server <address>* command; this will make your life a lot easier.
- When editing a filter (access list, prefix list, or route map), the easy way to do it is to edit the filter in a text editor, then issue the *no access-list <number>* command and paste the new access list in the Telnet window.
- When editing a filter, the right way to do it is first to create the new filter under a new name or number and then change all references from the old to the new name or number. This way, there is never a time during which the filter isn't active.
- If you want to see a specific part of the configuration, such as the BGP-related part, use *show running-config | begin bgp*, and the router will skip directly to the first occurrence of the indicated keyword. (This isn't available yet in IOS Version 12.0.)
- You can interrupt any running commands and return to the router's prompt by typing the escape sequence Ctrl-^ (Control-Shift-6).

For more information on Cisco IOS and security for Cisco routers, see the books *Cisco IOS in a Nutshell* by James Boney and *Hardening Cisco Routers* by Thomas Akin, both published by O'Reilly.

APPENDIX B

Binary Logic, Netmasks, and Prefixes

A good understanding of netmasks and prefixes is essential when managing networks using VLSM and CIDR. For this purpose, we must look at IP addresses and netmasks the same way routers do: in binary format. This isn't as complicated as it sounds; binary representation is not very different from our regular decimal numbers; it just uses a smaller set of digits. There are only two values that can be expressed by a single binary digit ("bit" for short): 0 and 1. This may seem like a huge limitation, but it's not so bad; after all, our regular digits only have room for the values 0 to 9. For larger numbers, we have to use two or more of them. In binary, we just start using double digits sooner: at two rather than at ten. Table B-1 shows how this works out when counting in both decimal and binary.

Table B-1. Counting in binary and decimal formats

Decimal	Binary
0	0
1	1
2	10
3	11
4	100
5	101
6	110
7	111
8	1000
9	1001
10	1010
11	1011
12	1100

The basic method of expressing numbers is the same in binary as in decimal: the value of a digit in a multidigit number depends on its place relative to the other digits. This isn't the only imaginable way to express numeric values; for instance, Roman numerals use a different mechanism. Figure B-1 illustrates the similarities between decimal and binary.

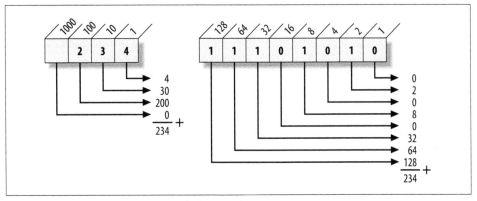

Figure B-1. Decimal versus binary multidigit numbers

The decimal value 234 has three digits. The 4 digit on the right is worth its value times one,[*] the next digit (3) has a "multiplier value" of 10 and the third digit (2) one of 100. The next digit would be worth its value times 1000 and so on. This works exactly the same way for the binary value 11101010, but this time we actually have to perform the calculation, because the result isn't immediately obvious as it is with decimal numbers.

Two other ways to represent numbers are in common use: octal (base 8) and hexadecimal (base 16). They both have the advantage that a single digit represents a fixed number of bits. In octal, the digits 8 and 9 aren't used, so the are eight possible single-digit values. Eight values can be encoded using exactly 3 bits, so a single octal digit represents 3 bits. Our example binary number 11101010 (234 decimal) is now converted as 11 = 3, 101 = 5, and 010 = 2 for a result of 352 in octal. In hexadecimal ("hex" for short), you count all the way up to 15 before running out of digits. The letters A through F stand in as the extra digits for the single-digit numbers beyond 9. 11101010 is transformed as 1110 = 14 = E and 1010 = 10 = A into the hexadecimal number EA.

With binary numbers, math becomes much simpler, but that's something for a book on building CPUs. In routing, we are not interested in performing computations in binary, we just want to be able to quickly compare IP and network addresses and

---

[*] The number each digit is multiplied by is the base (10 for decimal, 2 for binary) to the power of the digit's position, counting from the right and starting at zero. The rightmost digit is always worth just its face value because any positive number to the power of zero is one.

prefixes. For this we use logical operations. In logic, we work with true and false, represented by the bit values 1 for true and 0 for false. There are four logical operations:

AND
> Both things must be true. The result of a binary AND operation is 1 if both input bits are 1, and 0 in all other cases.

OR
> One or both things must be true. The result of a binary OR operation is 1 if one or both of the input bits is 1, and 0 when both input bits are 0.

EOR or XOR (exclusive OR)
> One thing must be true, the other false. The EOR operation returns 0 if both input bits are 1 or both input bits are 0, and it returns 1 if one of the input bits is 1 and the other is 0.

NOT
> true is false, and false is true. The NOT operation (sometimes written as "!") takes only one input bit. If the input is 0, the output is 1; if the input is 1, the output is 0.

Table B-2 shows the logical bit operations with all possible combinations of input bits.

Table B-2. Logical operations on bits

Operation	Input 0, 0	Input 0, 1	Input 1, 0	Input 1, 1
AND	0	0	0	1
OR	0	1	1	1
EOR	0	1	1	0
NOT	NOT 0 = 1		NOT 1 = 0	

When a CPU performs logical operations on multibit values, it starts by taking the first bit of both input bytes, and the result of the operation on these bits is the first bit of the output byte. The result of the logical operation on the second bit of both input bytes becomes the second bit of the output byte, and so on. Using these operations, it's possible to determine whether two hosts are in the same subnet by first stripping away all the host information by doing an AND operation between the IP address and the subnet mask. Because all the host bits are zero in the subnet mask, they will also be zero in the result. The bits in the network and subnet part of the subnet mask are one, so in the result, these bits are the same as the corresponding ones in the IP address. The resulting IP address with the host bits set to zero is the network address. If we perform this operation on two IP addresses and their subnet masks, we can then compare the network addresses, and if those are the same, the hosts belong to the same subnet:

```
if ((HOST1 AND NETMASK1) == (HOST2 AND NETMASK2))
   local;
else
   use default gateway;
```

Figure B-2 shows how an AND operation uses the subnet mask to turn IP addresses into network addresses so they can be compared.

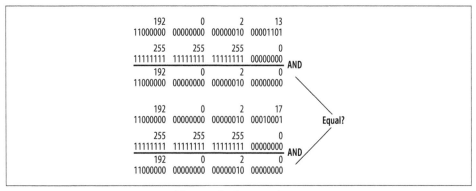

Figure B-2. AND operation on IP address and subnet mask

The result of both calculations is `192.0.2.0`, so the hosts are in the same subnet and can reach each other without involving a router. If the subnet information was entered in prefix notation, it would have to be converted to a mask first. This is easily done by inserting the appropriate number of 1 bits from left to right into an empty 32-bit memory location, or by looking the mask up in a table similar to Table B-3.

Table B-3. Prefix lengths and network masks

Prefix	Mask (binary)	Mask (decimal)	Mask (hex)
/0	00000000 00000000 00000000 00000000	0.0.0.0	00000000
/1	10000000 00000000 00000000 00000000	128.0.0.0	80000000
/2	11000000 00000000 00000000 00000000	192.0.0.0	C0000000
/3	11100000 00000000 00000000 00000000	224.0.0.0	E0000000
/4	11110000 00000000 00000000 00000000	240.0.0.0	F0000000
/5	11111000 00000000 00000000 00000000	248.0.0.0	F8000000
/6	11111100 00000000 00000000 00000000	252.0.0.0	FC000000
/7	11111110 00000000 00000000 00000000	254.0.0.0	FE000000
/8	11111111 00000000 00000000 00000000	255.0.0.0	FF000000
/9	11111111 10000000 00000000 00000000	255.128.0.0	FF800000
/10	11111111 11000000 00000000 00000000	255.192.0.0	FFC00000
/11	11111111 11100000 00000000 00000000	255.224.0.0	FFE00000
/12	11111111 11110000 00000000 00000000	255.240.0.0	FFF00000

Prefix	Mask (binary)	Mask (decimal)	Mask (hex)
/13	11111111 11111000 00000000 00000000	255.248.0.0	FFF80000
/14	11111111 11111100 00000000 00000000	255.252.0.0	FFFC0000
/15	11111111 11111110 00000000 00000000	255.254.0.0	FFFE0000
/16	11111111 11111111 00000000 00000000	255.255.0.0	FFFF0000
/17	11111111 11111111 10000000 00000000	255.255.128.0	FFFF8000
/18	11111111 11111111 11000000 00000000	255.255.192.0	FFFFC000
/19	11111111 11111111 11100000 00000000	255.255.224.0	FFFFE000
/20	11111111 11111111 11110000 00000000	255.255.240.0	FFFFF000
/21	11111111 11111111 11111000 00000000	255.255.248.0	FFFFF800
/22	11111111 11111111 11111100 00000000	255.255.252.0	FFFFFC00
/23	11111111 11111111 11111110 00000000	255.255.254.0	FFFFFE00
/24	11111111 11111111 11111111 00000000	255.255.255.0	FFFFFF00
/25	11111111 11111111 11111111 10000000	255.255.255.128	FFFFFF80
/26	11111111 11111111 11111111 11000000	255.255.255.192	FFFFFFC0
/27	11111111 11111111 11111111 11100000	255.255.255.224	FFFFFFE0
/28	11111111 11111111 11111111 11110000	255.255.255.240	FFFFFFF0
/29	11111111 11111111 11111111 11111000	255.255.255.248	FFFFFFF8
/30	11111111 11111111 11111111 11111100	255.255.255.252	FFFFFFFC
/31	11111111 11111111 11111111 11111110	255.255.255.254	FFFFFFFE
/32	11111111 11111111 11111111 11111111	255.255.255.255	FFFFFFFF

When a router searches through the routing table and has to compare a packet's destination with routing table entries to determine how a packet should be forwarded, it can use a similar mechanism as for determining whether a host belongs in a subnet. However, this isn't the most efficient way to do it, so router vendors implement smart algorithms to reach the same result faster.

In networking, it's often necessary to transmit multibyte values, such as 16-bit integers. Such an integer consists of two bytes: one holding the most significant part, the other holding the least significant part. The most significant byte holds the bits with the highest "multiplier value," or the ones on the left when written down. There are two ways to transmit this 16-bit value: with the least significant byte first or with the byte with the highest value first. In IP, we always transmit the most significant byte first. This transmission order is called *network byte order*, or *big-endian* and matches the way numbers are written down for human consumption. Most CPUs store multibyte values in memory the big-endian way, but some CPUs, most notably Intel's 8086 series and its descendants, use little-endian. Figure B-3 shows the IP address 172.25.234.59, the network mask 255.255.224.0 (/19), the subnet mask 255.255.255.128 (/25), and their relationships in binary representation, in network byte order.

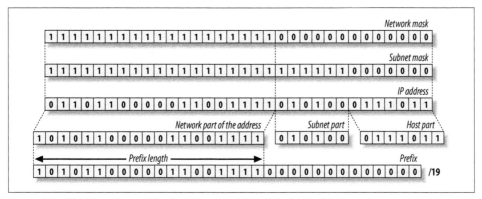

Figure B-3. IP address, net- and subnet masks, and prefix relationships

The IETF-mandated bit numbering is 0 for the most significant bit of the most significant octet, counting up to the least significant bit of the least significant octet, which would be bit 7, 15, or 31 in 8-,- 16-, or 32-bit values respectively.

For historic reasons, the word "octet" is often used instead of "byte" to indicate an 8-bit value.[*]

The way in which the bits within a byte are transmitted doesn't matter (and differs from one datalink protocol to the next), because the hardware always puts the bits back in the original order upon reception. The hardware doesn't know if two bytes are part of a multibyte value or are two unrelated bytes that just happen to be next to each other, so it can't reorder the bytes if necessary; this issue has to be dealt with in software.

---

[*] Also for historic reasons, the word "historic" is often used when "historical" would be more appropriate. (RFC 2026).

APPENDIX C

Notes on the IPv4 Address Space

Up until 1993, address space was assigned using classful mechanisms: everybody needing 254 addresses or less got a Class C network, everybody needing 16384 addresses or less got a Class B network, and everyone needing more than 16384 got a Class A network. About half the Class A and two thirds of the Class B space were assigned this way. Use of the Class C space was limited at this time: only 192.0.0.0/8 and 193.0.0.0/8 were in use to some degree at that moment. Then, after the introduction of Classless Inter-Domain Routing, most new allocations to ISPs and assignments to end users were taken from Class C space, which consequently started to run out quickly around the turn of the millennium. Today, most new address space is allocated as classless blocks from Class A space. During the mid-1990s, most allocations were /19 or larger blocks, but this was changed to /20 later. Thus, prefixes longer than /20 anywhere other than in 192.0.0.0/7 are almost always the result of poor aggregation, which may or may not be for good reasons. Table C-1 shows an overview of the IPv4 address space.

Table C-1. Overview of the IPv4 address space

Address range	Class
0.0.0.0/1	A, classful networks with mask 255.0.0.0 (/8)
128.0.0.0/2	B, classful networks with mask 255.255.0.0 (/16)
192.0.0.0/3	C, classful networks with mask 255.255.255.0 (/24)
224.0.0.0/4	Class D range, meant for multicast use
240.0.0.0/4	Class E range, reserved for future applications

The Internet Assigned Numbers Authority keeps a full list of IPv4 address assignments with a /8 granularity at *http://www.iana.org/assignments/ipv4-address-space/*. Table C-2 lists special addresses and ranges.

Table C-2. Table C-2. Overview of the IPv4 address space

Address range	Purpose
0.0.0.0/0	The whole Internet, used for default routes
0.0.0.0/8	Reserved; would clash with default route
10.0.0.0/8	Reserved for private use (RFC 1918)
127.0.0.0/8	Reserved for loopback addresses
127.0.0.1/32	The loopback address
169.254.0.0/16	For link-local use (when nothing else available)
172.16.0.0/12	Reserved for private use (RFC 1918)
192.0.2.0/24	Test network, reserved for testing and examples
192.168.0.0/16	Reserved for private use (RFC 1918)
233.0.0.0/8	GLOP multicast addresses (RFC 3180)
255.255.255.255/32	Broadcast address

Some network administrators prefer to do ingress filtering on source addresses from the reserved and private ranges. This won't buy you much; regular traffic from those addresses will be negligible because there can't be any return traffic. Also, filtering private address space will catch less than a percent of all packets with randomly spoofed source addresses. However, when you peer with other network over an Internet Exchange, you may want to filter explicitly on source addresses from these ranges and use *log-input* in the access list. This way, you can easily determine which peers don't employ any egress antispoofing filters: it is likely you'll see some packets from badly configured DHCP (in the 169.254.0.0/8 range) and NAT setups (usually in the 192.168.0.0/16 range).

Filtering out all nonassigned /8s gets rid of about a third of the packets with randomly spoofed source addresses, but you have to carefully keep those filters current because new ranges are deployed regularly. As for egress filtering, regular antispoofing egress filters will filter out packets with these addresses as the source address, and you can route the ranges to the null interface when they are the destination. Routing to the null interface rather than filtering is more efficient, and the result is the same.

Glossary

Advertise

Announce.

Aggregate

1. To announce a single, shorter prefix in place of several longer prefixes.

2. A shorter prefix that replaces several longer ones.

Announce

To send out BGP route updates indicating that a certain destination network (prefix) is reachable as part of the local AS.

Anycast

Packets sent to an anycast address are delivered to a single member of the associated anycast group the address belongs to. IPv6 anycast addresses follow regular unicast semantics, i.e., a system doesn't know it is sending a packet to an anycast address rather than a regular unicast address.

AS

Autonomous System.

AS number

Autonomous System number, a 16-bit value used in BGP (and EGP) processing for detecting routing loops and applying policies.

AS path

A list of AS numbers including the source of a route announcement (on the right), the next hop AS (on the left), and all ASes in between.

Autonomous System

"An AS is a connected group of one or more IP prefixes run by one or more network operators which has a *single* and *clearly defined* routing policy" (RFC 1930).

Bandwidth

Information transfer capacity, usually measured in (kilo-, mega-, or giga-) bits per second.

BGMP

Border Gateway Multicast Protocol. Protocol for interdomain multicast routing. Has no direct relationship to BGP.

BGP or BGP-4

Border Gateway Protocol (RFC 1771). BGP Version 4 is the routing protocol currently used for interdomain routing in the Internet.

BGP4+

BGP-4 with multiprotocol extensions (see MBGP).

Black hole

A router or AS announcing routes but not delivering packets forwarded according to those routes to their destination.

Black-hole (v)

To manipulate routing information to make packets flow to a place where they will be discarded.

Broadcast address
1. Address to which all stations listen.
2. IP address that turns packets addressed to it into datalink layer broadcasts.

The IPv4 global broadcast address is 255.255.255.255, and all addresses with all one bits in their host part are subnet broadcast addresses.

CIDR
Classless Inter-Domain Routing (RFC 1519). CIDR uses explicit network masks or prefix-length suffixes with network addresses rather than relying on implicit classful network size information. This makes it possible to have the network/host distinction on arbitrary bit boundaries.

Classful
Taking a network's A, B, or C Class into account, so the number of addresses per network can only be 16 million, 16834, or 256, and other values aren't possible.

Classless
Not taking a network's A, B, or C Class into account.

CLNP
IP-like protocol implementing CLNS, standardized by ISO as part of the OSI effort.

CLNS
1. Connectionless-mode network service, ISO terminology for a datagram network.
2. OSI CLNP.

Community
Optional transitive 32-bit attribute in BGP conveying user-defined information (RFC 1997).

Confederation
A set of ASes representing themselves to ASes outside the set as a single AS. This is done to overcome the iBGP full-mesh requirement (RFC 3065).

Datagram
Self-contained packet consisting of user data and routing (address) information.

Domain
OSI term for a network or AS.

EGP
Exterior Gateway Protocol.
1. Any protocol used for interdomain routing.
2. An early interdomain routing protocol (RFC 904).

Egress filtering
Filtering outbound packets or routes.

Gateway
1. System interconnecting dissimilar networks or applications.
2. A router.

Gbps
Gigabit(s) (1,000,000,000 bits or 119 megabytes) per second.

Global routing table
The set of routes visible to all BGP-running systems worldwide.

ICMP
Internet Control Message Protocol (RFC 792). Protocol carrying IP error and control information.

IDR
Interdomain routing: routing between ASes.

IDPR
Inter-Domain Policy Routing. A link state interdomain routing protocol with extensive policy support.

IDRP
BGP-like interdomain routing protocol for OSI networks.

IETF
The Internet Engineering Task force. From the IETF web site: "A large open international community of network designers, operators, vendors, and researchers concerned with the evolution of the Internet architecture and the smooth operation of the Internet."

IGP
Interior Gateway Protocol. Any routing protocol used within a single organization or AS.

Ingress filtering

Filtering inbound packets or routes.

Interdomain

Between ASes.

IP or IPv4

Internet Protocol Version 4 (RFC 791). Network-layer protocol used in the world-wide Internet and many private networks.

IPng

Internet Protocol Next Generation.

1. IPv6.

2. Any protocol put forward as a replacement for IPv4.

IPv6

Internet Protocol Version 6 (RFC 2460). New version of IP designed to overcome IPv4 shortcomings, mainly the limited number of available addresses.

IS-IS

Intermediate System to Intermediate System. OSI link-state interior routing protocol that can also be used for IP routing (RFC 1195).

Kbps

Kilobit(s) (1000 bits or 125 bytes) per second.

Layer, and layers 2, 3, and 4

The word "layer" usually refers to one of the layers in the OSI model. Layer 2 is the datalink layer and is responsible for getting packets from one system to the next. Layer 3 is the network layer and handles addressing and routing. Layer 4 is the transport layer, handling end-to-end issues such as reliability.

Longest match first

Rule stating that if an IP address potentially matches multiple prefixes in the routing table, the longest prefix should be considered to match.

Mask

String of bits in which each bit indicates whether this bit position is or isn't part of something. Net and subnet masks are written down in IP-address notation.

MBGP

Multiprotocol BGP: BGP-4 with multiprotocol extensions (RFC 2858).

Mbps

Megabit(s) (1,000,000 bits or 122 kilobytes) per second.

More specific

When there are two routes matching a certain destination, the one with the longest prefix is more specific.

Multicast

Packets sent to a multicast address are delivered to all members of the indicated multicast group.

Multihoming

Connecting to something (typically the Internet) over more than one connection.

Netmask

Mask indicating which bits are part of the network (1) and host (0) portions of an IP address. See *mask*.

Network

1. Collection of connected systems.

2. The connections between such a collection of systems.

3. Range of IP addresses sharing a common purpose, such as the range of addresses used by a single organization.

Network address

IP address with all the bits in the host part set to 0.

NLRI

Network Layer Reachability Information. Usually a single prefix, sometimes the term "NLRI" is used for more than one prefix.

Octet

8 bits or a byte.

OSPF

Open Shortest Path First (RFC 2328). Link state interior routing protocol.

OSPFv6

OSPF modified for use with IPv6 (RFC 2740).

Path

1. An AS path.

2. A physical path through a network.

3. A route.

Peer

1. A BGP neighbor: a router with which the local router has a BGP session with.

2. An AS with which the local AS peers.

Peering

Exchanging routing information and traffic with another AS without having a customer/service provider relationship in either direction.

Prefix

Network part of an IP address. Written down as a network address (possibly omitting trailing zeros), followed by a slash and the number of bits belonging to the network address. A longer prefix has more bits and is more specific; a shorter prefix has a smaller number (fewer bits).

Private addresses

Addresses in the ranges reserved for private use without global connectivity: 10.0.0.0/8, 172.16.0.0/12, and 192.168.0.0/16 (RFC 1918).

Private AS numbers

AS numbers in the range reserved for private use without global visibility: 64512–65535 (RFC 1930).

Queuing delay

The time a packet has to wait in a queue before it can be transmitted over an interface.

RFC

Request For Comment. A document published by the IETF (*http://www.ietf.org/rfc.html*), with or without any official status.

RIP

Routing Information Protocol (RFC 1058, RFC 2453). A simple distance-vector interior routing protocol.

RIPng

RIP modified for use with IPv6 (RFC 2080).

Route

Reachability information consisting of at least a destination network/prefix/NLRI, along with a next hop IP address and/or output interface.

Route reflector and route reflector client

A route reflector client has iBGP sessions with only one or more route reflectors rather than with all BGP routers within an AS. The route reflector "reflects" route information it receives over BGP to its clients (RFC 2796).

Router

1. A special-purpose device for layer 3 (usually IP) forwarding and associated tasks, such as running routing protocols.

2. Any system performing layer 3 forwarding.

Routing policy

A policy outlining the distribution of routing information between the local AS and other autonomous systems, in accordance with existing transit/customer and peering relationships.

Single-homing

Being connected (to the Internet) over a single connection.

Spoofing

Sending out packets with falsified information, such as a source address that doesn't rightfully belong to the sending host.

Subnet

1. A single datalink-layer network used for IP.

2. The range of IP addresses associated with a single datalink-layer network.

Subnet mask

Mask indicating which bits of an IP address are used to number hosts (the 0 bits) and which are part of the network or used to number subnets (the 1 bits).

Supernet

Collection of classful networks forming a single, larger network.

Switch

A device forwarding packets or non-packet data at the datalink or physical layer, such as Ethernet, ATM, or SONET. A switch operates transparently to higher layers.

TCP

Transmission Control Protocol (RFC 793). Reliable transport protocol used for many applications on the Internet.

Telco

Telephone company. Often used for companies selling leased line or dark fiber services, whether they also provide telephony services or not.

TCP/IP

The IP protocol suite, including IP, ICMP, TCP, and UDP.

Transit

A service in which a service provider network provides access to all destinations connected to the Internet.

UDP

User Datagram Protocol (RFC 768). Transport protocol implementing only multiplexing functions and an optional checksum to give applications direct access to IP's unreliable datagram service.

Unicast

Unicast packets are addressed to and received by a single destination host. In other words, "regular" IP packets, as opposed to anycast, multicast, or broadcast.

Index

A

Active state, 22
  (see also BGP, states)
address announcements,
        troubleshooting, 176–178
address assignment, policies, 62
address blocks
  allocation and assignment, 61
  announcing, 76
address families, 26
Address Family Identifier (AFI), 27
address space
  IPv4, 256
  PA (Provider Aggregatable), 62
  provider independent, 63
administrative distance, 34
Advanced Research Projects Agency Network
        (ARPANET), 1
AFI (Address Family Identifier), 27
American Registry for Internet Numbers
        (ARIN), 61
antispoofing filters, 248
APNIC (Asia-Pacific Network Information
        Centre), 61
ARIN (American Registry for Internet
        Numbers), 61
ARPANET (Advanced Research Projects
        Agency Network), 1
AS (Autonomous System)
  black holes because of transit from
        nontransit AS, 183
  numbers, 70

paths
  inbound, 103
  manipulating, 103
  outbound, 110–113
  prepending, 110–113, 178, 216–219
  and routing protocols, 10
Asia-Pacific Network Information Centre
        (APNIC), 61
ATM, CRC errors, 172
attacks
  detecting, 138
  finding source of, 141
  protection against, 133, 143
  stopping, 141
authentication, 73
Autonomous System (see AS)
availability, calculating, 36–38

B

backbone links, 57
backup
  connections for customer, 116, 224–225
  for fiber paths, 53
bandwidth, 39
  burst capacity, 40
  calculating requirements, 41–43
  minimum requirements, 39
  pricing, 41
  problems, 170
BGMP (Border Gateway Multicast
        Protocol), 28
BGP (Border Gateway Protocol), 10, 18
  configuration, 78, 80
  connectivity example, 12

We'd like to hear your suggestions for improving our indexes. Send email to *index@oreilly.com*.

multihoming
   benefits and risks, 13
   IPv6, 226
   traffic engineering, 95
multilateral peering, 234
multilayer switches, 45
Multiprotocol BGP (MBGP), 28
Multiprotocol Label Switching (MPLS), 31

N

name servers, 185
NANOG (North American Network
      Operators) mailing list, 240
NAPs (Network Access Points), original, 3
netstat command, 182
Network Access Points (NAPs), original, 3
network byte order, 254
network management suites, 154
network masks, 253
Network Operations Center (see NOC)
network partitions
   announcing addresses, 210
   problems with, 52
   using, 209–212
network performance, 169–173
network reliability, 36–38
Network Time Protocol (NTP), 160
network topology, 9, 54–60
networks, classification of, 5
next hop address, 180, 222
next-hop processing, 86
next-hop-self command, 86
no synchronization command, 86
NOC (Network Operations Center)
   compared with help desk, 148
   contact methods, 149–151
   hardware facilities, 151
   purpose of, 147
   types, 147
North American Network Operators
      (NANOG) mailing list, 240
notification message, 22
NSFNET, 2
NTP (Network Time Protocol), 160
numbered configuration, 76

O

open message, 20
Open Shortest Path First (see OSPF)
OpenConfirm state, 22
   (see also BGP, states)

OpenSent state, 22
   (see also BGP, states)
optimum switching, 47
OSPF metrics, overriding, 208
OSPF (Open Shortest Path First)
   and BGP, 201, 224
   as IGP, 198–207
   and SPF algorithm, 10, 199
   (see also IGPs)
outbound communities, 113–115
outbound route filters, 213–215
outbound traffic, troubleshooting, 179

P

PA (Provider Aggregatable) address blocks
   obtaining, 64
   and route announcements, 62
packet flood, 137
   (see also attacks)
packet sniffing, 130
partial mesh topology, 57, 59
password encryption, 135
passwords, 129–131, 245
path MTU discovery, 212
path prepending, 110–113, 178, 217–219
peer groups, 188
peering, 5
   business case, 229
   over direct connection, 229
   over an IX, 229
   multilateral, 234
   politics of, 233
   scenarios, 228
peers, filtering routes to, 213–215
performance problems, 169–173
PGP authentication, 73
physical network problems, 167–169
ping with options, 172, 212
port filtering, 142, 185
power failure
   avoiding, 50
   troubleshooting, 169
prefix lengths, and network masks, 251
prefix lists, 83
prepending paths, 110–113, 217–219
priority queueing, 125
process switching, 47
protocol
   BGP, 19
   distance-path, 10
   exterior gateway, 10
protocol (*continued*)

About the Author

Even before dropping out of high school, **Iljitsch van Beijnum** was intrigued by the way computers communicate. His old Commodore 64 home computer has the solder marks to prove it. Working in a low-level computer support job turned out to be too frustrating with lots of interesting networking stuff around, but with no real access to any of it. So he decided to go to college, studying computer science at the Haagse Hogeschool in The Hague and also, for a year, philosophy at Leiden University. Before he could graduate, a new challenge presented itself: the Internet. Working for a small local ISP, Iljitsch started to learn about Cisco routers and the myriads of interesting protocols running on them, most notably BGP. When this ISP literally went south, he and four other people started one of their own: Pine Internet. But the work there didn't include enough BGP, so he moved on to first being a senior network engineer for UUNET Netherlands and then to working as a freelance networking consultant.

When he's not working on a router configuration or his web site, *http://www.bgpexpert.com/*, Iljitsch enjoys gazing at tall buildings, watching sitcoms on TV, and reading thought-provoking books. In recent years, his taste in this area has expanded from science fiction from the 1960s to such classic literature as that of Dante and Kafka.

Colophon

Our look is the result of reader comments, our own experimentation, and feedback from distribution channels. Distinctive covers complement our distinctive approach to technical topics, breathing personality and life into potentially dry subjects.

The animal on the cover of *BGP* is the slender-horned gazelle (*Gazella leptoceros*). It is the palest of all gazelles and has slightly enlarged hooves for walking on sand. Both sexes have horns: in males, they are about a foot long, slender, and slightly "S" shaped. In females, they are significantly smaller and slimmer, about 8 inches long.

Females and young live in groups of 10 to 30. Adult males establish territories late in the year and mate with females that enter these territories. Females give birth in May or June and wean their one offspring approximately three months later. Gazelles weigh approximately 60 pounds and live about 14 years.

Due to the extreme heat of its desert environment, the slender-horned gazelle feeds mostly at night and in the early morning. Their water needs are small; morning dew on the vegetation they eat suffices. Their main cooling mechanisms are a reflective white coat and a specially adapted nasal passage.

The slender-horned gazelle lives in isolated pockets throughout the central Sahara Desert and has been classified as endangered because of excessive hunting for the animal's meat and horns.

Mary Anne Weeks Mayo was the production editor, and Leanne Soylemez was the copyeditor, for *BGP*. Tatiana Apandi Diaz and Jane Ellin provided quality control. Phil Dangler provided production assistance. Lynda D'Arcangelo wrote the index.

Ellie Volckhausen designed the cover of this book, based on a series design by Edie Freedman. The cover image is an original antique engraving. Emma Colby produced the cover layout with QuarkXPress 4.1 using Adobe's ITC Garamond font.

David Futato designed the interior layout. This book was converted to FrameMaker 5.5.6 by Joe Wizda with a format conversion tool created by Erik Ray, Jason McIntosh, Neil Walls, and Mike Sierra that uses Perl and XML technologies. The text font is Linotype Birka; the heading font is Adobe Myriad Condensed; and the code font is LucasFont's TheSans Mono Condensed. The illustrations that appear in the book were produced by Robert Romano and Jessamyn Read using Macromedia FreeHand 9 and Adobe Photoshop 6. The tip and warning icons were drawn by Christopher Bing. This colophon was compiled by Mary Anne Weeks Mayo.

Milton Keynes UK
Ingram Content Group UK Ltd.
UKHW052224060824
446577UK00016B/161

9 780596 002541